John Betjeman and Cornwall

"Betjeman might have been a child of the suburbs, but his heart and soul lay in Cornwall." **Richard Morrison, writing in *The Times*, 25 August 2006**

Quintessentially English, Betjeman was an 'outsider' in England - and doubly so in Cornwall where, as he was the first to admit, he was a 'foreigner'.

And yet, as this book describes, Betjeman also strove to acquire a veneer of 'Cornishness', cultivating an alternative Celtic identity that he wove during sojourns in Ireland and other Celtic countries. He likewise rooted his religious identity in Cornwall, finding inspiration in 'Celtic Christianity' and Cornwall's Anglo-Catholic tradition. North Cornwall, in particular, was for Betjeman a place of 'liberation', where he found relief from the many conflicting pressures in his life. But he was also active in Cornish affairs, insisting that Cornwall was not part of England, and championing Cornish environmental concerns that anticipated today's focus on sustainability.

Philip Payton is Professor of Cornish & Australian Studies in the University of Exeter and Director of the Institute of Cornish Studies at the University's Cornwall campus. He is the author of numerous books on Cornwall and the Cornish.

Other books from University of Exeter Press by Philip Payton:

A.L. Rowse and Cornwall: A paradoxical patriot (2005)

Making Moonta: The invention of 'Australia's Little Cornwall' (2007)

University of Exeter Press also publishes the annual series 'Cornish Studies', edited by Philip Payton; *Cornish Studies 18* will be published in 2010.

John Betjeman and Cornwall

'The Celebrated Cornish Nationalist'

PHILIP PAYTON

UNIVERSITY
of
EXETER
PRESS

Paperback cover images The photographs by Jane Bown show John Betjeman in 1972 at the Camel estuary, near Trebetherick, North Cornwall; they are copyright Guardian News and Media Ltd 2006.

First published in 2010 by
University of Exeter Press
Reed Hall, Streatham Drive
Exeter EX4 4QR
UK
www.exeterpress.co.uk

British Library Cataloguing in Publication Data
A catalogue record for this book is available from the British Library.

Hardback ISBN 978 0 85989 847 8
Paperback ISBN 978 0 85989 848 5

Mixed Sources
Product group from well-managed
forests and other controlled sources
www.fsc.org Cert no. SA-COC-002112
© 1996 Forest Stewardship Council

Typeset in Perpetua 11½ point on 14 point by Carnegie Book Production, Lancaster
Printed in Great Britain by Short Run Press Ltd, Exeter

For Brigid and Unity,
and in fond remembrance of the Withered Arm
and The Route of the 'ACE'

'In time, perhaps, books about Betjeman will be as frequent as
books about [T.S.] Eliot, if less solemn'.
William Plomer, writing in the *Guardian*, 7 April 1961

'Clearly Sir John Betjeman was not a poet to be talked about
in the same breath as, say, T.S. Eliot and it is unlikely that he
will be studied on university Eng Lit course and "explained"
in academic theses and treatises'.
Huddersfield Daily Examiner, 21 May 1984

Contents

Illustrations

Preface

I was one of the 8,000-strong 'Betjemaniacs' gathered at Carruan farm in Cornwall in August 2006 to celebrate the hundredth birthday of Sir John Betjeman, the late Poet Laureate. Situated high above Polzeath, with tremendous views out to the azure Atlantic and the great headland of Pentire, Carruan was, with its exhilarating sense of space, an inspirational choice for this great event. I stood in the pasty-queue with the Archbishop of Canterbury, watched the poetic performance of Bert Biscoe, and browsed among the bookstalls in the hope of finding second-hand copies of rare Betjeman books to add to my collection. Here was that Patrick Taylor-Martin volume that had eluded me for years, and *Betjeman's Britain* – compiled by Candida Lycett Green, Betjeman's daughter – together with more recent editions of old favourites.

As I browsed and mused, so the idea formed – dimly at first, half-baked – that perhaps the task would (maybe even should) fall to me to tackle the complex subject of John Betjeman and his long relationship with Cornwall. So many others had written about Sir John, and all acknowledged the centrality of Cornwall in his make-up, yet none had elaborated in depth or at length the real significance of Cornwall in his life and work. This, then, would be my challenge. Next morning, at my desk in the Institute of Cornish Studies at Tremough, the University of Exeter's Cornwall Campus, I recounted the preceding day's events to my colleague, Bernard Deacon. Unprompted, he suggested that a 'Cornish biography' of John Betjeman was long overdue. I was the one to do it, he insisted, and so the project was born.

Thanks to the exhaustive and indispensable three-volumed narrative biography by Bevis Hillier, the general facts of John Betjeman's life are already well known and readily accessible. Candida Lycett Green's editions of her father's letters are a further boon for the Betjeman scholar, as are the recent edited volumes by Stephen Games, with their thoughtful introductions and excellent selections from Betjeman's many wireless and television broadcasts. Kevin Gardner, first with his *Faith and Doubt of John Betjeman: An Anthology of Betjeman's Religious Verse* (2005), then his *Poems in the Porch: The Radio Poems of John Betjeman* (2008), and now his *John Betjeman: Writing the Public Life* (2010), has added an academic dimension to Betjeman studies. So have Dennis Brown's *John Betjeman* (1999), Timothy Mowl's *Stylistic Cold Wars: Betjeman versus Pevsner* (2000) and Greg Morse's *John Betjeman: Reading the Victorians* (2008), while William S. Peterson's *John Betjeman: A Bibliography* (2006) provides the definitive guide to all Betjeman's creative work.

Beyond this rich literature, to which must be added, of course, Betjeman's own prodigious output, is the large Betjeman Archive at the Tom Brown's School Museum in Uffington in south Oxfordshire, formerly Berkshire. Duplicating much of the material from the Betjeman Archive in the McPherson Library at the University of Victoria in British Columbia, Canada, together with copies of other Betjeman material in various libraries in North America and the United Kingdom, the Uffington collection also includes a fascinatingly diverse mix of original Betjeman correspondence, personal papers, notebooks, appointment diaries, newspaper cuttings, and ephemera of all types – including a stash of envelopes, addressed in Betjeman's hand and bearing Manx postage stamps! There is also personal correspondence from Penelope Betjeman to her husband. I have been fortune enough to have had this extremely important Uffington collection put at my disposal, through the assistance of the Friends of the Tom Brown's School Museum and the permission of Candida Lycett Green, and I am especially grateful to Sharon Smith of the Friends for making all the necessary arrangements for me to visit the Museum on several occasions and to undertake extended research there.

I am also grateful to Candida Lycett Green for her warm enthusiasm for my project, and to the Betjeman Estate for permission to draw upon John Betjeman's published and unpublished work, as detailed in the text. Tom Williams at Aitken Alexander Associates was ever patient and diplomatic in dealing with my many enquiries. My wife Deidre, as always, accompanied me on my Betjeman adventures, to Uffington and to the many places in Cornwall associated with the late Poet Laureate, and several of her photographs grace the pages of this book. We visited Blisland and St Ervan, went to Padstow on May Day, and walked the old railway track-bed from Wadebridge to Padstow by the widening Camel estuary, as well as returning many times to St Enodoc and Daymer Bay.

Many others helped with the project, and those deserving especial mention include Elizabeth Bartlett (who lent me an important Betjeman letter in her possession), Bruce and Trish Bennett (who joined us from Australia to visit St Enodoc), Emma Bennett (with her interesting 'take' on Betjeman, du Maurier and Rowse), Bert Biscoe (who allowed me to quote extensively from his poem, 'Mercifully Preserved'), Hilary Bracegirdle and Angela Broome at the Royal Cornwall Museum in Truro, Julia Eddy, Christine Faunch (who arranged my visits to the Betjeman Working Library in the Special Collections at the University of Exeter), John Fleet (who first opened my eyes to the significance of the St Ervan episode), D.H. Frost, Jessica Gardner, Ian Grant, Lucy Guenole, Máiread Nic Cráith, (who assisted with the Irish language), Helena Hammond, John Heald, John Hurst, Alan M. Kent, the late Patricia Lay (McCooey), Catherine Lorigan, Judy Martin, David Milsted, Anne Pender, Donald R. Rawe, Jonathan Steddal (who kindly lent several photographs for this book), Moire Tangye, Ella Westland, James Whetter, Nicholas J.A. Williams, and Colin Wright (who drew my research to the attention of the Betjeman Society). My Visiting Fellowship in 2007 in the Humanities Research Centre at the Australian National University provided the opportunity to conduct the initial research for this project, and in 2008 I was invited to present a paper on 'John Betjeman and Australia' to a literary colloquium in honour of Bruce Bennett at the National Library of Australia in Canberra. At the University of Exeter, Cornwall Campus, students and staff were likewise helpful, including several cohorts of my second-year undergraduate 'Celtic Literatures' course and my colleagues Catherine Brace, Bernard Deacon, Adeline Johns-Putra, Nick Groom, Mandy Morris, and Garry Tregidga. At University of Exeter Press, Simon Baker and Helen Gannon smoothed the way to publication, putting my anxieties to rest and providing the friendly, reassuring atmosphere for which the UEP team is justly renowned.

Philip Payton
Bodmin, Cornwall,
12 July 2010.

PREAMBLE

'The Sky Widens
to a Sense of Cornwall'

The centenary of John Betjeman's birth in 2006 rekindled both academic and popular interest in the life and career of John Betjeman, the late Poet Laureate. This prompted a variety of publications, notably A.N. Wilson's new biography *Betjeman* and an abridged version (*John Betjeman – The Biography*) of Bevis Hillier's magisterial three-volumed biographical study.[1] But although these works alluded generally to Betjeman's intimate and enduring relationship with Cornwall, none thought to investigate the relationship in detail or to offer explanations for its complexity.

Richard Morrison, writing in *The Times* on 25 August 2006, saw that 'Betjeman might have been a child of the suburbs, but his heart and soul lay in Cornwall'.[2] This book seeks to ask how and why this should have been so. It casts Betjeman as part of a wider twentieth-century social and literary movement – including the likes of J.B. Priestley and H.V. Morton – which was increasingly critical of what it saw as a jaded, over-urbanized England and went instead in nostalgic search of an 'other', more elusive but primordial Englishness. Betjeman's 'other' was Cornwall, on which he first alighted unwittingly as a small boy when visiting with his parents. Thereafter, the book argues, from this early childhood acquaintance until his death, Cornwall became a constant in Betjeman's life. It was significant in his religious life as well as in other aspects of his existence, both creative and personal, and moulded a great many aspects of his personal identity. This book, then, seeks to better understand Betjeman and his life and work, through a detailed examination of his intimate relationship with Cornwall.

The book also seeks to better understand modern Cornwall itself, exploring Betjeman's literary links with the Celtic Revival that was busily 're-inventing' Cornwall, and demonstrating the extent to which his sympathy for revivalist imaginings of Cornwall was reflected in his own work. Here Betjeman's experiences elsewhere in the 'Celtic world' – his

imagined Welsh descent, his intimate knowledge of Ireland, his fondness
for Scotland and the Isle of Man, even his enthusiasm for Australia – had
a bearing on his own construction of Celtic Cornwall. It also influenced
the way in which he thought about these islands, eschewing any notion
of any unified 'Britishness' and stressing instead the separate identities of
their constituent nations.

   Likewise, this book sheds light on the contested 'outsider-insider' nexus,
an important element of identity formation in twentieth-century Cornwall
as mass tourism, second-homes and in-migration all became controversial
aspects of Cornish life. Betjeman was an 'outsider' in Cornwall who aspired
to be an 'insider', a paradox that he felt acutely and never quite resolved
to his own satisfaction. This was a position shared by others (Daphne du
Maurier even joined the Cornish nationalist party, Mebyon Kernow) but
was an intriguing reversal of the predicament experienced by Betjeman's
Cornish companion, A.L. Rowse, the 'insider' who famously strove to
become an 'outsider'. To that extent, this book revisits the themes of place,
identity and (auto)biography elucidated in my earlier *A.L. Rowse and Cornwall:
A Paradoxical Patriot*, and may, perhaps, be considered a 'natural' companion
to that volume.

*   *   *

In his poem 'Old Friends, which appeared in the collection *High and Low*
in 1966, John Betjeman imagined himself arriving at Trebetherick late one
summer's evening after a long drive down from somewhere up-country. As
he drove through the North Cornwall countryside, familiar since his early
boyhood, he glimpsed the Atlantic coast near Polzeath that for him was
'home'. 'The sky widens to a sense of Cornwall', he wrote, 'A sense of sea /
Hangs in the lichenous branches and still there's light'. As the sun set gently
into the west, he pondered a 'glowing ... mackerel sky' that 'faded to a
purple pink', and suddenly at that late hour experienced an inner loneliness,
a melancholy that matched that eerie twilight 'still and deep'. Why, he
asked, 'Do my spirits sink?'. The 'gathering dark is full of the thought of
friends / I shall see no more', he wrote, his mourning for his chums from
those early Cornish days made more acute by the familiarity now close at
hand: 'There's Doom Bar; Bray Hill shows plain' and 'two miles off I hear
St Minver bells'.

   And yet, as Betjeman mused on those long departed friends, his gloom
gave way at last to a more serene contemplation, an intense awareness of

a benign, timeless eternity, where he and Old Friends would meet once
more:

> Are they one with the Celtic saints and the years between?
>> Can they see the moonlit pools where ribbonweed drifts?
> As I reach our hill, I am part of a sea unseen –
>> The oppression lifts.[3]

As Frank Delaney once observed, 'Cornwall yields up Betjeman, vivid
and immediate, in all his loneliness, his fears, his religious supplication, his
wistful yearning for old and warm times'. But Cornwall was 'Betjeman's
holy well', he added, the source of literary inspiration as well as sanctuary
from an often hostile world, although there was also a 'haunting, primeval
Celtic Cornwall', he said, a place of 'menace' and 'apprehension' that would
by turns unsettle and excite.[4] In 'Old Friends' there are glimpses of each
of these 'Cornwalls'. There is Cornwall as a place of loneliness and loss,
of strangeness and vulnerability. But there is also the Cornwall of hope
renewed, of welcoming familiarity, of freedom, of endless possibilities, and
ultimately of religious redemption. And Cornwall in these several moods is
always 'Celtic', the land of holy saints as well as brooding menace, with an
alluring sense of 'difference' that holds Betjeman perpetually in its thrall.

In this book, we revisit these several Cornwalls and explore their
intimate connections with Betjeman's life and work. North Cornwall, in
particular, with its literary associations of Tennyson and Hardy, Robert
Stephen Hawker and Sabine Baring-Gould, the rural fastness of Arthur
and the saintly children of King Brychan, is explored at length. This was
the 'Betjemanland' where John Betjeman felt most at home, where he had
holidayed as a small boy, where he spent weeks and months over subsequent
years, and where he died in 1984. It was, he imagined, the most deeply
'Celtic' part of Cornwall, with a separateness all of its own. Nonetheless,
with the help of Cornish friends, most especially the historian A.L. Rowse,
Betjeman lifted his sights to other Cornwalls, exploring distant churches
and hidden villages in far-off parishes, acquiring an unrivalled knowledge
of the Duchy (as he liked to term it) in all its diversity, quite literally from
the Tamar to Land's End, an expertise he demonstrated authoritatively in
his Shell Guide to Cornwall in 1964.

However, beneath Betjeman's enthusiasm for his 'own' North Cornwall,
and his wider devotion to all things Cornish, was a deeper search for personal
identity. Never sure of his English credentials – the Betjemanns were a

German family (not Dutch, as his mother tried to reassure him) – Betjeman had followed in the footsteps of English writers such as H.V. Morton who in the years after the Great War had attempted to 're-invent' Englishness afresh, locating the 'real' England deep in the countryside. Indeed, Betjeman was to emerge as the foremost literary champion of this nostalgic Englishness. In prose and poem, and in radio and television broadcasts, he portrayed an idyllic rural England of remote branch line railways, homely Women's Institutes, and ancient parish churches. England took him to heart and he became the nation's favourite poet, appointed Poet Laureate in 1972. But, just as his own 'Englishness' was in doubt, so this 'real' England was now under threat – from rapacious developers bent on pulling down the best of old England in the interests of making a quick profit, and from bureaucrats and centralists in 'Whitehall' who were complicit in this march of so-called 'progress'. Here Betjeman found himself involved in numerous public campaigns designed to thwart such 'development', earning a reputation as a passionate conservationist but also demonstrating his ability as a shrewd, tough political operator, cunning (and subversive) enough to take on the establishment and win.

Yet, for all this intimate embrace of Englishness, Betjeman remained an 'outsider' – not least in his own estimation – and in the midst of this quest for the 'real' England he sought an alternative identity. Clutching at a Welsh twig in his family tree, he discovered an authentic 'Celticity' that somehow legitimated his sense of belonging in Cornwall, and lent a feeling of common cause with the Cornish and other Celtic peoples. At Oxford he tried to learn Welsh and later, during the Second World War, he learned Irish when in Eire as part of the United Kingdom's diplomatic mission. Already deeply enamoured of Ireland, his experiences there in the war years broadened his understanding of Irish culture and politics, prompting a sympathy for Irish neutrality and the wider aims of Irish nationalism. He began to argue that the Act of Union in 1801 between Britain and Ireland, like the later partition of Ireland, had been a catastrophic mistake.

Part of this complex alternative identity was Betjeman's identification with 'Celtic Christianity', especially in its Cornish guise, where he was attracted by the twin components of Anglo-Catholicism and Celtic revivalism. A chance encounter as a youth with the rector of St Ervan, deep in the North Cornwall countryside, opened his eyes to a world of Celtic saints and the Holy Grail, as did Arthur Machen's book *The Secret Glory*, thoughtfully lent to Betjeman by the kindly rector. That Machen was a Welshman, as was the hero of the novel – Ambrose Meyrick – added to the book's significance in

Betjeman's estimation, and in its pages he found himself enwrapped in the mysteries of the 'Ancient Mass of the Britons' and the 'Celtic Church'.

After the war, a practising Anglo-Catholic and a growing devotee of Pan-Celticism, Betjeman redoubled his Cornish enthusiasms, eventually buying a house at Trebetherick and spending increasing amounts of time each year in Cornwall. But he also pursued his other Celtic affiliations, including new-found interests in Scotland and the Isle of Man, and – only slightly tongue-in-cheek – adopted in his writings a variety of Celtic personae: he was, variously, Séan O'Betjemán (Irish), Ewen Quetjeman (Manx), Iain MacBetjeman (Scots), and, of course, 'Jan Killigrew Trebetjeman', the adopted Cornishman. In childhood and adolescence, holidays in Cornwall had offered 'liberation' – from his school, and later from his parents – and in the post-war years Cornwall became ever more important to Betjeman as a place of healing and escape. First, there was respite from the pressures of journalistic work in London, and then later, and more significantly, he sought solace in Cornwall with his companion Lady Elizabeth Cavendish as his marriage to his wife Penelope faltered. Later still, as he became increasingly ill, Cornwall was for Betjeman a place of rest, recuperation and reflection.

However, Betjeman was by no means a recluse, and although he sometimes sought anonymity at Trebetherick, this did not prevent his adoption of various Cornish causes. His experiences in Ireland had nurtured his understanding of Irish nationalism, a sympathy he translated easily to Cornwall. Cornwall was not England, he insisted; it was a country and not a county; it was a Celtic nation, and so on. Although often protesting that he was merely a 'foreigner' in Cornwall, he nonetheless went out of his way to cultivate a sense of belonging. He was an early advocate of 'sustainable tourism' in Cornwall (to the alarm of an embarrassed National Trust, taken aback by the strength of his language), and was likewise an ardent supporter of the Cornish anti-nuclear movement. He also took on the china clay industry in Cornwall, leading the campaign to stop the dumping of china clay waste along St Austell Bay. He had become, as he put it, 'John Trebetjeman, the Celebrated Cornish Nationalist', and, by and large, Cornish nationalists tended to agree.

As this book argues, John Betjeman was ahead of his time. Even at the height of the war, he denied the existence of a homogenous 'British' people, insisting instead upon separate treatment for each of Britain's constituent nations. Significantly, as well as anticipating the 'end of Britishness' debate of recent years, he had placed consideration of Cornwall centre stage in this new appreciation of the territorial complexity of these islands. Indeed, his search for personal and religious identity, and with it his formidable literary output, had had, as it turned out, profound cultural and political implications – for Cornwall, and for the United Kingdom as a whole.

CHAPTER ONE

'That bold coast-line
where he was not born'

John Betjeman as 'foreigner'

In death, as in life, John Betjeman was master of the unexpected. Always the consummate performer, even on his funeral day he contrived – or so it seemed – to provide a spectacle to grip his audience; a drama as apt as it was memorable. Many knew of Betjeman's long-held wish to be buried in the small churchyard of St Enodoc, amidst the sand dunes (*towans*, in the Cornish language) and golf-links along Daymer Bay, at the mouth of the Camel estuary on the North Cornwall coast. It was a spot that he had known and loved since early childhood. His mother, Bessie, was buried there, and in the tiny church itself was a memorial to his late father Ernest. 'I knelt in darkness at St Enodoc',[1] Betjeman had recalled in his autobiographical *Summoned by Bells*, remembering his early youth and the instinctive reverence he had felt in the dim, damp, oil-lit interior of the little nave. He had also 'visited our local Holy Well', he said, in 'quest of mystical experience' and elusive Celtic saints, and knew that, only half a century or so before, the church, with its small wizened tower, had been all but engulfed by the encroaching dunes, the vicar lowered through the roof on a rope to conduct his services – or so it was reported.[2] Enchanted by the location – 'Bléssèd be St Enodoc',[3] he wrote – Betjeman had long since decided that this should be his final resting place: 'To-day a pair walks newly married / Along the path where I'll be carried'.[4]

'the wild Atlantic coast that had inspired him since boyhood'

John Betjeman had died peacefully at Treen, his house at Trebetherick, near St Enodoc, on the morning of 19 May 1984. His funeral took place a few days later, on 22 May. In spring, as Simon Jenkins has observed, this is a 'tranquil coastline',[5] in contrast to the Atlantic cliffs beyond the estuary where even on calm days there is a constant swell and the waves crash upon jagged rocks. In its seclusion, protected by tamarisk hedges and sunk in its sandy hollow beside 'turfy hills'[6] (as Betjeman described them), St Enodoc in May can seem almost Mediterranean, a suntrap where the light is fierce, the sky is bright blue clear, and the sea sparkles. Betjeman, however, knew how fickle this North Cornwall coast could be, even along sequestered Daymer Bay, with sudden raging storms the stuff of nightmares, even in spring:

> But in a dream the other night
> I saw this coastline from the sea
> And felt the breakers plunging white
> Their weight of waters over me.[7]

These were days and nights when 'trees outside were stripped of leaves / And heavy seas were roaring'.[8] Such, indeed, was 22 May, when gusts of almost gale-force intensity ripped inland from the Atlantic, driving near-horizontal rain down the Camel estuary and across the dunes and links of St Enodoc. Instead of the warmth and sunshine that might have been expected, here was a wintry chill and constant downpour, the sky darkened by black, fast-moving clouds. It was, as the *Western Morning News* observed in its account of the funeral, a gothic scene that Betjeman himself would have found powerfully evocative. It was if he had arranged it all deliberately, orchestrating an unforgettable melodrama that somehow suited the occasion, matching Betjeman's sense of theatre and his profound awe of the Cornish coast in all its moods. 'It seemed fitting', wrote the *Western Morning News*, 'that Sir John's funeral was conducted in almost gale force conditions because their fury ... had great appeal for him'.[9] The *Daily Express* thought likewise. Here, it said, was 'the wild Atlantic coast that had inspired him since boyhood'.[10]

For the six pall-bearers there was the difficult task of confronting the elements as they bore Betjeman's coffin along the rough path to the church, picking their way carefully and already soaked through by the incessant downpour. Jonathan Stedall, the film maker, was one of the six and recalled years later how they 'had to carry the coffin over half a mile through a ferocious Atlantic gale, arriving at the church – as someone said – looking like a gang of Cornish wreckers'.[11] It was, as one observer wrote, a windswept

1. Sir John Betjeman's funeral at St Enodoc, 22 May 1984. Jonathan Stedall,
the film-maker, is the leading pall-bearer on the coffin's left; at the rear
is Penelope Betjeman, Sir John's widow.

scene that would have caught Betjeman's imagination, 'the kind of weather
that might have triggered another poem'.[12] It was as though, Jonathan Stedall
imagined, 'nature itself acknowledged that the life which was now complete
had been, despite Betjeman's somewhat cosy and cuddly image, a powerful
and radical one'.[13] For the mourners, there was also the struggle against the
'horizontal monsoon'[14] (as the *Guardian* described it), streaming rainwater
disguising their tears as they made for the temporary refuge of the church's
interior. Once inside the little building there was darkness, relieved only by
the oil-lamps, candles and the verger's torch. Betjeman's wife, Penelope, and
his devoted companion, Elizabeth Cavendish, were among the small group
of relations and friends present. The two women had not met before, and
they did not speak. 'Dear Lord and Father of Mankind, Forgive Our Foolish
Ways', sang the congregation, and after the service the coffin was carried
in still torrential rain to Betjeman's grave, near the lych gate, where Sir
John was laid to rest.[15] All in all, it had been a remarkable pageant, surreal
even in its intensity, as individualistic and incomparable as Betjeman had

appeared in life. Betjeman was dead, lamented the *Sunday Telegraph*, 'and has been mourned by the great writers of this country and by lovers of the countryside, old churches and old locomotives'.[16] His legacy was unique; but how would it be contemplated by future generations?

For A.L. Rowse, Betjeman's mercurial long-time Cornish friend, there was no doubt about how Sir John should be remembered and his life understood. 'John Betjeman was from his schooldays an "original"', he wrote in his portrait of the 'The Real Betjeman', an essay penned in the aftermath of the Poet Laureate's death in 1984 and first published shortly thereafter.[17] As he added, Betjeman was 'always recognised as such: there was [not], and never has been, anybody quite like him'. Indeed, he mused: 'Where on earth he came from, that personality utterly *sui generis*, heaven only knows'.[18] The appeal to heaven was apposite – Betjeman, for all his religious doubts, had in life deferred constantly to the destiny meted out by the divine 'Management' up above – and the sense of uncertainty and individualism was also spot-on. Betjeman's was an 'elusive personality', Rowse thought, 'a man of genius – all was not as meets the eye', and there was 'much ambivalence about him, much that was paradoxical, ironic, not easily penetrable … idiosyncratic'.[19]

Here was a brief character sketch that in its emphasis upon ambiguity went a long way towards delineating the essential Betjeman, as Rowse himself boasted in his essay. It was a picture that would be recognized readily by those who had met John Betjeman, or had read his work or heard him on the wireless or seen him on television. It would also put right, Rowse thought, those people 'who did not really know him, or thought they knew him, or did not know him at all'.[20] Yet Rowse also thought Betjeman an enigma. 'From what curious ancestry did John come', he asked rhetorically, contemplating Betjeman's complex background and his seemingly unique blend of traits and talents: 'where on earth did his spirit come from?'.[21] Betjeman was a fleeting 'one-off' in this world, Rowse thought – like 'the bird flying from the dark into a lighted hall and out again into the night'[22] – a singular individual who had made his home briefly on this planet, to startling effect, and then had disappeared again as mysteriously as he had arrived. It was a seductive picture, enticingly persuasive in its portrayal of Betjeman as ultimately beyond explanation. It was a conceit with which Betjeman had himself happily colluded:

> An only child, deliciously apart,
> Misunderstood and not like other boys,

Deep, dark and pitiful I saw myself
In my mind's mirror, every step I took
A fascinating study to the world.[23]

'How will future historians and critics see him?'

Michael Williams, Cornish author and publisher, also echoed Rowse's assessment. Writing in 1985 in his brief study *People and Places in Cornwall*, Williams observed that 'Sir John [Betjeman] defied neat easy classification. He was ... a considerable all-rounder: architectural critic, social historian, conservationist, short-story writer, railway enthusiast, countryman, humourist, churchman and eccentric – he was all of these – and a good deal more'.[24] And yet, as Williams admitted, it was often difficult to grasp and make sense of these kaleidoscopic and sometimes conflicting personae. There were so many sides to Betjeman, he thought, in his personality as well as in his interests, enthusiasms and obsessions. He had, as Williams put it, 'refused to live in a narrow limiting groove'.[25] And as Williams pondered this multi-faceted Betjeman, he too wondered: 'How will future historians and critics see him?'.[26]

Perhaps surprisingly, part of the answer was that John Betjeman, for all his singularity, was best understood as belonging to a wider social and literary movement, one of profound importance for the twentieth century. Despite his undoubted individual genius, and for all Rowse's insistence that he was beyond explanation, Betjeman was inescapably and emphatically a child of his times. Born in London in 1906, the young Betjeman was exposed to an intellectual climate that had been in the making since the mid-nineteenth century and was soon to reach its apogee. Put simply, this was an anti-industrialism that regretted the profound ills (as it saw them) of urban industrial society, and looked instead to the redeeming qualities of rural life and the timeless (but now threatened) characteristics of the 'real' England embedded in the countryside. Charles Dickens had exposed the 'Gradgrind' greed of smoky northern mill-towns, while William Wordsworth had offered an alternative England of dreamy romantic landscapes among the Fells and Lakes. The high-minded Celtic-Arthurian themes depicted by pre-Raphaelite painters like Edward Burne-Jones and John William Waterhouse hinted at a wider 'Celtic Twilight' revivalism, a medieval rural idyll oppositional in every way to modern industrial Englishness, while the uncomplicated back-to-the-land socialism advocated by William Morris – doyen of the Arts & Crafts movement – proposed a simpler, saner way forward for human (especially English) society. A central figure in this anti-industrial movement, William Morris had devoted himself to a life of craftsmanship and design, imagining an ideal world in which 'people lived in little communities ... and had few wants; almost no furniture for instance, and no servants, and studied ... what they really wanted'.[27]

The Edwardian England of John Betjeman's early childhood had already absorbed much of this anti-industrialism, and there was everywhere a demand for progressive change – Votes for Women (which Betjeman's mother, Bessie, espoused), Home Rule for Ireland back on the agenda with a vengeance, and the incipient challenge to Liberal Nonconformity by the new secular socialism of Labour. But industrialism was by no means dead, and there were new material advances that matched this progressive Edwardian mood. The motor-car, for example, still an unlikely and unreliable novelty at the turn of the century, was by 1910 (the year Edward VII died) an innovation of promise that opened new vistas and offered new horizons for those who could afford it. The aeroplane had also arrived.[28]

But these inventions helped make possible the greatest industrial nightmare of all – the Great War of 1914–18. To some, such as the novelist D.H. Lawrence, the war was somehow the inevitable, even logical, conclusion to the process of relentless de-humanization inherent in industrialism. Lawrence had seen the German Army exercising in the field in Bavaria before the outbreak of hostilities, and he knew at once that future conflicts would be total wars of huge destructive force. He said so in an article in the *Manchester Guardian*. This would be 'a war of machines', in which men would be 'no more than the subjective material' – cannon fodder – for the all-engulfing 'machine' of the modern battlefield.[29] Lawrence had already determined to turn his back on industrial England, and to try to construct elsewhere an alternative utopian community of like-minded souls. At first he looked to Florida for the chance to create this *Rananim*, as he called it, seeing in America a fresher, more open society. But, with a war on, he had had to settle for Cornwall instead, moving initially to Porthcothan, near Padstow in North Cornwall (not far from where the Betjeman family holidayed at much the same time), and then further down the Cornish coast to Zennor in West Penwith.[30] Although Lawrence was soon to abandon this short-lived *Rananim*, finding it insufficiently remote from England's reach and so fleeing overseas, his portrayal of Cornwall as an alternative Celtic 'other' anticipated the twentieth-century influx of those seeking a new post-industrial way of life west of the Tamar.[31]

Searching for Englishness

Nonetheless, in contrast to Lawrence's angry repudiation of England and Englishness, there were others who sought not to abandon England but rather to rediscover its essential qualities afresh. Such critics voiced disappointment and disapproval of what they saw as a jaded, over-urbanized, worn-out, war-weary England, an industrial England that had lost its way and was out of touch with its historical and cultural roots. They turned instead to the 'real' England outside the urban and industrial conglomerations, seeking solace and renewal in the countryside beyond. Here the enduring, though often forgotten, values of genuine Englishness were to be found, embodied in the sturdy men and women of country crafts and agricultural labour. It was a vision that harked back to William Morris, and after the horrors of the Great War there were many who returned to his healing prescriptions. But it was also the stuff of a new generation of writers, notably the prolific H.V. Morton, who sought to 'rediscover' the English countryside and to locate there the essence of England's national identity. Morton, and others like him, went off in literary search of this elusive but more authentic 'other' England. At first glance, it seemed like a quaint adventure, a shamelessly nostalgic journey in pursuit of forgotten villages, with their rustic 'characters' and fresh-faced milkmaids, their ancient churches and tumbled-down cottages. But behind the lyrical, whimsical prose was a serious ideological commitment, one which sought to refashion and re-found national identity firmly in the countryside.[32]

J.B. Priestley, meanwhile, had embarked on an *English Journey*.[33] This admitted the existence of other possible 'Englands', including the industrial cities from which he sprang, but, as John Baxendale has noted, 'Priestly loved the English countryside ... [and] deplored the impact upon it of nineteenth-century industrialism and twentieth-century suburbanisation'.[34] And like William Morris, he was a radical, and he too admired the skills and artistry of craftsmen and artisans, such as the Cotswold stonemasons whose buildings radiated warmth and appeared to grow naturally out of the surrounding landscape. In an article in 1926 Priestley had described a 'Toy Farm', given to a little girl for her seventh birthday, and in this essay he revealed his sophisticated view of the English countryside. In addition to the barns, haystacks, fences, trees and a wide assortment of implements and animals, there were five people in the farm set: 'and very fine people they are too'.[35] There was, Priestley explained, a man in his shirt-sleeves who 'perpetually pushes a crimson wheelbarrow', two carters — whips in hand and decked out in smocks and small round hats – 'whistling tunes that we shall never catch', and the farmer himself: 'bluff, whiskered', with his scarlet waistcoat, white cravat, green breeches and stout walking stick. And there was also his wife: 'neat and buxom in a blue bonnet, a pink gown, and snowy apron'. As Priestley observed, even though they were only two inches high, and made merely of painted tin, these characters – 'ever confident, ruddy, smiling in perpetual sunshine' – seemed 'to stare at us out of a lost Arcadia'. It was for this reason, Priestley supposed, that adults were also drawn to the toys, finding in this miniature Arcady a vision of rural England that appealed directly to their souls. As he put it, 'there are special reasons why we should find the toy farm so enchanting'. The farmer and his wife were 'the happy epitome of all farmers and their wives', he said, the jolly whistling carters 'images of an old dream of the countryside'.

But, Priestley admitted, these toys characters were 'unmistakably idealised', not 'the countrymen we know' but the product instead of 'the countryside that has always existed in our imagination, so clean, trim, lavishly coloured'. The real countryside was, for town-dwellers, that place where 'the tram-lines come to an end and the street lamps fade out', an altogether less attractive place of dirty straw, mud, manure, of the 'clumsy and endless obstetrics' of 'actual lumbering beasts', where agricultural communities struggled against the financial odds to make a living. Town-dwellers drew a veil over this reality, he said, 'in revolt against the ugly mechanical things of today', in repudiation of the 'wilderness of bricks and mortar' in which they lived. And yet, he pondered, the idealized countryside which the 'townee' sought was not merely a product of latter-day urban yearnings but reflected something far more fundamental in the human psyche. Long before there were towns and cities, he said, the countryside had been celebrated by poets who lived 'among real shepherds and dairymaids' as the source of enduring beauty and the antidote to pain and suffering. Priestley acknowledged this as an essential truth, 'from which there is no escape except into brutishness'.[36]

This profound sense of the countryside was echoed in H.V. Morton's *In Search of England*, first published in 1927, the year after Priestley's essay, when John Betjeman was just twenty-one. As Simon Jenkins has remarked, Morton fretted over 'the loss of country innocence, the decay of country values and the final triumph of the urban cosmos over what is most true to the national character'.[37] Morton saw that 'Political power is today all on the side of the cities', and that rural society was beset by financial problems: 'mortgages on farms; no fluid capital; the breaking up of famous estates'.[38] He regretted that 'Since the so-called Industrial "Revolution" ... English country life has declined, agriculture has fallen on bad times, and the village has been drained to a great extent of its social vitality'.[39] The answer, he thought, was for urban England to re-discover the countryside, to begin to understand not only the problems of rural life but also the deep-rooted contribution of the countryside to the fabric of England's 'common racial heritage', as he put it.[40] Like Priestley, he detected 'an ancient instinct', a 'deep love for the country' in urban dwellers, and in his book *In Search of England* he attempted to show his readers how they might follow their instinct and fulfil this love.[41] In doing so, he did not wish to abandon modernity altogether: indeed, the method of rediscovery was to be 'the King's highway' and 'the cheap motor-car'.[42] But he did seek a 'long-overdue interest in English history, antiquities, and topography ... a new enthusiasm' which would bring together town and country in a new harmonious relationship.[43]

Despite the underlying seriousness of his book, Morton admitted that he had 'pitched [it] in a much lighter key',[44] making it a delightful celebratory tour around England, full of telling incidents and characters, and laced with humour. But it was significant, as Simon Jenkins has observed, that Morton's first encounter on this journey was with a bowl-turner, 'a craftsman, the lover of his job, the proud creator of beautiful, common things; a voice that is now smothered by the scream of machines'.[45] Here was more than a touch of William Morris and Arts & Crafts, as there was in Morton's support for what he termed the '"Back to the Land" cry'.[46] And the further into England that Morton ventured, the more lyrical and purple became his prose. At Winchester, for example, he imagined 'the Kings of Wessex riding through a country that was not yet England; we saw the long boats of the pirates pointed to our shores; we saw Roman cities desolate on their hills. Darkness and fighting'.[47] But he also witnessed, he said, 'the monk from Rome come walking over English meadows; Saint Augustine, preaching beside pagan wells, bringing the Cross from Rome again, telling the world's greatest story to king, to noble, to common man. So the seed of all cathedrals was sown'.[48]

There was more than a sprinkling of country characters to give colour and life to Morton's story – such as the 'old man [who] tries to tell me something'[49] in Zomerset, the impenetrable dialect of the Exmoor hills – but the people encountered in his journey are not all rustics. There was a light-hearted eroticism to be found in the countryside, he suggested, in comely girls with happy smiles – some well-bred and well-dressed, like the 'county' girl en route to a point-to-point meeting who had run out of petrol

for her car. She was 'distinctly charming', Morton said, especially when she
flickered her eyes 'in a way she knew was fascinating', and she was 'neat
as a doe ... in a brown tweed costume – with speckly stockings ending in
brogues'. She wore a smart hat with a diamante arrow, 'shot by an unerring
Bond Street jeweller', and there was a 'tight string of small pearls around
her neck'. Morton gave this attractive young lady two gallons of petrol,
pretending to convince himself that he would have done so even if she had
been 'spotty, or possessed rabbit teeth or legs like a Norman nave'.[50] As he
no doubt mused, the charms of the countryside were many and varied.

'an emblem of Englishness'

In H.V. Morton's light-but-serious approach there was much that anticipated
John Betjeman's style, that 'given to guying things that he really held
seriously'[51] as Rowse was to write so perceptively. There was also much else
that Morton and Betjeman had so obviously in common: the resort to prose-
poem to evoke the beauty and heritage of the countryside, the reverence for
religious history in the landscape – the 'preaching beside pagan wells', the
saints 'telling the world's greatest story' – and the appreciation of young,
pretty, sporty country girls. Although Betjeman had been only eight years
old when the Great War had broken out in 1914, even his young life was
touched by the war: a neighbour's son had been killed at Ypres, and another
wounded. He himself had been teased and bullied on account of his 'German'
surname. 'Betjeman's a German spy', chorused his schoolboy tormentors,
'Shoot him down and let him die'.[52] Not surprisingly, then, he grew up as
part of that post-war generation susceptible to the ideas of writers such as
Priestley and Morton. Indeed, he was shortly to join their ranks.

Betjeman was to evoke the English countryside as assuredly and effortlessly
as had H.V. Morton. 'England stands for the Church of England, eccentric
incumbents, oil-lit churches, Women's Institutes', he declared, 'modest
village inns ... branch-line trains, light railways, leaning on gates and looking
across fields'.[53] Even 'Metro-land', the outer-London suburbia that he grew
to love, was endowed by Betjeman with 'country' qualities – garden suburbs
quite distinct from industrial, urban inner-cities. And like Morton he too
feared for the future of English country life and values. As Stephen Games
has observed, 'His England was in peril',[54] threatened by a fifth-column of
planners and developers who conspired to pull down beautiful old buildings
in the heart of country towns, and who would sweep away ancient hedgerows
and copses in a frenzy of new road construction. Later, in the 1960s, there

would be the assault on England's railway system, the dreaded 'Beeching Axe' which, in its shameless disregard for rural communities, would at a stroke obliterate so many of Betjeman's beloved country branch lines, with no thought for possible demographic change or potential future traffic growth, let alone the implications for England's natural and cultural heritage. Betjeman's response to these destructive forces, as Games has argued, was to offer 'an alternative vision',[55] to resort to the powerful weapon of nostalgia as he lent his support to the myriad campaigns and numerous organizations aiming to preserve the best of rural England or to avert the wanton demolition of architectural gems up and down the country. Far from being the establishment figure that many had supposed, Betjeman was often a thorn in the side of that establishment, subversive even, as he questioned and disrupted the planners and the policymakers, mobilizing popular protest against those who would ride rough-shod over public opinion.

As David Milsted has observed, John Betjeman's evocation of England and Englishness also appealed strongly to 'the English trait of nostalgia', where 'the most characteristic English patriotism is a deep loyalty to a Country of the Past', where 'the past was nearly always better' and 'Much of what we celebrate and cherish is (and always has been) perceived as going, or already gone'.[56] Moreover, Milsted added, this patriotism and its yearning for the past was 'unashamedly rural', inextricably entwined in 'a landscape and the ways of life that go with it; a landscape that has been created, and tended, and loved, by English people'.[57] In deploying 'nostalgia', Betjeman had both responded to and helped shape this English patriotism, building on the work of H.V. Morton and others, with their happy knack of making rural England accessible to even armchair travellers. But he had also tapped into a deeper vein of English national consciousness; exploiting, moulding and re-inventing it in accordance with the demands of the twentieth century. And England reciprocated. 'Sir John Betjeman is a national institution',[58] wrote Patrick Taylor Martin in 1983 – CBE in 1960, Knighted 1969, Poet Laureate in 1972 – and was 'one of those national eccentrics on whom the English dote'.[59] He was, according to Norman Vance, 'an emblem of Englishness'.[60]

There was also a strong 'practical' dimension to Betjeman's nostalgia, not only in his support for this or that canal, railway or architectural preservation society, but also in his work over several decades as journalist and architectural critic. There was too an 'intellectual' element, as the young Betjeman struggled to compose his own personal aesthetic and religious identity, attempting to locate himself within contemporary cultural shifts and trends. There was, for example, the enduring influence of William Morris

and the Arts & Crafts movement. Betjeman became a lifelong devotee of
William Morris (he was a founder member of the William Morris Society)
and remained a constant advocate of Arts & Crafts. He greatly admired
Morris' house at Kelmscott, on the upper Thames in Oxfordshire, as he told
listeners in a BBC radio broadcast in 1952.[61] Although Morris had died before
the turn of the century, the house was still full of his memories and artefacts,
not least when Betjeman visited in the 1930s and found to his delight that
Morris' daughter, May, still weaved her father's old designs, the characteristic
floral patterns of Morris' prints and papers. When, in 1934, Betjeman and
his wife Penelope rented Garrards Farm at Uffington in Berkshire, they
chose Arts & Crafts furnishings, and curtain designs by Charles Voysey.
Betjeman also applauded the influence of Arts & Crafts design in 'superior'
suburban developments, such as Bedford Park, Chiswick, laid out in 1876 by
Richard Norman Shaw 'for artistic people of moderate incomes'.[62] Here in
this aesthetic enclave, wrote Betjeman in 1960, '[W.B.] Yeats as a young man
lived with his artistic father ... [and] gentle craftsfolk survived making Celtic
jewellery in their studios'.[63] Nearby was the *Tabard Inn*, 'where supporters
of William Morris could learn of early Socialism'.[64] Likewise, Betjeman
admired the architectural and design work of Charles Rennie Mackintosh
and Charles Voysey, both with their Arts & Crafts roots, and was similarly
appreciative of Sir Edwin Lutyens – creator of the extravagant yet restrained
Castle Drogo on the Dartmoor hills – because he too had been once an Arts
& Crafts man, a devotee of essential 'Englishness'.

Early experiences at Oxford, where as an undergraduate he had attended
High Mass at Pusey House, had also pointed Betjeman towards Anglo-
Catholicism. Here was another 'nostalgia', a yearning for the sacred and
for a faith, based not on dogma or fundamentalist readings of the Gospel,
but rather on the beauty and mystery of the Mass as it was practised in
High Church Anglicanism. Ancient parish churches – or clever Victorian
imitations of England's medieval architectural treasures – were redolent of
two thousand years of Christian history, and of Christianity's rootedness
in England and the English countryside. 'The steps to truth were made by
sculptured stone', wrote Betjeman, 'Stained glass and vestments, holy-water
stoups, / Incense and crossings of myself'.[65] This was a religious affiliation
that, for Betjeman, was a natural complement to his enthusiasm for Arts &
Crafts. Much of the best of modern ecclesiastical architecture, he argued,
was in the Arts & Crafts tradition, and, moreover, created in the name
and cause of Anglo-Catholicism. Ninian Comper – then England's greatest
living church architect, as Betjeman claimed – had always insisted that 'a

church should bring you to your knees when you first enter it',[66] and that 'the first requisite' [67] in the creation of religious atmosphere in a church was a knowledge of architectural tradition and an ability to evoke a humbling sense of eternity. As Betjeman was to observe, Comper had achieved all this in a string of architectural triumphs across England, and was knighted in 1950 at the age of 86 in recognition of his accomplishments.

'Herr Doktor Professor '

As Betjeman had argued, there was embodied in Ninian Comper's Anglo-Catholicism a particular vision of England and the English spirit. Yet not all approved of Comper's architectural style or his religious sympathies, and chief among his critics was Nikolaus Pevsner, the Jewish refugee who had fled the Nazi regime, arriving in Birmingham in 1933 and thereafter carving out for himself a distinguished academic career in English art history. He went on to become Professor of History of Art at Birkbeck College (University of London) and Professor of Fine Art at Cambridge, as well as a Gold Medallist of the Royal Institute of British Architects. In 1952, in a twin attack upon Comper the church architect and Betjeman as his admirer and apologist, Pevsner dismissed perfunctorily 'those who confound aesthetic with religious emotions'.[68] It was a barb aimed at the central tenet of both men's religious and architectural convictions, and it found its mark, perpetuating an enmity between Betjeman and Pevsner that had already begun to colour their respective careers. Pevsner was the German-born émigré ('Prussian', as Betjeman incorrectly dubbed him), the 'foreigner' who had the temerity to write in intimate historical detail about every English county (whether he actually knew them intimately or not), the 'Herr Doktor Professor' [69] who, Betjeman protested, brought a humourless, dry-as-dust academic approach to what otherwise might be interesting and entertaining subjects.

There were professional rivalries and matters of conscience behind this 'Betjeman versus Pevsner' feud. But part of Betjeman's hostility lay in his own search for Englishness, and in his nagging uncertainty about his English identity. In attacking Pevsner, and in responding so woundedly to Pevsner's criticisms, Betjeman had betrayed his own insecurities. Betjeman had nailed his flag – and his conception of Englishness – firmly to the mast of William Morris; seeing in Morris, Philip Webb, Richard Norman Shaw, Charles Voysey and others of that tradition the future of 'authentic' English architecture. Pevsner, by contrast, steeped in Bauhaus and the

Continental tradition, was a devotee of the Modern. Pevsner's guides to *The Buildings of England* – those county-by-county architectural studies – became bestsellers, even finding their way onto Betjeman's bookshelves (despite his much avowed disapproval of their methods), affording Pevsner a significant place 'on the edge of an English identity',[70] as Timothy Mowl has put it. Yet Pevsner's principal aim in architectural criticism was to encourage in England the adoption of the Continental Modern Movement, and to eschew the 'vernacular' style of Voysey and the other Arts & Crafts derivatives. In this he failed. As Mowls concluded: 'It was Voysey that England would follow, not the Modern Movement: the vernacular roofs and the Tudor gables [even now] are still going up'.[71] For Betjeman, this might have been evidence enough that his vision of his England had prevailed, that his view of Englishness had triumphed over that of the 'foreigner'.

But, as always, Betjeman was more complicated than that. To begin with, Betjeman was so often racked with uncertainty. Despite the apparent constancy of his Anglo-Catholicism, and of his enduring admiration for Ninian Comper, Betjeman had wrestled with both his religious affiliations and his architectural allegiances. In the early 1930s, during his time on the staff of the *Architectural Review*, he had temporarily embraced Quakerism. In many ways the antithesis of Anglo-Catholicism, it nonetheless offered a pacifism that was attractive to many of that persuasion, those who shrank (as Betjeman did) from the recent horrors of the Great War and prayed that they might never again be repeated. At the same time, incredibly, Betjeman also appeared to waver in his architectural instincts – especially his admiration of the medieval and the Gothic, the neo-Classical and the Georgian – to advocate instead the functional 'cold steel and concrete' logic of Modernism, bowing to Continental fashion and adopting the stylistic preferences and current editorial policy of the *Archie Rev* (as it was known).[72]

Yet not even Betjeman was persuaded by this aesthetic and religious *volte face*. An unconvincing attempt to detect in the work of Richard Norman Shaw and Charles Voysey a kind of halfway-house between Arts & Crafts and Modern was soon abandoned as nonsense, while Modern itself was increasingly dismissed as 'Continental' and 'un-English' – especially as it became ever more explicitly the preserve of Nikolaus Pevsner. Likewise, Betjeman had also found himself drifting towards a contradictory and untenable 'Anglo-Catholic Quaker'-ism[73] (as Mowl has described it), and even Betjeman at his most ambivalent could not quite square his new role as Anglican churchwarden at Uffington in Berkshire with his membership of the Society of Friends. He resigned from the Quakers, and Anglo-Catholicism was restored, to his own relief. As Patrick Taylor Martin has so rightly observed, 'for Betjeman it was the Englishness of Anglo-Catholicism ... which was important'.[74] Moreover, as Dennis Brown has added, this was an ancient, elemental 'Englishness far older than the British Empire, rooted in Christian belief'.[75]

'quintessentially English and completely an outsider'

Such experiences confirmed Betjeman in his 'English' prejudices and in the 'English' pre-occupations of so much of his subsequent writing and media performances. His BBC film *A Passion for Churches*, for example, made in 1974, might just as easily have been entitled – as Greg Morse has observed wryly – *A Passion for England*.[76] Indeed, as John Betjeman became an ever more familiar household name in England, between the wars and after – with articles and book reviews in magazines and newspapers, volumes of poetry and essays, and (increasingly) wireless and television broadcasts – so, in the eyes of his countless devotees, he appeared ever more quintessentially English: in manner, outlook, humour, and in his own sentimental obsessions as well as in his many anxieties. Moreover, Betjeman was to be celebrated routinely as the most successful twentieth-century purveyor of nostalgic constructions of England and Englishness, eclipsing even H.V. Morton, evidenced in a life-time's corpus of work, and culminating in his appointment as England's Poet Laureate in 1972, a position he held until his death. As A.N. Wilson has observed, 'at some visceral level he spoke for England',[77] and 'When he died, there was a palpable sense of national loss in England'.[78]

And yet, as Wilson has also observed, 'Betjeman was both quintessentially English and completely an outsider'.[79] He was never fully confident of his English credentials, his supposedly 'Dutch' surname – anglicized from Betjemann as enmity between Britain and Germany grew – only thinly disguising his family's German origins, leading among other things to those school-boy taunts ('Betjeman's a German spy') that caused such anxiety during the Great War. He was, he decided, 'an alien' in England, though his mother rushed to reassure him that 'you're English on your mother's side' ('Thank God').[80] But, much as he loved his mother, in this as in other things he did not quite trust her judgement or opinions, and, remarkably, remained convinced that at root he was an outsider in England. When, in the early 1930s, he began courting his wife-to-be, Penelope Chetwode, his disapproving future parents-in-law dismissed him perfunctorily as 'a middle class Dutchman',[81] adding further to his uncertainty and undermining his self-esteem. It was an insecurity that, as we have seen, underpinned his later hostility to Pevsner. Betjeman had devoted his life's work to an embrace of Englishness, to acquiring an English patina through constant celebration of the best of England, and here was Pevsner, the out-and-out foreigner, attempting to do the same in short order. It was if Betjeman's cover was about to be blown, his device exposed; or at least that another 'foreigner' with no English credentials at all was intruding on his 'turf' with the shameless intention of acquiring an *ersatz* Englishness.

Paradoxically, at the same time that Betjeman deployed such prickly defence of his own 'Englishness', he also sought an alternative identity, one that might compensate for the shaky foundations (as he saw them) of his English credentials, yet still root him firmly in these islands. This was a composite 'Celtic' identity, based – as we shall see in subsequent chapters – on his 'supposedly Welsh ancestry',[82] as Bevis Hillier has called it. John Betjeman's great-grandfather had married one Mary Annie Merrick in 1830, and family tradition insisted that they were descended from the Merricks – anciently Meyricks – of Bodorgan in Anglesey, North Wales, in Betjeman's imagination the most deeply Welsh part of that country. For Betjeman, if he was not really English, then here at least was a genuine Welshness, an authentic Celticity that would allow him to claim common kinship with Wales and the wider Celtic world. He attempted to learn both the Welsh and Irish languages, and in the inter-war period spent a good deal of time travelling in Ireland (more then than he did in Cornwall), later joining the British government's representative staff in Dublin during the war itself. He also professed a deep love of the Isle of Man, adopting Manx nationalist sympathies, and was likewise enthusiastic about Scotland – especially the Highlands and Islands.

Yet, more than any other Celtic country, it was Cornwall to which Betjeman turned. Over the course of his lifetime, he developed an intense sense of 'belonging' in Cornwall, returning there most years – especially after the Second World War – sometimes with multiple visits (at Christmas or Easter, perhaps, or during the summer holidays), and sometimes for extended periods. Cornwall featured prominently in his work – in articles, poetry and broadcasts – and Cornwall was the backdrop against which significant events of his life were performed, as a child and as an adult. It was here too that he developed many of his passions and enthusiasms, not least his embrace of Cornish-Celtic revivalism and its links with a Cornish Anglo-Catholic tradition that claimed direct descent from the ancient 'Celtic Christianity' of Cornwall. Eventually, he acquired a home of his own at

Trebetherick, and it was here that he passed away in May 1984, fulfilling his wish to die in Cornwall and to be buried at his beloved St Enodoc. Only the year before, in 1983, Patrick Martin-Taylor had observed that 'Cornwall, as much as north London, was the place where he had his roots. It was, moreover, the place in which he has been happiest'.[83] Nearly a quarter of a century later, Richard Morrison could make the same point with even greater conviction. 'Betjeman might have been a child of the suburbs', he wrote in *The Times* in August 2006, in an article commemorating the century of Betjeman's birth, 'but his heart and soul lay in Cornwall'.[84]

'There is a strangeness about Cornwall'

Like D.H. Lawrence, Betjeman had looked beyond England, if not to repudiate his (wavering) Englishness then at least to secure an alternative Celticity. Here he could fashion a contingent existence, sometimes 'English' and sometimes 'not', to be deployed as the situation demanded. It was an ambiguity characteristic of Betjeman, and, whatever anxieties may have lurked beneath the surface, he managed the apparent hybridity with aplomb, moving between identities with seemingly consummate ease. If there was a contradiction between his ardent celebration of Englishness and his adoption of an alternative Celticity, then no-one seemed to mind or notice. That he chose to perform this hybridity in Cornwall was significant. Cornwall shared too his uncertain identity, moving often imperceptibly between its twin personalities: 'in England' but not 'of England'. Betjeman was keenly aware of Cornwall's paradoxical status; as, indeed, are historians and commentators today. James Vernon, for example, has mused on the 'ambivalent position of Cornwall in the English imagination, and of England in the Cornish imagination – of the Cornish as English but not English', of 'Cornwall's place on the margins of England and Englishness'.[85] More recently, Bernard Deacon has offered a more sustained analysis of Cornwall's 'unsettling' hybridity, describing 'a kind of halfway house between English county and Celtic nation', where Cornwall's Janus-like identity is the result of the colliding influence of 'two traditions' over the past millennium – one 'Celtic', the other 'English' – presenting us now with a 'post-industrial paradox': Cornwall as 'nation, region and county all wrapped in one'.[86]

   H.V. Morton had also alighted upon the puzzling uncertainties of Cornish identity, as apparent in the 1920s as they are today, and in the midst of his journey *In Search of England* found himself in a Cornwall that seemed decidedly un-English. 'There is a strangeness about Cornwall', he wrote,

'You feel it as soon as you cross Tor[point] Ferry'.[87] Cornwall might be thought part of England but the evidence was all to the contrary. When he stopped for water for his car, the woman who came to his aid 'sang her words prettily, like the Welsh do ... these people possess a fine Celtic fluency'.[88] And there was Celtic music in the very place-names, he said: 'the saints have taken root like white daisies in a field. Is there a saintlier country on earth?'. He thought not: 'St Austell, St Anthony, St Mawes, and St Ives; St Agnes, St Neot, St Pinnock, St Eval, and St Columb – they ring like a peal of bells over a meadow. And what strange saints! Cornwall was converted by the Celtic Church, England by the Roman. These names preserved on the map of Cornwall are those of holy men from Wales and Ireland'.[89]

There was more. 'A man cannot leave Cornwall without thinking a number of things', wrote Morton. 'They [the Cornish] have been all over the world in ships', he said, 'They come home on leave from mines in Canada and Australia, and from voyages of the Fleet. Half of them seem to be naval reservists'.[90] And as he left Cornwall behind, he noted how the countryside appeared to change. 'Towards Devon the rugged Cornish rocks gave way to a smoother, more comfortable countryside, a homelier, less disturbing vista of green and red fields'. He thought himself 'In England once again' as he observed a farmer 'ploughing a real Devon field', and reflected that in Cornwall he had been in 'A different country'. He remembered an old man at Tregoney who had 'told me that he was "going up to England next week", and then corrected himself and said "Plymouth"'.[91]

Here, indeed, were themes that Betjeman would make his own: Cornish saints, names that ring like 'a peal of bells', the Celtic Church and links with Wales and Ireland, the Cornish as sea-faring folk and emigrants to far-flung corners of the world, Cornwall as separate from England, Devon as different from Cornwall. In celebrating Englishness, Morton had found space for an alternative Cornishness – perhaps complementary, perhaps competing – a literary device that Betjeman would seize upon avidly and wholeheartedly. Here were the means of reconciling his personal identities – not really English, not fully Celtic – an ambiguity he shared with his adopted Cornwall, and to which he could now give expression. In many ways, the ambiguity of Cornish identity was a metaphor for Betjeman's own uncertainty and ambivalence. To that extent, Cornwall was the ideal place in which to develop his genius.

And yet, if John Betjeman was an outsider in England, then he was doubly so in Cornwall. For all his Celtic affinities, and despite his devotion to Cornwall, he remained in many respects a 'foreigner'. In 1851 Wilkie

Collins, the novelist, had observed that Cornwall was 'a county where, it must be remembered, a stranger is doubly a stranger, in relation to provincial sympathies; where the national feeling is almost entirely merged in the local feeling'. As he explained: 'a man speaks of himself as Cornish in much the same way that a Welshman speaks of himself as Welsh'.[92] Fifty years later and things had not changed. W.H. Hudson, the naturalist, described that 'remote and most un-English county of Cornwall', noting that there were few 'Englishmen in Cornwall who do not experience that antipathy or sense of separation in mind from the people they live with, and are not looked at as foreigners'.[93] Betjeman would have agreed. He was, he admitted freely, a 'foreigner' in Cornwall, just like the other well-to-do up-country 'visitors' who, in the Edwardian period when he was a small boy, had begun to take holidays or acquire second homes in picturesque Cornish locations.

'not the same as being Cornish'

A.L. Rowse, always alive to the contested boundaries of Cornishness and Englishness, poured scorn on any suggestion that Betjeman might be considered 'Cornish' – or could even become Cornish by adoption – and protested that only an idiot could possibly mistake 'Betjeman' for a Cornish name. Nonetheless, Rowse was sympathetic to Betjeman's plight, and understood from his own experience the tensions inherent in Betjeman's search for personal identity.[94] John Betjeman 'was not all that English', Rowse agreed, reflecting on those 'German' origins, even though Englishness was 'the persona he so successfully – and genuinely – projected upon the public'.[95] As Rowse recognized, drawing upon his own uncertainties and the inner conflicts of his 'Cornish' and 'not-English' identity, Betjeman 'loved England with the self-conscious passion of one who does not inwardly belong, when the purely English take that kind of thing for granted'.[96] And so it was 'with the assumption of [Betjeman's] Cornishry', said Rowse: 'Betjeman was passionately devoted to that bit of the north coast of Cornwall around Padstow, Trebetherick and Rock' but 'That is not the same thing as being Cornish, though we are grateful to him for his love of Cornwall'.[97]

Yet, like his father, Ernest Betjemann, John Betjeman yearned to press his claim upon Cornwall, to find common cause with Cornwall and the Cornish, to protest his Celtic affiliations and sympathies. When Betjeman wrote of his father's wistful longing for Cornish credentials, he was also expressing his own predicament:

> My father's sad grey eyes in gathering dusk
> Saw Roughtor and Brown Willy hide the view
> Of that bold coast-line where he was not born –
> Not born but would he had been, would he had
> More right than just the price of them to wear [98]

This is a predicament that many early twenty-first century in-migrants or second-home owners in Cornwall would still recognize, and to that extent the experience of John Betjeman stands as an exemplar of a much wider phenomenon: the intense desire of those outsiders who have 'fallen in love with Cornwall' to construct conduits of legitimacy and belonging. These might be Cornish twigs somewhere distant in a family tree, or some other long-established connection with Cornwall, or even a sense – like Marion Bowman's 'cardiac Celts' [99] – that somehow deep in one's heart one feels profoundly 'Cornish'.

The Betjemann family had long nurtured such sentiment, for even before Ernest Betjemann's Cornish holidays and his subsequent acquisition of a holiday home on the North Cornwall coast, an earlier forbear – Gilbert H. Betjemann (1840–1921) – had alighted upon Robert Stephen Hawker's famous Cornish ballad 'Trelawny', composing a cantata, 'The Song of the Western Men', for the Highbury Athenaeum. Musician-in-Ordinary to both Queen Victoria and Edward VII, Gilbert H. Betjemann was in his day a noted violinist, composer and conductor. He was a cousin of John Betjeman's grandfather, and when a small boy young John was taken to see this elderly relation in Camden Town.[100] Young Betjeman was an intensely sensitive child, in those early years forming impressions and opinions that stayed with him for life. And there was nothing more stirring – nor more memorable – than Hawker's patriotic refrain:

> And shall Trelawny live?
>   Or shall Trelawny die?
> Here's twenty-thousand Cornishmen
>   Will know the reason why! [101]

It cannot be entirely coincidental that John Betjeman developed a lasting enthusiasm and affection for the life and work of Parson Hawker (1803–1875), who was the High Church vicar of Morwenstow (on Betjeman's beloved North Cornwall coast) for forty years until his death. There was an intimate and enduring connection between this Anglo-Catholic cleric and that wild

Cornish coast, Betjeman thought, a fancy that stayed with him throughout his life. 'Stormy nights, and a sea mountains high, and the thunder on the shore, heard three miles inland – those are the times', wrote Betjeman, 'when I like to think of Parson Hawker, the Cornish mystic and poet'.[102] It was, perhaps, in his family blood, a family not-quite-English seeking the solace of the Celtic 'other', and with it a chance to 'belong'. Or, at the very least, John Betjeman had inherited his family's deep enthusiasm for Cornwall, an enthusiasm that in his lifetime was to develop into something close to an obsession, forging a relationship with Cornwall that was to become fundamental to who he was and how he imagined his destiny.

But for all the sense that the Betjemann family had, through several generations, forged its special links with Cornwall, there was for John, as he built his own relationship, the uneasy, ever-present discomfort that he was somehow 'part of the problem'. For all his celebration of things Cornish, he fretted, he was still an interloper, part of a class that was by its presence and through its activities already 'ruining' Cornwall, his own work popularizing hitherto little known Cornish spots and encouraging their despoliation through the creation of mass tourism. Again, this is a predicament that remains familiar in early twenty-first century Cornwall, where those who trumpet the charms of Cornwall run the risk of colluding in its exploitation. Once more, Betjeman's personal experience points to a wider phenomenon. Posy Simmonds, who contributed the long-running 'Tresoddit' cartoon strip to the *Guardian* newspaper, saw that this was so. Based loosely on Padstow, her 'Tresoddit' was the refuge of polytechnic lecturers and similar folk who fled the pressures of metropolitan life. As Jonathan Stedall (who in 1991 made the BBC feature film *Tresoddit for Easter*) observed, the problem was that everyone was doing the same thing. The film, he said, was 'about escape and our search for some sort of earthly paradise'. But it also concerned 'Our tendency to destroy what we love'.[103] This, exactly, was Betjeman's point.

Moreover, as John Hurst has argued, Betjeman often seemed more concerned than Cornish-born writers about the 'ruination' of Cornwall. It 'is significant', Hurst wrote, 'that Betjeman is more explicitly concerned with "the matter of Cornwall" and with what is happening to Cornwall' than were indigenous authors such as Jack Clemo or Charles Causley. For these other poets, 'Cornwall is the air they breathe, the assumed subject, rather than the concern'.[104] Betjeman, however, was prepared to confront head-on the malaise overtaking twentieth-century Cornwall, to acknowledge 'with sharp honesty'[105] his status as outsider and his personal guilt. As Alan M. Kent has added, 'Betjeman realized that he himself was causing the destruction of Cornwall'. But he also 'criticized the direction that Cornwall was being forced to move in', offering a powerful critique of contemporary Cornwall that appealed to and was shared 'by Revivalists, nationalists and environmentalists alike in the post-war period'.[106] Likewise, Betjeman's Cornish poems were 'unashamedly anti-metropolitan' in tone, Kent has argued: Betjeman 'assumed the role of an early environmental campaigner and anti-developer', expressing 'concerns which were to become increasingly to the forefront of the Cornish agenda after his death'.[107]

'"Visitors", "foreigners", we're called by the Cornish'

Confessing his personal complicity and responsibility, Betjeman had lamented: 'The visitors have come to Cornwall. "Visitors", "foreigners" we're called by the Cornish. We litter the cliffs with our houses. We litter the cliffs with our shacks. When I was a boy all this was open fields'.[108] Yet he wanted to share the wonders of Cornwall with the like-minded, those who would also be stirred to a sensitive appreciation – and perhaps defence – of place and people. In a wireless broadcast in February 1949, for example, he could not resist singing the praises of Padstow – one of his favourite places on the North Cornish coast – but in the same breath he offered his apologies to the town for spilling its precious beans: 'Farewell, Padstow! Forgive me, a stranger, for telling some of your secrets outside your little streets. I have known them and loved them so long, I want others to enjoy, as I have done, your ancientness and beauty'.[109]

Earlier, in a broadcast in May 1938, Betjeman had played cat-and-mouse with his listeners, extolling the attractions of hidden coves and picturesque harbours, though taking care not to reveal their identities too closely: 'I shan't tell you where all the lovely places are: I want them for myself. But I'll let you know where to look: between Falmouth and St Ives, between Pentire and Tintagel, and right up in the north beyond Bude where Cornwall thins out into Devon and Hartland stretches on into the Atlantic'.[110] Put like this, it sounded rather like a harmless topographical game. But beneath the fun there were, as Betjeman had pointed out already, far more serious concerns. As well as the despoliation of place, there was also the deleterious effect of intrusive mass tourism upon the indigenous Cornish. As Betjeman explained:

> fishermen have become stage fishermen, who lounge on the quay to tell
> apocryphal tales of King Arthur and John Wesley at half a crown apiece

or take out London businessmen and make them seasick at ten bob an hour ... The avariceness which is the least charming thing in simple people has been exploited [in Cornwall] to the full. It's not their fault that this has happened: it's the fault of the visitors who have corrupted and uprooted them.[111]

Earlier still, in an article in the *Architectural Review* in April 1933, he had expressed similar sentiments in even more scathing terms. These were the days when, as his daughter Candida Lycett Green has admitted, Betjeman's style was often hectoring, even belligerent, and had not yet developed the familiar mellow quality so characteristic of his later work. 'There is a clipped and bossy tone in JB's early journalism', she agrees, 'the arrogance of youth'.[112] Thus, in the *Archie Rev*, Betjeman had poured scorn on the 'average visitor [to Cornwall] who confines his tour to the coastline that has been overrun with bungalows' and to the old fishing coves where:

> The village is bedizened with orange curtains and tea-rooms; the inhabitants, with true Brythonic ability for getting money out of arty visitors who see 'the picturesque' in their squalor, have become mere play actors, and in almost every seaport in the county ... the quay is littered with 'old salts' who find yarn-spinning more profitable than fishing, while their wives make Cornish teas for the foreigners.[113]

Betjeman was dismissive of narrow-minded and unadventurous tourists, incapable of penetrating the hidden hinterland beyond the coastal settlements, and who were all too ready to exploit the Cornish, taking advantage of their poverty and their lack of modern amenities. But he also criticized the Cornish for their easy collusion, for allowing themselves to be corrupted, though he recognized that in practice they had little choice and often resented the intrusion of the 'foreigners'. At times, he was aware of the latent – and occasionally not-so-latent – hostility of the locals in Cornwall:

> 'Come away, Henry, from those common little children. They're only visitors'.

> 'Don't have anything to do with those people, Bertie – they think they own the place'.[114]

2.   St Enodoc, with its wizened spire, and the Camel estuary beyond.

'Delectable Duchy'

Betjeman was also aware that cultural alienation was the handmaiden of
environmental destruction. In a television broadcast in 1964, he considered
that 'It's hard to say whether the china clay industry [which dominated the
St Austell district] or the tourist trade, we visitors, have done more harm
to the natural beauty of Cornwall'.[115] He protested that 'You can't blame us
for coming to Cornwall' – its charms were irresistible – but he regretted
that 'Here, where St Piran brought the gospel, we ... bring our caravans
and our signs of what we call civilization, that is to say transistor sets
and sanitation for ladies'. Was this 'Civilization or barbarism', he mused,
concluding with sad resignation: '[and] does it much matter?'.[116] A few years
later, however, Betjeman was writing in more confident tone. He wondered
now whether the tourist trade was actually sustainable in the long-run. His
poem 'Delectable Duchy' was a remarkably prescient commentary on the
future of tourism in Cornwall, anticipating the important ecological debates
of the early twenty-first century. First published in 1967 in the *Cornish
Review* as 'One and All' (the Cornish motto), the poem was later re-titled

'Delectable Duchy' for its appearance in Betjeman's collection *A Nip in the Air* in 1974.[117] This new title was an ironic play on Sir Arthur Quiller-Couch's affectionate pen name for Cornwall (already much co-opted by the tourist trade), and the poem contemplated all the changes for the worst that had overtaken the area around Trebetherick and St Enodoc, the places Betjeman had known since early childhood:

> Where yonder villa hogs the sea
> Was open cliff to you and me.
> The many coloured cara's fill
> The salty marsh to Shilla Mill.
> And, foreground to the hanging wood,
> Are toilets where the cattle stood.
> The mint and meadowsweet would scent
> The brambly lane by which we went;
> Now, as we near the ocean roar,
> A smell of deep-fry haunts the shore.[118]

To such vulgarity was added the gratuitous pollution inflicted by thoughtless trippers; the ugly detritus of the careless and the lazy:

> In pools beyond the reach of tides
> The Senior Service carton glides,
> And on the sand the surf-line lisps
> With wrappings of potato crisps.
> The breakers bring with merry noise
> Tribute of broken plastic toys
> And lichened spears of blackthorn glitter
> With harvest of the August litter.

And with the eventual departure of the summer hordes, Cornwall was left breathless, fighting to regain her composure and her dignity after repeated violation, indignant that she should be taken so much for granted:

> Here in late October light
> See Cornwall, a pathetic sight,
> Raddled and put upon and tired
> And looking somewhat over-hired,
> Remembering in the autumn air

The years when she was young and fair —
Those golden and unpeopled bays,
The shadowy cliffs and sheep-worn ways,
The white unpopulated surf,
The thyme- and mushroom scented turf,
The slate-hung farms, the oil-lit chapels,
Thin elms and lemon-coloured apples —
Going and gone beyond recall
Now she is free for 'One and All'.

Just like rural England, whose imminent demise Betjeman had lamented, Cornwall too was in danger of being overwhelmed forever, a bittersweet and vengeful inundation that would at last bring humankind to account:

One day a tidal wave will break
Before the breakfasters awake
And sweep the cara's out to sea,
The oil, the tar, and you and me,
And leave in windy criss-cross motion
A waste of undulating ocean
With, jutting out, a second Scilly,
The isles of Roughtor and Brown Willy.

Betjeman was convinced that it was his own generation that had done the damage in Cornwall, and he felt his guilt keenly: 'it was not the Victorian but our own age that ruined the wild west coast with bungalows and ... littered the roadside with shacks and hoardings, [and] turned old inns into glittering pretension'.[119] However, Betjeman, defiant as ever, believed that all was not yet lost. He had a deeper faith in Cornwall and its ability to endure, a faith quite literally, as it turned out, of religious intensity and proportion. Cornwall was still, he argued, despite all those recent depredations, 'like another country within our island, as yet not quite suburbanized, not quite given over to the chain store and the farming syndicate, the local-government official and his ally in Whitehall'.[120] Cornwall was still worth fighting for, he insisted. He said so loudly, and, as he admitted — only slightly tongue-in-cheek — he was well on his way to becoming: 'Jan Trebetjeman, the celebrated Cornish nationalist'.[121]

CHAPTER TWO

'Into Betjemanland'

Imagining North Cornwall

In the summer of 1957, the publisher John Foster White wrote to John Betjeman to seek his advice about where best to stay when visiting Cornwall. By now Betjeman was in his early fifties, his Cornish enthusiasms firmly imprinted in the public mind, his reputation as something of a Cornish expert well established: 'you could not have come to a better man for advice about Cornwall',[1] he replied, with some truth. He admitted reluctantly – grudgingly, almost – that Foster White ought to see the city of Truro, Cornwall's *de facto* capital. 'Truro is rather worth staying in', he said, 'because of the cathedral and a good deal of Georgian [architecture], but it is not much of a centre – at least, it is not for me'. As he explained, Truro was really South Cornwall. Its three little rivers were tributaries of the mighty Fal, which, with its many wooded creeks, flowed southwards to the Carrick Roads and emptied into the expanse of Falmouth Haven. This landscape was too gentle, he said: 'my heart is not in those warm tree-shaded creeks of South Cornwall, but among the cliffs and slate and moors of the north coast'. This was Betjeman's North Cornwall, bounded roughly by the Camel estuary in the west, the Tamar border with Devon in the east, and the southern slopes of Bodmin Moor to the south.

Bodmin, still the *de jure* 'county town', was best avoided, Betjeman told Foster White, despite the convenience of its railway stations, 'for it is thundered through by lorries and is little more than one street'. But its North Cornwall hinterland was altogether a different matter. 'I think I would advise Padstow as a good place to stay', he decided, 'It is a beautiful railway journey from Wadebridge and there is a ferry across to Rock and my own Trebetherick'. There was other good advice too: 'Avoid Newquay, and walk along the cliffs from Padstow to Stepper Point and look down the chasm of Butter Hole, and fear will set your knees a-trembling'. Padstow was 'not exactly on the sea', Betjeman admitted, located as it was on the Camel

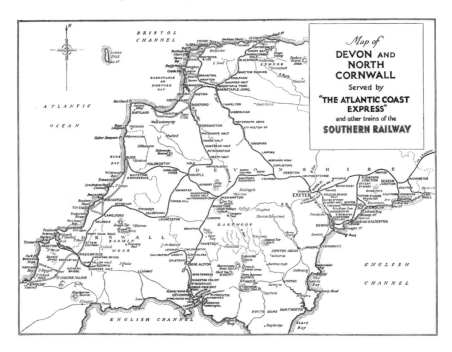

3.   The Withered Arm and the 'Route of the *ACE*' – the sprawling railway line
         into 'Betjemanland' and on to Wadebridge and Padstow.

estuary, but, he added solemnly, 'it is on the Southern Railway'. Elsewhere in
the locality there was Callington, a 'most unimportant town where nobody
ever stays', although the 'decayed port of Calstock near Callington is well
worth seeing'. Of all the towns in the district, he said, 'the most beautiful is
Launceston … and by far the most beautiful church in Cornwall is Blisland
on Bodmin Moor. You must see that'.[2]

In replying to John Foster White, Betjeman had written what amounted
almost to a mini manifesto for North Cornwall, asserting its superiority
over mild Truro-centric South Cornwall and evoking a wilder landscape
of rock-strewn moors and precipitous cliffs, punctuated here and there
with interesting or attractive towns and villages. He had also asserted a
proprietorial sense of ownership, or at least identification – it was 'my
Trebetherick' – and he had sketched the limits, more or less, of his imagined
North Cornwall: Launceston (which he always pronounced as 'Lanson',[3] in
the Cornish way) and Calstock on the Tamar, Blisland on Bodmin Moor,
and Padstow (almost) on the north coast, with Newquay altogether beyond
the pale – too developed and commercialized for Betjeman's taste, no

doubt, and also too near Truro perhaps. Additionally, he had singled out for especial praise the railway line running from Wadebridge to Padstow along the Camel estuary, and seemed rather pleased that this was the preserve of the 'Southern Railway' – or Southern Region of British Railways, as it had by then become.

'the most beautiful train journey I know'

Earlier, in February 1949, Betjeman had insisted in a radio broadcast that the 'five-and-a-half miles beside the broadening Camel to Padstow is the most beautiful train journey I know'.[4] As he explained, this was the final, triumphant stretch of the long 260-mile, six-and-a-half-hour journey from London Waterloo. This was the famous 'route of the *ACE*' – the *Atlantic Coast Express* – the Southern (formerly London and South Western) railway that crossed into Cornwall at Launceston, and continued down 'that windy single'[5] track by way of remote country stations – Egloskerry, Tresmeer, Otterham, Camelford, Delabole, Port Isaac Road and St Kew Highway – to reach the junction at Wadebridge and eventually 'the utter endedness of the line at Padstow'. He knew all these 'stations by heart', he said, 'the slate-and granite-built waiting rooms, the oil lamps and veronica bushes, the great Delabole Quarry, the little high-hedged fields; and where the smallholdings grow fewer and the fields larger and browner, I see the distant outline of Brown Willy and Rough Tor on Bodmin Moor'.[6]

Westwards, beyond the moor, 'the train goes fast downhill through high cuttings and a wooded valley', said Betjeman, and then 'We round a bend and there is the flat marsh of the Camel, there the little rows of blackish-green cottages along the river at Egloshayle and we are at Wadebridge, next stop Padstow'. After that was the glorious run along the Camel estuary. 'See it on a fine evening at high tide with golden light on the low hills', he urged, 'the heron-haunted mud coves flooded over, the sudden thunder as we cross the bridge over Little Petherick creek, the glimpses of slate roofs and a deserted jetty among spindly Cornish elms, the wide and unexpected sight of open sea at the river mouth'. And then Padstow at last, with its 'smell of fish and seaweed, the crying of gulls, the warm West Country air and the valerian growing wild on slate walls'.[7]

In its territorial extent, this railway mirrored – almost defined – Betjeman's North Cornwall, as Betjeman himself recognized. This, indeed, was 'Betjemanland', as T.W.E. Roche dubbed it in his little book *The Withered Arm*, published in 1967, a nostalgic railway enthusiast's volume that

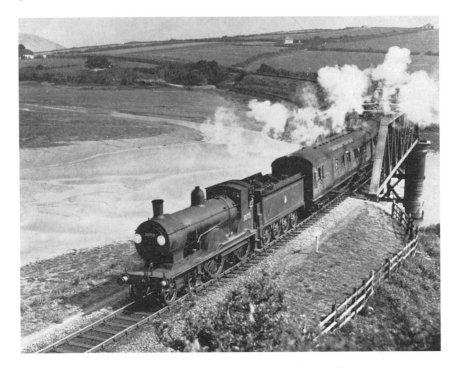

4. 'the most beautiful train journey I know'. A Southern Railway train crosses
Little Petherick bridge, alongside the Camel estuary, as it approaches Padstow and
the end of the line from Waterloo.

celebrated the former Southern Railway lines in North Cornwall and West
Devon. Known by its detractors (and affectionately by its friends) as the
'Withered Arm', this sprawling branch railway system left the Waterloo-
Exeter-Plymouth main line at Meldon junction, west of Okehampton, and
traversed the wild Devon-Cornwall borderland to Halwill Junction. There
the line divided, one branch continuing on to Bude, the other turning south-
westerly, crossing 'Into Betjemanland' (as Roche put it) at Launceston and
continuing on by the route Betjeman had described to Padstow. There was
also a short branch that ran south from Wadebridge along the Camel valley
to Bodmin, with mineral line spurs to Wenford Bridge and Ruthern Bridge
and a connection to the Great Western at Bodmin Road via the little station
of Bodmin General.

    The Withered Arm 'sought out the high places and the lonely places', said
Roche, and 'penetrated into King Arthur's land'. It was 'a railway of great
distances, whose towns were far apart and population sparse', he added.[8] It
was also a border railway:

Launceston was of course one of the most important places on the North Cornwall line, the frontier town between England and Cornwall, with a sense of division about it – here the Celtic land really began, here lush Devon was left behind and austere Cornwall lay ahead. The fact that the GWR had a terminus here accentuated this – it had reached the foreign land but could go no further.[9]

Betjeman thought so too: 'Travellers coming out of Devon ... lift up their hearts at the sight of Launceston ... the Tamar is crossed and here at last is the Duchy'.[10] Celebrating the Betjeman connection, Roche quoted (not altogether correctly) from Betjeman's verse autobiography *Summoned by Bells*, evoking the journey to Padstow made via the lonely wayside stations of North Cornwall. 'Dare one hope that Egloskerry and Tresmeer will have their nameboards preserved for posterity since their names were immortalised by Betjeman?',[11] he asked rhetorically.

Exactly what Betjeman made of Roche's booklet we cannot know: whether he was irritated by the careless misquotations, flattered by the references to his identification with North Cornwall, or charmed by Roche's elegant portrait of this far-flung railway 'where there were always green coaches proudly flaunting the legend "WATERLOO" to remind one of links with the outside world'.[12] But we do know that Betjeman was a committed railway enthusiast, if not of the 'loco-spotting' kind (with an encyclopaedic knowledge of numbers, names and classes), then certainly as an informed

5. Launceston Castle: 'Travellers ... lift up their hearts at the sight of Launceston ... the Tamar is crossed and here at last is the Duchy'.

observer conversant with railway history and architecture, and as a seasoned railway traveller with a deep love of branch lines and obscure tramways. As he himself put it, 'The study of railway stations is something like the study of churches';[13] and over the years he contributed learned articles on railway subjects to a number of magazines and journals.[14] He understood the significance of railways in the landscape, and their importance in shaping and defining local identities. He was also on friendly terms with leading writers on railway history, from whom he learned a good deal. L.T.C. Rolt, for example, author of major biographies of Trevithick, Brunel and the Stephensons, together with volumes such as *Railway Adventure* (about the restoration of the narrow-gauge Talyllyn Railway in North Wales) and *Red for Danger* (a history of railway accidents), was instrumental in persuading Betjeman to join the Talyllyn preservation society.[15] Likewise, the distinguished railway historian and artist C. Hamilton Ellis sent Betjeman a signed copy of his history of *The Midland Railway*, which was placed in his working library. 'To John Betjeman who saw beauty in sulphurous fumes, and once loved a red engine',[16] wrote Ellis affectionately in his flyleaf inscription.

Within Betjeman's library there was also a copy of *The Withered Arm*.[17] Whatever his opinion of the book, Betjeman shared Roche's informed enthusiasm for this particular railway and, like Roche, delighted in the separate identity that it lent North Cornwall, distinguishing it from the rest of Cornwall where the rival Great Western held undisputed sway. 'I like to think', he said, 'how annoying it must be to tidy-minded civil servants to have to put up with green Southern Railway engines [*sic*; he means 'carriages'] coming right into this brown-and-cream Great Western district of Cornwall'.[18] He had travelled to North Cornwall by train for family holidays, as a small child and later as an adult, the day-long journey from London part of the ritual of 'going to Cornwall', the slow progress and the continued dividing of trains at windswept junction stations west of Exeter seeming to add to the sense of penetrating a far-off land. 'Can it really be', Betjeman asked, 'That this same carriage came from Waterloo?'.[19] When he wrote his book on London railway termini, Betjeman discussed Waterloo.[20] He enthused about the suburban 'Southern Electric' network and the fast main lines to Portsmouth and Southampton. But somehow Padstow, Wadebridge and the North Cornwall had slipped from view, as though these were quite separate places divorced from the everyday life of metropolitan Waterloo, a gulf that mirrored his own sense of there being a vast chasm between the two main orbits of his existence: Cornwall and London.

'the emptying train ... that puffs out of Egloskerry to Tresmeer'

This was a gulf that reflected the uncertainties of Betjeman's personal identity – or identities – and which, when he was steeped in writing *London's Historic Railway Stations*, allowed him temporarily to forget 'the long express from Waterloo / That takes us down to Cornwall'; the 'emptying train, wind in the ventilators' that 'Puffs out of Egloskerry to Tresmeer'.[21] But when his thoughts returned to things Cornish, as they always would, he could conjure afresh distant North Cornwall and its railway, just as he had done in *Summoned by Bells*:

> On Wadebridge station what a breath of sea
> Scented the Camel valley! Cornish air,
> Soft Cornish rains, and silence after steam ...
> As out of Derry's stable came the brake
> To drag us up those long, familiar hills,
> Past haunted woods and oil-lit farms and on
> To far Trebetherick by the sounding sea.[22]

Others have recognized Betjeman's intimate connection with the 'route of the *ACE*' and the North Cornwall line. The railway author Stephen Austin, for example, reminds readers that this was 'a favourite journey of Sir John Betjeman'.[23] It was an association that Betjeman was happy to acknowledge. 'Best of all', he said in a broadcast on railways in 1940, 'I know that station [Wadebridge] in Cornwall I loved as a boy – the oil lights, the smell of seaweed floating up the estuary, the rain-washed platform and the sparkling Cornish granite and the hedges along the valleys around'.[24] He also had a particular affection for St Lawrence Platform, he insisted, an obscure halt on the western outskirts of Bodmin, on the short stretch of railway joining the Great Western mainline at Bodmin Road to the Wadebridge-Bodmin branch.[25] Sometimes, he explained, his journey to Cornwall was made on the Great Western Railway from Paddington via Exeter and Plymouth, instead of the usual Waterloo route. On such occasions, he changed at Bodmin Road station: 'A slow branch line went [from there] to the Great Western terminus at Bodmin, then backed out and stopped at a very unimportant place on a hillside called St Lawrence Platform'. Thence 'it rushed through the woody Camel valley, not stopping at oil-lit halts owned by the London and South Western, until here we were at Wadebridge at 7.51 pm'.[26]

At times, Bodmin Road (now Parkway) could be as important for Betjeman as Wadebridge station as gateway to 'his' North Cornwall. In September 1958, for example, he wrote to his friend Peggy Thomas in playful mood, regretting that pressure of work in London had required him to leave Cornwall so soon after his summer sojourn. He longed 'to live there forever', he said, and he imagined a fanciful railway idyll in which they might all find congenial employment, enabling them to stay permanently in Cornwall. 'Perhaps we could set up at Bodmin Road station', he suggested improbably, 'you in the refreshment room because of drink, Lynam [Peggy's husband] in the signal box because of administrative ability, me in the booking office because I'm literary'. Others friends would also be given appropriate tasks: 'Edward to do the lamps and odd jobs because he's so clever with his hands, Douglas to look after the down platform as head porter and Ted as outside boy, pushing trolleys to Bodmin and greeting motor cars on arrival'. And they would all work together in perfect harmony: 'We won't have a station master, as we'll be one glorious Soviet'.[27]

As T.W.E. Roche has shown, the Betjeman connection had added lustre to the North Cornwall railway system and its sense of 'difference' – the notion that the 'Betjemanland' it encompassed was somehow apart from the rest of Cornwall. It was a construction with which Betjeman was happily complicit, eager to present 'his' North Cornwall as somehow superior, and anxious to do his bit to elaborate and evoke this 'difference'. However, the Southern Railway (and its forerunner, the London and South Western) had colluded in this imagining of North Cornwall long before the district had acquired its Betjemanesque associations. It was an imagining to which Betjeman, as railway enthusiast and Cornish *aficionado*, was susceptible, and which he was to inherit and eventually make his own.

Although the London and South Western Railway (LSWR) had absorbed the existing Bodmin and Wadebridge line as early as 1846, its principal network did not cross the Tamar until later, reaching Bude in 1898 and Padstow in 1899. This newly penetrated North Cornwall, with Tintagel castle at its heart, was of course King Arthur country, as Tennyson had already made plain to the reading public in his recent and hugely popular *The Idylls of the King*. It was a potent link that the LSWR was not slow to exploit. In the early years of the Great War the LSWR produced *By the Cornish Seas and Moors: Holidays in King Arthur's Land*, a publication designed to lure visitors to the mysteries of Arthurian North Cornwall, and in 1918 it introduced the first of a new fleet of 'King Arthur Class' locomotives, built to haul its Cornish expresses westwards from Waterloo.[28] Names such

NORTH CORNWALL
BY
SOUTHERN RAILWAY

6.   John Betjeman's North Cornwall: the classic Southern Railway poster, from a
painting by Norman Wilkinson PRI entitled 'Pentire Head near Padstow'.

as *Merlin, Lyonesse, Excalibur, Pendragon, Iseult, Sir Cador of Cornwall* and, of
course, *Tintagel*, as well as *King Arthur* himself and *Queen Guinevere*, were
entirely redolent of this western land, affording a *frisson* of excitement and
anticipation in passengers as they commenced the long journey to King
Arthur's kingdom. Disappointingly, these locomotives were actually too
heavy to work over Meldon viaduct and into Cornwall itself, handing over
their trains to lesser, more anonymous engines at Exeter for the final legs
of the journey. However, in 1945 new 'West Country Class' locomotives,
with names drawn judiciously from the locality – *Launceston, Boscastle,
Camelford, Calstock, Bodmin, Wadebridge, Padstow* – were permitted to haul
their expresses all the way to Padstow, a publicity coup that precipitated
a new post-war wave of public enthusiasm for the Withered Arm and the
route of the *ACE*.[29]

The LSWR had become part of the Southern Railway in 1923, and in
1925 J.B. (later Sir John) Elliot was appointed to lead this new company's
Public Relations department. He set to with a will. The 10.00 a.m. train

from Waterloo was soon named the *North Cornwall Express*, and in July 1926 the 11.00 a.m. departure became the *Atlantic Coast Express*. Capitalizing on the positive public response to these and other initiatives, the Southern Railway commissioned S.P.B. Mais, the popular topographical writer and broadcaster, whose work had more than a hint of H.V. Morton, to produce accompanying booklets. His *Let's Get Out Here* appeared in 1936, a guide to walks from the route of the *Atlantic Coast Express*, to be followed by a volume simply entitled *ACE*, with evocative drawings by the noted Anna Zinkeisen depicting Celtic legends, like St Brannock and the Devil.[30] Such publicity insisted that 'the strangely compelling atmosphere of the Duchy begins to make itself felt almost as soon as the ATLANTIC COAST EXPRESS begins to leave the purple Tors of Dartmoor in the rear'. It was explained: 'At one moment you are in comfortable Devon with its terra-cotta warm loam, white cottages and thickly wooded coombes, all typically English, the next you are on strange soil'. Here the traveller is 'suddenly thrown back five thousand years in the British region where the successive centuries have failed to efface all trace of legend and romance. There is rich haunting music in the very place names. What play Homer and Milton, had they known of them, would have made of Tresmeer and Egloskerry'.[31]

'King Arthur is not dead!'

It was, of course, left to John Betjeman to conjure with these two place-names, soon to be made famous in *Summoned by Bells*. But, as we have seen, the Southern Railway, and the LSWR before it, had done much to construct North Cornwall as a place apart long before it became Betjemanland; apart from England but also from the rest of Cornwall. There was the Arthurian connection, felt more strongly here than in other parts of Cornwall, which fostered this sense of 'apartness'. To this was added an increasingly vibrant Cornish-Celtic revivalism which also saw North Cornwall as a special place, a remote fastness of ancient Celticity, largely untouched by modernity, industry and urbanization. Indeed, the early revivalists had made much of the Arthurian association, co-opting the notion of Arthur the once-and-future king as a metaphor for their project to invent Celtic Cornwall anew. Joseph Hambley Rowe, for example, one such revivalist – bard *Tolzethan* of the Cornish Gorsedd at its foundation in 1928 – was also a keen Arthurian. When, in September 1904, Henry Jenner had secured Cornwall's admission as a Celtic nation into the Pan-Celtic Congress, meeting that year in Caernarfon, Hambley Rowe sent him a congratulatory telegram, composed in the Cornish language. 'Tintagel byth agan cres fenten an breder!', he exclaimed, 'May Tintagel be our centre, our fountain of the brothers!', insisting on a special place for Tintagel in the pantheon of things Cornish and, indeed, in the wider Celtic world.[32]

Later, in 1930, Hambley Rowe was secretary of the Arthurian Conference, held that year in Cornwall, and he persuaded the Cornish Gorsedd to hold its bardic ceremony on 29 August, to coincide with the conference. Then as now, the assembled bards enquired imploringly: 'Where shall we find King Arthur? His place is sought in vain./ Yet dead he is not, but alive, and he shall come again'. The answer, deeply allegorical, was that 'Still Arthur watches our shore, / In guise of a Chough there flown; / His Kingdom he keeps his own, /Once King, to be King once more'. 'King Arthur is not dead!' roared the bards in response, and they swore their perpetual loyalty to 'Cornwall, our Motherland' on Excalibur, the Sword of Arthur. Cornwall, the bards sang in patriotic unison, was the 'Kingdom of King Arthur, the Saints and the Grail'.[33] It was a heady mix. It was especially so in North Cornwall, and among those smitten by its seductive power would be John Betjeman.

By the time of Betjeman's birth in 1906, the Cornish-Celtic revivalist project to re-invent Cornwall was already well underway. It was, in many ways, a response to the difficult position in which Cornwall had found itself. In the face of the decline of Cornish mining in the second half of the nineteenth-century – the collapse of copper in 1866, the faltering of tin in the 1870s and the decades thereafter – the crisis facing Cornwall was not only social and economic but also cultural. In the hey-day of Cornish mining, Cornwall's identity was founded firmly on industrial prowess, based on the sure knowledge that Cornwall led the world in deep hard-rock mining and associated steam engineering. It was a self-belief that the Cornish had taken the world over, insisting on the mining frontiers of America, Australia and elsewhere that the 'Cousin Jacks' – as they called themselves – were inherently superior in mining skills to competing ethnic groups. When, in a relatively few years, all this seemed to have fallen away, there were those – responding to the enormity of the situation in which they found themselves – who looked back over the debris of de-industrialization to a time when Cornwall was more purely 'Celtic'. This was an overwhelmingly rural Cornwall, it was argued, Cornish-speaking, and steeped in a 'Celtic Christianity' planted in the Cornish countryside by saints from Wales and Ireland and Brittany. In 1904, two years before Betjeman's birth, Henry Jenner's *Handbook of the Cornish Language* was published, firm evidence that the Revival was already taking root in Cornwall.[34]

Significantly, the large tract of North Cornwall defined by the Southern Railway system had been always, notwithstanding the massive slate quarry at Delabole (which the railway skirted closely) and the remains of old metal mines at St Teath and elsewhere, the least industrialized part of Cornwall. It lent itself easily, therefore, to the revivalist project. Much of it was moor or high wind-swept plateau, with few towns of any size. The landscape was a pattern of far-flung farmsteads and lonely churchtowns, where distances seemed considerable and where the population was sparse, the latter partly a result of rural depopulation in the mid-nineteenth century when the agricultural districts of North Cornwall experienced what was called at the time a 'Rage for Emigration' to the United States and Canada. From Padstow alone, 6,200 emigrants sailed for Canada between 1831 and 1860, to destinations such as Prince Edward Island, Quebec and Manitoba. Others went to the farming country of south-east Wisconsin in the United States, where in the 1840s and 1850s hundreds, possibly thousands, of emigrants from parishes across North Cornwall – from St Gennys, Trevalga, Poundstock, Warbstow, Laneast, Egloskerry, Tresmeer, Tremaine, Stratton and elsewhere – played their part in pushing forward the American agricultural frontier.[35] A century later, and the effects of such population loss were still plain to see, a survey by the University College of the South West (the embryonic University of Exeter) in 1947 remarking on the 'bleak, lonely areas ... where the village nucleus may consist merely of an isolated church, with perhaps a few cottages; where the parish is less of a community than a widespread powdering over the landscape of scattered farms'.[36] It was a landscape punctuated by the tall towers of those ancient churches, with their saintly Celtic dedications, and in the churchyards or in remoter spots down dark lanes or on moorland tracks were the ancient crosses and holy wells that were for the Cornish-Celtic revivalists the stuff of Celtic Cornwall. Perhaps here, more than anywhere else in Cornwall, it was possible to construct an imagined landscape of remote Celtic rurality.

Betjeman certainly thought so. 'The first whorls of the Celtic Revival had risen at Tintagel with Tennyson's *Idylls of the King*', he insisted, explaining to his readers that the 'Cornish Celtic Revivalists, poetical and artistic, took an interest in the old Cornish language which was akin to Breton and Welsh ... and in the legends of the Celtic saints'.[37] But mention of Tennyson showed that for Betjeman this was also a literary landscape, and within this imagined space he placed those figures who, for him, gave North Cornwall its particular literary identity. Alfred Lord Tennyson had first visited North Cornwall in 1848, returning several times as he absorbed the local topography and soaked up the atmosphere of the wild cliffs and seascapes, essential background work for his *The Idylls of the King*, which was finally completed in 1885. According to Betjeman, Tennyson was not just the 'greatest Victorian poet' but 'the greatest English poet who ever lived'.[38] He regretted that popular estimations of Tennyson were liable to reduce him to a stereotypical 'May Queen, the Lady of Shalott, and Guinevere standing on a craggy piece of Cornish cliff'. The 'true beauty of Tennyson', insisted Betjeman, lay in his 'description of the landscape, his lyrical qualities, his observation of the minutest forms of nature, and a sense of sky and space'.[39] And part of this beauty had been crafted in and inspired by North Cornwall: the first *Idylls* appeared in 1859, the second – *The Holy Grail and other Poems* – in 1869, *Gareth and Lynette* in 1872, and the final poem *Balin and Balan* in 1885. It was a cycle that was to have a profound effect upon Betjeman, especially, as we shall see in chapter four, in his fascination with the story of the Quest of the Holy Grail.

'When I set out for Lyonesse'

Likewise, Thomas Hardy was to be a constant source of inspiration for John Betjeman, and Hardy-esque associations littered Betjeman's imagined North Cornwall. If Tennyson had been the greatest poet, said Betjeman, then Thomas Hardy was among the first rank of novelists – certainly in the first half of the twentieth century, when there had been two really great writers of fiction in the British Isles, he thought, Hardy and James Joyce.[40] But Betjeman claimed particular affinity with Hardy because he was also a poet. Moreover, Hardy had been an architect – a profession about which, of course, Betjeman knew a great deal. And, again like Betjeman, in his personal life, as well as in his professional activities, Hardy had had his own intimate connections with North Cornwall: he met his first wife there (glimpsed as the heroine Elfride in his novel *A Pair of Blue Eyes*) and, years later, after her death, it was on that coast that he wrote some of his finest verse.

Thomas Hardy first visited North Cornwall in March 1870, making the long journey from Dorchester in his native Dorset to remote St Juliot, a few miles inland from Boscastle, where the parish church was in danger of imminent collapse. His task was to plan and then execute its restoration. During this and subsequent visits he stayed at the vicarage, where he met and fell in love with Emma Gifford, the vicar's sister-in-law. The Giffords were a Devon family but had moved to Kirland House, near Bodmin, in 1860. Helen, Emma's elder sister, married the Revd Cadell Holder, vicar of St Juliot, in 1867, and the two women then went to live at his vicarage, one as wife, the other as house-keeper.[41] Emma was a keen horsewoman, and from this remote vantage point took every opportunity to explore the hinterland on horseback, riding fearlessly on the cliff-tops to majestic Beeny Cliff, or seeking out hidden places such as Valency Valley and the waterfall of St Nectan's Kieve. Soon she knew the locality well, and on the second day of Hardy's visit drove him through Boscastle and Tintagel to inspect the slate at Penpethy quarry. During their subsequent courtship, she showed him other places – the magnificent beach at Trebarwith Strand, the castle ruins at Tintagel – and they picnicked in the Valency Valley, deliciously alone. Later, they stayed with friends at St Benet's Abbey at Lanivet, outside Bodmin, straying as far as the Luxulyan valley as they set out together to discover inland Cornwall. Emma Gifford and Thomas Hardy married in September 1874, settling in Dorset, but, alas, the early passion of their courtship did not survive the passage of the years. Eventually, they were living separate lives within the confines of their house. Yet when Emma died in November 1912, after thirty-eight years of marriage, Hardy was overcome by grief – and guilt.

In March 1913 Hardy journeyed to St Juliot, visiting again the scenes of his courtship all those years ago, and penning his remarkable collection of expiatory verse. In 1870 he had written his celebrated poem 'When I set out for Lyonesse', not published until after Emma's death, deploying the legendary Lyonesse of Arthurian lore as his metaphor for North Cornwall. It was a love poem not matched until his new 'Poems of 1912–13', as he called them, in which he poured out remorse and regret, revisiting in verse the places in North Cornwall where he and Emma had first fallen in love. In 'Beeny Cliff', for example, he remembered 'O the opal and the sapphire of that wandering western sea / And the woman riding high above with bright hair flashing free – / The woman whom I loved so, and who loyally loved me'. In another poem, 'A Dream or No', he pondered: 'Does there even a place like Saint Juliot exist? / Or a Valency Valley / With stream and leafed alley, / Or Beeny, or Bos with its flounce flinging mist?'. And in 'She opened the Door' he could reflect sadly: 'She opened the door of the West to me / With its loud sea-lashings, / And cliff-side clashings / Of waters rife with revelry'.[42]

Later, Hardy turned to drama as his medium, in 1923 publishing *The Famous Tragedy of the Queen of Cornwall*, a reworking of the ancient story of the star-crossed lovers, Tristan and Iseult, interlaced now with Arthurian imagery, where Tristan becomes Tristram and the wizard Merlin lends a hand. There are in fact two Iseults – Queen Iseult, wife of King Mark of Cornwall, and Iseult of the White Hands in Brittany – and in the complex plot of this violent tragedy, with its suicide and murder, Tristram becomes entangled with both women. As in much of Hardy's work, there is a strong autobiographical strand: Tristram is apparently Hardy, and the two Iseults were, as Kenneth Phelps has remarked, 'women intensely involved emotionally in Hardy's life'.[43] Phelps has argued convincingly that the Queen is Emma Gifford, while the second Iseult represents Florence Dugdale, Hardy's second wife whom he married in February 1914 while still in bleak despair after Emma's death.

Oddly enough, in a much earlier work, the short story 'A Mere Interlude', first published in 1885, Hardy had also examined the theme of marital discord, dwelling (as Frank Ruhrmund has put it) on the maxim 'marry in haste, repent at leisure'.[44] But this time the tale is told from the woman's (Emma's?) perspective. Once more, the location is Cornwall, although the action is moved to Penzance (Pen-zephyr) and St Mary's (St Maria's) on the Isles of Scilly (the Isles of Lyonesse), where Baptista Trewethen makes the mistake of agreeing to marry David Heddegan and subsequently learns the terrible error of her decision: 'In the long vista of future years she saw nothing but dreary drudgery ... without prospect of reward'.[45]

These amatory conflicts, played out against their Cornish backgrounds, resonated with John Betjeman, mirroring as they did the angst, guilt, and uncertainties of his own private life (see chapter six). That Hardy had wandered the cliffs of North Cornwall in 1913, deep in poetic contemplation, a mere handful of miles from where the young Betjeman holidayed with his family at much the same time, would also have struck Betjeman as remarkably apposite. Hardy and Betjeman trod the same lanes of North Cornwall, and visited the same places. At St Juliot, wrote Betjeman, displaying the intimacy of his own local knowledge, the 'fast Valency river goes under elms to the sea; the valley widens with its rounded pastoral hills. On the northern slope, with a few landward-leaning elm trees round it, is the church'.[46] Here, he added, 'Two old granite crosses guard the churchyard, one at the north and the other at the south, whence there is a wide view down the valley to the sea'. Inside the church, Betjeman noted, Hardy had had erected a wall tablet of polished granite, commemorating his first wife, Emma, and 'at this place he wrote "A Pair of Blue Eyes" and some of his best poems'. The cliff scenery of St Juliot parish was 'some of the grandest on the North coast', added Betjeman, and at 'Pentargon the Valency River falls eighty feet down a cliff face ... On a hot still day it is as Hardy shows it:

Beeny did not quiver
          Juliot grew not gray,
Thin Valency's river
          Held its wonted way.
Bos seemed not to utter
          Dimmest note of dirge,
Targan mouth a mutter
          To its creamy surge.'.[47]

Betjeman knew all the North Cornwall churches well. Charles Henderson, the Cornish antiquarian and author of the authoritative *The Cornish Church Guide*, published in 1928, thought that, at St Juliot, Hardy had performed 'an injudicious "restoration"' which had 'made the building dull'.[48] He objected especially to the 'destruction of the north transept [which] has altered the plan' of the church. Betjeman leapt to Hardy's defence, insisting that the 'effect of Hardy's interior is pleasant and Cornish'.[49] Although, in later life, an embarrassed Hardy liked to distance himself from such early 'restoration' work, Betjeman felt that his efforts were far more sympathetic than those of the notorious Victorian restorer, J.P. St Aubyn, who had dealt with neighbouring Lesnewth church 'far more violently'.[50] At St Juliot, Hardy had taken care to preserve seventeenth-century bench-ends, Betjeman noted approvingly, and in general his approach had much in common (Betjeman argued) 'with the advanced architects of his time, that is to say, Norman Shaw and Philip Webb ... and the Arts and Crafts as practised by William Morris'.[51]

'all lend strength to the legend of King Arthur'

The Arts & Crafts movement sat well in North Cornwall, Betjeman thought, and indeed many of those metropolitans of 'a more sophisticated taste, inspired by the Morris movement and a love of the simple life', had by the late nineteenth century 'found solace' among 'the rugged fishermen of Cornwall'.[52] The movement's penchant for pre-Raphaelite Arthurian themes fitted neatly with Tintagel and its supposed Arthurian affiliations, and had much in common with romantic Celtic revivalism. After the Great War, Frederick Thomas Glassock had descended on Tintagel. A partner in the custard company of Monkhouse & Glassock, he had funds enough to spare and indulged his Arthurian enthusiasms lavishly, constructing two halls dedicated to the remembrance and celebration of Arthur. The first was

built in 1930, the second in 1933. Seventy-three stained glass windows ('fit
for a cathedral'[53], as Brenda Duxbury and Michael Williams noted), all in
pre-Raphaelite style and designed by Veronica Whall (a pupil of William
Morris), depicted Arthurian themes, and a Fellowship of the Order of the
Round Table was founded to perpetuate Arthurian values and the code of
chivalry. The second hall was consecrated by the Bishop of Truro, Walter
Frere, lending it an Anglo-Catholic legitimacy, although the unexpected
death of Glassock on board the *Queen Mary* en route to America in 1934 did
much to dampen interest in his enterprise. Nonetheless, the halls survived,
as a tourist attraction and as a venue for Freemasonry.[54]

Betjeman was in two minds about Tintagel. He deplored the cheap
commercialization of 'this popularised parish',[55] as he called it, writing in
1964 that the best time to see it was 'out of season and on a stormy day'.[56]
Then the 'gift shops in the village, the more modern village and boarding
houses, and council estates, seem flimsier and more futile', he said, while 'the
car parks are mostly wind whipped ponds, the litter baskets are emptier, the
mown grass round the Ministry of Works excavations reverts to nature and
the thunder of the Atlantic is loud as the wind'. On such days, 'Even the
late Victorian bulk of King Arthur's Hotel ... looks temporary'.[57] Observed
in this way, the clutter of modern tourism was simply a veneer, beneath
which was the 'real' Tintagel of timeless grandeur and enduring significance.
It was this Tintagel that exercised its appeal for Betjeman, as it had done for
previous generations, including Tennyson, long 'before the London and South
Western railway reached Camelford in the eighteen nineties'.[58] The location
was stupendous, with its towering cliffs and raging seas, and the sense of
history was overwhelming. There were Iron Age forts and an ancient burial
barrow on the cliff tops, Betjeman reported, and – reflecting the scholarly
opinion of the time – he noted that on the island were archaeological
'remains of the cells of Celtic monks and their oratory'.[59] Here, indeed,
with its 'Celtic cells and chapels', was a 'holy island ... a sort of Lindisfarne
of Cornwall: Tintagel'.[60]

Yet more compelling still, said Betjeman, were the ruins of Tintagel castle
itself, the fortress built by the 'Norman Earls of Cornwall ... early in the
thirteenth century ... in order to keep watch on the Celts'.[61] As Betjeman
explained, it was Geoffrey of Monmouth who 'c.1150 either invented or
perpetuated the legend that the British chieftain Arthur, the hammer of
the pagan Saxons, was born here ... in the sixth century'. Ever since, he
added, 'the legend has grown', and such was its persuasive power that even
when 'a thirst for accuracy is assuaged by the excellent guide book to the

ruins produced by the Ministry of Works', one could not 'help reverting to a credulous and reverent mood'. As he put it:

> The black jagged slate of which the Norman castle is built, the loop holes for arrows, the mighty inaccessible cliffs of black slate, the way, above the tide line, the slate has been scooped by wind and rain into ridges and basins, the short wind-shorn turf, the touching remains of the early Christian cells and the ever present merciless roll of the heaving Atlantic all round hundreds of feet below and the pillars of slate above, the cliffs which look as though man had built them, the wild sweeps of shadowy cliff on either side disappearing into the horizon, all lend strength to the legend of King Arthur.[62]

Arthurian traces also peppered the countryside beyond. Near Bossiney, for instance, was the 'romantic St Nectan's Kieve', said Betjeman, which could be 'only approached on foot'.[63] Here there were 'Legends of a Celtic hermit [St Nectan] ... and Knights of the Holy Grail'. In St Breward parish, on Bodmin Moor, was the mysterious 'King Arthur's Hall', probably (said Betjeman) the creation of Bronze-Age people who 2,000 years BC built the numerous hut circles that dotted the banks of the nearby De Lank river and the slopes of Rough Tor.[64] Further up the coast, towards the Devon border, was Morwenstow, and here the Arthurian association was not so much topographical as personal – in the shape of the Revd Robert Stephen Hawker, vicar of that parish from 1834 until 1875, whose literary life as poet reached its apogee in 1864 with his 'The Quest of the Sangraal', an epic tale of Cornwall, King Arthur and the Quest of the Holy Grail.

This was the same Hawker whose 'Song of the Western Men' had been the subject of Gilbert H. Betjemann's cantata (see p. 20), and whose Anglo-Catholicism and romantic associations with the wild North Cornwall coast had already caught the imagination of young Betjeman. Along with the Revd Sabine Baring-Gould, whose writings had also enchanted the youthful Betjeman, Hawker was responsible for crafting a literary-religious vision of North Cornwall that ranged across the Arthurian tradition, Celtic Christianity, and a haunted landscape shot through with the perpetual struggle between good and evil. It was a vision, as we shall see, that was to have a profound effect upon John Betjeman, furnishing new dimensions to his imagined North Cornwall and providing the basis for his own religious belief.

CHAPTER THREE

'The oldest part of Cornwall'

Hawker, Baring-Gould
and 'Betjeman Country'

'This, in modern verse, is ... Betjeman country', wrote J.C. Trewin – the Cornish writer and critic – in 1948: 'He is freeman of Polzeath, master of Trebetherick, lord of St Enodoc'.[1] But, in Betjeman's own estimation, North Cornwall was first and foremost the domain of Robert Stephen Hawker (1803–1875) and Sabine-Baring Gould (1834–1924). It was these two High Churchmen who had sketched the religious identity of North Cornwall, with its saints and holy wells and ancient crosses, and whose meld of Anglo-Catholicism and Celtic Christianity would exercise its enduring appeal for John Betjeman. More than any other writers, Hawker and Baring-Gould inspired the imagination of young Betjeman – the former in his remote rectory deep in North Cornwall at Morwenstow, the latter at his rectory in equally remote Lew Trenchard, just across the Devon border.

So remote was Morwenstow, thought Betjeman, that it seemed 'not only the end of Cornwall, but ... the end of the world'.[2] It was a scattered parish of lonely farms, high hills and steep, wooden combes, bounded in the west by precipitous cliffs and the Atlantic ocean. The village itself was little more than an inn, a few cottages and the church. Yet everywhere, said Betjeman, were echoes of Robert Stephen Hawker. 'His strong Celtic, catholic and compassionate personality pervades this remote parish', he wrote, 'particularly its church and glebe'. On the nearby cliffs was 'the hut where he watched the Atlantic in all its moods which he described so well in his verse', and 'under a ship's figure-head in the churchyard he buried the bodies of drowned sailors: in the church itself (St Morwenna), he first introduced Harvest Festival, now popular throughout the world'.[3] In fact, the church's modern dedication, like that of the nearby holy well, was to St John the Baptist, and had been since about 1285 when it had replaced the

earlier Morwenna.[4] However, from the mid eighteenth century, there had
been attempts to revive the Morwenna association, and Hawker embraced
this re-dedication with enthusiasm. He explained that Morwenna was one of
the twenty-four saintly children of King Brychan, who had come to Cornwall
from South Wales in the sixth century or thereabouts and whose dedications
studded the North Cornwall landscape – Adwen at Advent, Clether at St
Clether, Endelienta at St Endellion, Issey at St Issey, Juliot at St Juliot and at
Lanteglos-by-Camelford, Keria at Egloskerry, Mabyn at St Mabyn, Nectan at
St Necton's Kieve, Teath at St Teath, Wenna at St Wenn. Likewise, Hawker
took care to respell the then prevailing 'Moorwinstow' as Morwenstow (or
Morwenstowe) to emphasize the Morwenna connection.[5] He also celebrated
the connection in verse. In 1836, soon after moving to Morwenstow from
his curacy in neighbouring North Tamerton, Hawker published 'The Western
Shore' (a poem he had originally entitled 'Cornwall'), with its proud
evocation of St Morwenna:

> Welcome! Wild rock and lonely shore,
> Where round my days dark seas shall roar;
> And thy gray fane, Morwenna, stand
> The beacon of the Eternal Land![6]

Reviving the cult of St Morwenna, and remembering the saintly deeds
of Brychan's many offspring, reflected the aspirations and pre-occupations
of the emerging Cornish-Celtic revivalist movement. Hawker was part of
that revival ('perhaps modern Cornwall's first nationalist',[7] in the estimation
of John Theobold), and looked unashamedly to 'Keltic Cornwall'[8] – as he
termed it – for both literary and religious inspiration. He embraced the
anti-industrialism of the Revival, and like other early revivalists looked to
pre-industrial Cornwall for models for the future. Out of step with the
utilitarian, technological, Nonconformist character of much of nineteenth-
century Cornwall, Hawker nonetheless anticipated the post-industrial search
for 'Celtic-Catholic Cornwall' that was to characterize the revivalist movement
in the late nineteenth and twentieth centuries. 'Who is to come down with
succour?', he asked, 'What angel could arrive with duties to perform for that
large Blaspheming Smithery, once a great Nation, now a forge for Railways'.[9]
Such sentiments found little support and struck few chords in Cornwall at
the height of its mining and engineering prowess. But in the rural fastness of
Morwenstow, deep in North Cornwall, early Cornish-Celtic revivalism had
planted a seed that would shortly bear fruit abundantly.

7. Robert Stephen Hawker, vicar of Morwenstow, in characteristic garb and pose.

Part of that fruit was the growing entwinement of Anglo-Catholicism with 'Celtic Christianity'. Here the Anglo-Catholic 'Tractarian' tradition in Cornwall was to become linked explicitly and inextricably with Cornish-Celtic revivalism, with Hawker an early advocate and practitioner. Taking its name from the *Tracts for Our Times*, collected and published in the 1830s by John Henry Newman, the Tractarian or Oxford Movement gave new impetus to the High Church element of the Anglican Church. There was renewed emphasis on the Catholic nature of the Church, together with an insistence that the Sacraments should be honoured more frequently and with greater reverence and ceremony. There was to be more attention to ritual and the performance of the liturgy, with more ornament and colour, and – above all – the wearing of vestments by priests. Candles, flowers on the altar, holy water, incense, and church decoration – from the Stations of the Cross to newly-erected rood screens – were all encouraged. There was more than a hint of medievalism here, of the celebration of the Church's ancient glory, including the study of the lives of the saints. In Cornwall, where Methodism had made spectacular strides in the late eighteenth and nineteenth centuries, the Anglican Church was galvanized anew by the enthusiasm of the Tractarians, shedding its erstwhile apathy and inadequacy to embrace an Anglo-Catholicism that (as H. Miles Brown has described it) moved emphatically 'in the direction of sincere religious devotion, self-sacrifice, and love of people'.[10]

Hawker was one of those moved by the new spirit abroad in Cornwall. In 1844 he was elected Dean Rural of Trigg Major in North Cornwall, and on 5 March (St Piran's Day) that year gathered his clergy together at Poundstock in that deanery, initiating a revival of rural synods, a practice that would soon become commonplace across Cornwall and Devon. In 1847 a visitor to Morwenstow noted that Hawker was wearing a chasuble (he was one of the first to revive this vestment), and at the christening of the local squire's son he was dressed in 'an alb, a purple velvet cope, and a stole said to be the exact copy of that worn by St Cuthbert'.[11] Betjeman, with his own Anglo-Catholic sympathies and his love of theatre, approved of such display, and said so. Hawker was 'an old-fashioned High Churchman', he wrote admiringly, although, as an ardent Celtic revivalist and Tractarian innovator, Hawker was also 'well in advance of his times'.[12] As Betjeman explained, 'His Church was his home ... he thought himself back in the Eternal Past and lived in the old Celtic church of Cornwall, that Church which had Christianised the western parts of these islands long before St Augustine came to Canterbury'.[13] Hawker had imagined the modern Anglican Church in Cornwall to be the direct descendent and inheritor of this 'Celtic Christianity', brought to Cornish shores by dark-age saints from Wales, Ireland and Brittany. 'To Hawker', Betjeman said, 'Morwenstowe (sic) was the shrine of St Morwenna, the Celtic saint who founded her church there'.[14]

Hawker was an eccentric much given to practical jokes, added Betjeman, such as the time when he pretended to be a mermaid, 'and dressed himself up in seaweed and little else and sat singing on the rocks at Bude and combing his hair'.[15] He went up to Oxford at the age of nineteen, shortly after marrying a bride aged forty-one. When she died aged eighty in 1863 he was devastated, although only a year later, when he was sixty, he married a Polish girl of twenty and fathered three daughters in quick succession: Morwenna (his precious saint), Rosalind (an old family name), and Juliot (after the church that Hardy was soon to restore). Hawker was also full of paradoxes. High Tory in many of his prejudices – he smiled patronisingly on those would-be Cornish emigrants to North America who imagined a classless New World where they might improve their social station[16] – he nonetheless was reputed to have voted in the Liberal interest at each election. Yet elsewhere he claimed that 'I have no Radical or Liberal tendencies in my nature ... my mind is cast in the Old Conservative mould'.[17] And although he felt keenly the gulf between his Anglo-Catholic theology and the religious (and superstitious) beliefs of the common folk of his parish, mostly Methodists, this did not prevent him, Betjeman explained, from 'giving away all the little money he had in tips and buying drink and food for his workers'.[18] Moreover, 'He was a champion of the poor people – against the rich farmers'. Betjeman recalled Hawker's hatred of the Poor Law system and the Workhouse:

> The poor have hands, and feet, and eyes – he wrote
> Flesh, and a feeling mind:
> They breathe the breath of mortal sighs
> They are of human kind.[19]

Hawker's essential humanity was also evident, Betjeman argued, in his insistence – contrary to (alleged) Cornish custom – that shipwrecked sailors be given Christian burials. When the *Caledonia* was wrecked on Vicarage Rocks in 1843, Hawker was aroused at day-break and sped to the scene in 'cassocks and slippers',[20] as Betjeman described it, running across his glebe to the cliff-top a quarter-of-a-mile away, and then descending the terrifying three-hundred feet to the beach below. He supervised the retrieval of the battered bodies and their interment in the churchyard. 'To this day you may see the wooden figurehead of the "Caledonia" in Morwenstowe churchyard', wrote Betjeman, 'over the grave of her crew'. Moreover: 'You can see too, that the really big things of life, birth and death, were ever-present with Hawker ... he lived in an atmosphere of eternity'.[21]

'From Padstow Point to Lundy Light / Is a watery grave, by day and night'

Morwenna, Juliot and all the children of Brychan had brought an everlasting Celtic Christianity to North Cornwall, Hawker believed, endowing the landscape with a Christian benevolence that was timeless and omnipresent: 'Gabriel shall beam forth and Lord Michael shine', he wrote.[22] And yet, as the constant threat of shipwrecks along that treacherous coast evidenced,

this was also a wild and dangerous country. It was Hawker who had coined
the rhyme:

> From Padstow Point to Lundy Light,
> Is a watery grave, by day and night.[23]

As Betjeman observed, Hawker imagined the stormy Atlantic in perpetual
war against that coast:

> War, 'mid the ocean and the land!
> The battlefield, Morwenna's strand,
> Where rock and ridge the bulwark keep,
> The giant warders of the deep.[24]

There were ruthless smugglers too, such as the incorrigible (even if
apocryphal) Tristram Pentire who confessed to Hawker to being 'drunk
all night and idle abed all day, cursing, swearing, fighting, gambling, lying,
and always prepared to shoot the gauger [excise man]'.[25] His marauding
smuggling gang, including the notorious Will Pooley, who was hanged
at Bodmin, and on whose grave (it was said) grass refused to grow, had
terrorised the locality even in recent times, according to Hawker.

Here, then, was another darker, more violent, Morwenstow: wrecks were
commonplace along that stormy shore, with drowned mariners routinely
washed-up on rocks and beaches, while desperate smuggling bands plumbed
new depths of depravity. Hawker also fretted at the casual immorality
he encountered in his parish, especially what he took to be the universal
unchastity of 'chapel girls'. Local humour insisted that the only virgin to
be found in Morwenstow was the female figurehead from the *Caledonia*,
and Hawker was inclined to agree. He railed against 'that father of English
fornication John Wesley',[26] and complained bitterly of 'Cornwall and Wales,
the thick places of Methodism'.[27] In these two countries the Methodists
had lured the good people away from their ancient Celtic church, with
dire results. As Hawker put it, 'John Wesley ... corrupted and degraded
the Cornish Character ... Nothing ever conceived in the Roman Catholic
church ever approached the tremendous blasphemies of Methodism'.[28] As he
admitted:

> I've no respect for Calvin's Face,
> Nor Whitefield's locks of gray,

John Wesley's Picture hath no Place
Where I kneel down to pray! [29]

For Hawker, Methodism represented a contemporary affront to the dignity of North Cornwall, the hallowed land of Celtic saints. Yet more sinister and deep-seated was a lingering pre-Christian paganism – Devil worship, ill-wishing, the evil-eye, and the like – which Hawker imagined to be ingrained in the countryside all round. As Betjeman explained, abroad in Morwenstow parish were 'evil superstitions with which Parson Hawker had to contend', and at times Hawker felt himself surrounded and besieged. 'Life was war for him', said Betjeman, 'war against the Devil, who was almost a tangible person in evil cottages where witches lived, witches who were consulted by his parishioners'.[30] It was a perpetual contest, in which there could be no let-up, and it made for an atmosphere of constant struggle and confrontation. It was no surprise, perhaps, that Parson Hawker turned eventually to opium.

'From grey Morwenna's stone to Michael's tor'

In this war between good and evil, Hawker also turned to the high allegory of Arthurianism, with its heady mix of medievalism and epic drama. For Hawker, 'Keltic' Cornwall – 'From grey Morwenna's stone to Michael's tor' [St Michael's Mount] [31], as he put it – was the central, linking strand of the King Arthur legend, with Tintagel as its focus. Following his first marriage in 1823, he and his wife Charlotte had honeymooned at Tintagel ('Dundagel', as Hawker had it), arousing his interest in the locality and its Arthurian associations. He met Tennyson during the latter's visit to Cornwall in 1848. 'We then talked about Cornwall and King Arthur',[32] Hawker recalled, the two men swapping notes and forging something of a mutual admiration society. Thereafter, Arthurian allusions peppered Hawker's work. In the 'Doom Well of St Madron', for example, first published in 1855, King Arthur tests the loyalty of Guinevere and his knights by requiring them to plunge their hands into St Madron's well. They set out, these 'Dundagel men' and 'Proud Gwennivar', passing 'Routorr side' and making for St Madron in the far west, with 'twice six knights of the stony ring, / They girded and guarded their Cornish king'. Arriving at the holy well, Arthur commands them to plunge their arms into the water: '"Now off with your gauntlets", King Arthur cried, / "And glory or shame for our Tamar side".' Sir Gauvain (*sic*), Sir Lancelot, Sir Kay and the others do as they are bid, with no visible result, but when it is Sir Mordred's turn, the waters 'bubbled and boiled like a cauldron of hell'. Here Mordred is revealed as 'Sir Judas'.[33] Here was affirmation of the mystic qualities of Celtic Christianity, with its saints and holy wells, and here too was the perpetual struggle between good and evil – personified in the revelation of Mordred's treachery, that central tenet of the Arthurian story.

When Charlotte died in 1863, Hawker in his grief embarked upon his greatest work, 'The Quest of the Sangraal', conceived as a memorial to her life and in remembrance of those days long ago when they had lodged for a month at Tintagel. Ever since, he explained, he had nurtured the idea of writing a great Arthurian epic, and now the moment had arrived. It was to be about the Sangraal – the Holy Grail – first brought to Glastonbury by Joseph of Arimathea but lost 'when the land became sinful'. Then, said Hawker, a 'search for it was proclaimed at Dundagel by King Arthur to his Knights of the Round Table'. It was a Quest full of Christian symbolism: 'The Sangraal has always been regarded as the type of the gospel', argued Hawker, 'and the loss and recovery are emblems of the failure of our light and its restoration'.[34] In Hawker's poem, it is Merlin who prophesies the Quest and Arthur's destiny:

> 'All gone! But not for ever: on a day
> There shall arise a king from Keltic loins
> Of mystic birth and name, tender and true;
> His vassals shall be noble, to a man:
> Knights strong in battle till the war is won:
> Then while the land is husht on Tamar side,
> So that warder upon Carradon
> Shall hear at once the river and the sea –
> That king shall call a Quest: a kindling cry:
> 'Ho! For the Sangraal! Vanished Vase of God'''.[35]

For Betjeman, 'The Quest of the Sangraal' brought together in brilliant synthesis all that he admired in Hawker's life and work, not least his literary-religious imaginings of North Cornwall. As Betjeman explained in a BBC broadcast in October 1945, 'Hawker's angels, his faith, and the ancient Celtic church of which he was a member are expressed in that magnificent poem of his about the Holy Grail, the Cup which Our Lord used at the Last Supper'.[36] It was a poem 'about King Arthur and Tintagel, just like Tennyson's *Idylls of the King*'. But there was also a remarkable admission. For all his admiration of Tennyson, Betjeman considered that 'The Quest of the Sangraal' was the superior work. 'Much as I revere Tennyson', he confessed, 'I feel that on this theme Hawker was the finer poet – and small wonder for Tennyson's theology was so liberal that his Belief was as vague as Hawker's was sacramental and defined'.[37] Interestingly, Tennyson had agreed that 'Hawker has beaten me on my home ground'.[38] But Betjeman's judgement was not purely on literary merit, for he recognized – and empathized with and approved – that entwinement of Anglo-Catholicism and Celtic Christianity that had underpinned all of Hawker's work.

Sabine Baring-Gould – squarson of Lew Trenchard

Hawker had not actually been born in Cornwall. For all his immersion in and championship of Cornish themes, and for all his proprietorial sense of 'belonging' in Morwenstow, he actually hailed from Plymouth, across the Devon border, and had been baptised at neighbouring Stoke Damarel. Hawker never claimed to be Cornish, and in a sense he never had to – for his allegiances, loyalties, affections and personal identities were plain for all to see. Betjeman no doubt took comfort from this; an 'outsider' who also hoped to acquire 'insider' credentials, just as Hawker had done. Likewise, Betjeman was drawn to the Revd Sabine Baring-Gould, another of those early Celtic revivalists and 'a thorough Tractarian, an old-fashioned High Churchman'[39] (as Betjeman put it), who was not Cornish-born and yet developed an intense passion for Cornwall and things Cornish. In fact, Baring-Gould had been born in Exeter of an old Devon family and, although he had spent part of his early childhood at Bratton Clovelly and at Tavistock, both close to the Cornish border, he had for the most part grown up overseas, travelling in continental Europe with his parents. Graduating from Cambridge in 1860, he became curate at Horbury Brig in Yorkshire in 1864, moving to East Mersea in Essex in 1871, and returning finally to his native Devon in 1881 where, inheriting his family estates, he became 'squarson' – squire and parson – of Lew Trenchard, a tiny village and parish a few miles from the Cornish border.

Acutely aware of the proximity of Cornwall, Baring-Gould imagined his part of Devon as almost an extension of North Cornwall – as well he might; Launceston and the Tamar were but a short distance away, while Lew Trenchard, tucked in against the western slopes of Dartmoor, was cut off from the rest of Devon by the great expanse of moorland heights. In the Prayer Book Rebellion of 1549 and in the Civil War, the Dartmoor tinners

8. Sabine Baring-Gould, squarson of Lew Trenchard, in middle age.

of that locality had shown more in common with the neighbouring Cornish than with their compatriots in the rest of Devon. After all, Dartmoor was part of the territory of the Duchy of Cornwall, and the Dartmoor tinners were subject to the peculiar laws and customs of their Stannaries, an echo of the Stannary Law and Parliament that exercised similar authority west of the Tamar. The rise of the Bible Christian denomination (a Methodist sect) in the North Cornwall-West Devon border district after 1815 had perpetuated this sense of 'greater Cornwall', notwithstanding the objections of Parson Hawker, as had the spread of copper mining from Cornwall across the Tamar to the district around Tavistock in the mid-nineteenth century. Later, when the Diocese of Truro was created in 1877, several Devon parishes east of the Tamar were included in this new Cornish see. In many ways, Devonshire was a marcher county, a borderland between 'Celtic' Cornwall in the west and lowland England in the east. Baring-Gould certainly thought so, and he imagined that this was reflected in the ethnic composition of the local population. 'In my own county of Devon', he explained, 'we have on one side of Dartmoor a people ... [who] are more than half Celts'. This was the western side, of course, and applied especially to Lew Trenchard, where in the veins of these vigorous 'half Celts' a 'volatile sparking ichor exists to a good extent'. In marked contrast, he said, 'on the other side of the moor the population is heavy, unimaginative, and prosaic – the dreadfully dull Saxon prevails there'.[40]

Betjeman may not have shared this racial stereotyping. But he certainly felt the transition from lowland England to Celtic Cornwall that seemed to take place as the train skirted the Dartmoor tors west of Okehampton, or as the car sped towards the Tamar, the countryside somehow taking on a sterner face, cob and thatch giving way to granite and slate. For all his insistence that Cornwall 'is separated from England by the picturesque Tamar Valley',[41] he too felt that there was a debatable land east of the river, not exactly Cornwall but not 'proper' Devon either. 'Somehow Devon in my mind is associated most kindly with the softer, less granite-hewn parts of it', he wrote, those areas east and south of Dartmoor where 'very green grass' complemented the rich red soil, a 'sunny colouring', as he put it, which 'makes people love the face of Devon'.[42] Yet Betjeman also admired the austere, grey churches of Dartmoor and western Devon. 'I find the granite churches of the Dartmoor district as impressive, rude and small as they are, as some graceful lace-like cathedral made of softer stone',[43] he wrote, expressing his incredulity that anyone would have the inclination let alone skill to carve this notoriously hard and difficult stone.

Among these churches was Sabine Baring-Gould's Lew Trenchard. 'Lew Trenchard is a wooded kingdom on the western edge of Dartmoor', Betjeman explained, and 'the loveliest thing in the village is the church of St Petroc'.[44] He thought it 'almost overwhelming in its beauty'. It was only 'a small building', he admitted, 'But when you open the door the full glory of a great rich Devonshire screen bursts upon you. Encrusted with saints and vines and leaves, it cuts across the whole church and through it you may glimpse the altar and monuments'. It was, indeed, a memorial to Baring-Gould's Anglo-Catholic tastes and to his profound sense of vocation in that district. As Betjeman recalled, Baring-Gould had always admitted his mission in life: 'I felt that I had work to do, not like that of Newman in England at large, but at Lew Trenchard the small'.[45]

St Petroc, as Betjeman knew, was chief among Cornish saints (along with St Piran), and was especially associated with North Cornwall. Padstow was anciently Petrockstowe, and Trebetherick itself was named after the saint. Bodmin, with the largest parish church in Cornwall, was also dedicated to St Petroc, as was Little Petherick near Wadebridge, that 'shrine of Anglo-Catholicism'[46] as Betjeman called it, its interior by none other than Ninian Comper. Sometimes, as Betjeman also knew, such dedications had spilled across the Tamar into neighbouring parts of Devon, such as at that other

Petrockstowe, a small wayside halt on the lonely branch line from Halwill
Junction to Torrington. Lew Trenchard was another example, Betjeman
imagined, but here he was mistaken. The modern dedication, from about
1742, was to St Peter but (rather like Hawker and St Morwenna), Baring-
Gould had detected an earlier Celtic connection, or so he said.[47] The
adoption of St Petroc as patron, and the commissioning by Baring-Gould
of rood screed paintings of Celtic saints – Itha, Rumon, Urith, Samson,
Geraint, Nona, David, Bridget, Paddern, Cuby, and of course Petroc – was
part of his strategy to 're-Celticize' the church at Lew Trenchard.[48] But in
reality there was little or no evidence to substantiate this earlier dedication,
and it appears that in this as in much else Baring-Gould had used his vivid
imagination to make it up.

Betjeman had been caught out, but he should have known better. He,
more than anyone, knew that Baring-Gould was notoriously unreliable.
Baring-Gould had written a biography of Hawker, *The Vicar of Morwenstow*,
first published in 1876, which was full of error and invention, and he had
produced a monumental 16-volume *Lives of the Saints* that, with its sloppy
and sometimes false scholarship, had infuriated serious hagiographers and
antiquarians. Yet, as Betjeman acknowledged, there was a compelling
quality in much of Baring-Gould's writing, an ability to captivate, inspire
and enthuse. His books were eminently readable, Betjeman said, and 'must
have been the inspiration of many young children and nourished the first
love and pride in Devon and Cornwall that those children remember. I was
one such child'.[49] It was fashionable now for scholars to look down upon
Baring-Gould, he added, but 'I suspect that many of those archaeologists and
historians who despise him today took up their careers on account of Baring-
Gould's enthusiasm'. At any rate, Betjeman was happy to acknowledge that
it was his 'books of antiquarian lore ... [that] first stirred me to marvel at
rough pieces of granite, hewn centuries ago, seen lying in tamarisk-sheltered
churchyards or in similar manner on Bodmin Moor'. It was 'Baring-Gould
who brought to life for me the strange-named saints of little holy wells. He
peopled high Cornish lanes with ghosts and hinted at curses and tragedy
round some sheltered, feather-grey slate manor house of Elizabeth I's time,
now a decrepit-looking farm'.[50]

Among those irritated by Baring-Gould's sometimes extravagant flights
of fancy was the Revd Gilbert Hunter Doble. Made a bard of the Cornish
Gorsedd at its inception in 1928, taking the bardic name *Gwas Gwendron*
(Servant of Wendron), Canon Doble was a noted Celtic hagiographer. He
produced an impressive series of studies of the lives of Cornish saints,

focussing especially on their links with the other Celtic lands, particularly
Wales and Brittany. In a radio broadcast in July 1949 Betjeman dwelt on
those 'Strange and sweet-sounding saints of Cornwall'.[51] He deferred to
Doble's superior scholarship in such matters but not without first recording
his indebtedness to Baring-Gould. 'The late Revd S. Baring-Gould, the
most readable and enjoyable writer on the Celtic Church is, alas!, regarded
as unreliable', he said regretfully, though adding swiftly that 'To him I owe
all my early enthusiasm'. But for authenticity, he said, he turned to 'The
late Canon Doble, a scholar who did more than any man to find out about
Cornish saints, [and who] wrote mainly for scholars ... If a wireless talk can
be dedicated to anyone's memory, this should be to that of Canon Doble,
vicar of Wendron'.[52]

In the Roar of the Sea

Half-a-dozen or so years later, Betjeman was asked to write an 'Introduction'
to *Onward Christian Soldier: A Life of Sabine Baring-Gould*. This was a biography
by William Purcell, an Anglican clergyman now involved in religious writing
and broadcasting, occupations that had endeared him to Betjeman. As before,
Betjeman dwelt on the twin characteristics of Baring-Gould's work: its
sheer attractiveness, and its dubious reputation. As he explained, when he
was a boy in North Cornwall forty years before, it was impossible not to
have heard of Baring-Gould. From folk-lore and folk-song to archaeology,
hagiology, theology, antiquities and much more, Baring-Gould had always had
something to say, and his was then a household name in Cornwall. He 'was
a born story-teller and popularizer', said Betjeman, 'who enjoyed making
entertaining what others made dull'.[53] And yet, as Betjeman admitted, 'Such
a man, so readable and simple, is bound to have his detractors'. Baring-Gould
had his set his novel *In the Roar of the Sea* (about the legendary smuggler,
Cruel Coppinger) in the area that the young Betjeman knew best, around
Polzeath and St Enodoc. Although admitting that it was by no means the
best of Baring-Gould's fiction, Betjeman insisted that it had 'that quality
of all his novels, remarkable narrative power', and that no-one who had
started to read the book would 'put it down unfinished'. The book was still
in print, he said, 'for the summer reading of visitors to the north coast of
Cornwall', although literary critics and local historians combined to dismiss
it 'as romantic piffle'. Even he, he admitted, had had his 'own faint doubts
as to the authenticity of the tale when first I read it'. To begin with, 'there
was no cottage-like vicarage with roses round the door near St Enodoc,

and Pentire Glaze farm, which was pointed out to me as the home of Cruel Coppinger, did not seem to me to be as old or imposing as the novel had led me to expect'. As Betjeman concluded, it was 'only too likely, as Canon Doble suspected, that Baring-Gould, when stumped for a legend ... would invent one on the very slenderest evidence'.[54]

Betjeman forgave Baring-Gould his shortcomings: 'However inaccurate he may be, he loves the stories he tells and the places he describes'. Moreover, Betjeman recognized the powerful influence that Baring-Gould had had on his own imaginings of North Cornwall: 'I am far more indebted to him for a romantic sense of place and local legend than I am to any other writer'.[55] *Cornwall*, the second volume of Baring-Gould's *A Book of the West*, first published in 1899, had provided the eager young Betjeman and his 'enquiring turn of mind'[56] (as he put it) with a wealth of such material. Along the river Inny, for example, were the chapel and holy well of St Clether, both sixteenth century but 'kindly restored'[57] (as Betjeman noted) by Baring-Gould in 1895. Baring-Gould had spun a captivating tale about this sequestered spot, explaining in great detail how St Clether had come from Wales to help tackle 'the God-forsaken condition of North Cornwall'.[58] It was a story that Betjeman remembered fondly; and he thought the hidden, wooded valley of the Inny among the 'remotest and loveliest'[59] in all Cornwall. There was much else to engage young Betjeman. Hawker, for example, had described the twenty-four children of King Brychan. But Baring-Gould said that Welsh genealogists had counted no fewer than forty-nine offspring from this 'much-wived man', while 'the Irish, the Cornish, and the Bretons attribute to him several more'.[60] Again, Betjeman was enchanted by this extravagant tale: years later, King Brychan and his 'sainted children'[61] were duly found a place in *Summoned by Bells*.

Similarly enthralling, Betjeman thought, were Baring-Gould's tales of St Petroc. According to Baring-Gould, Petroc was one of those many saints who had come to North Cornwall from South Wales, forsaking his native Gwent and landing at Padstow. He remained there for thirty years, before embarking upon a pilgrimage to the East, visiting India and other distant lands. Eventually, he returned to Cornwall, settling now at Bodmin, where he founded his monastery, and it was from there, Baring-Gould explained, that he had embarked on his 'many excursions through Devon'.[62] In his wanderings, St Petroc had been attended by a faithful wolf. The wolf had been a guard for Petroc's sheepskin and his staff. But it was not a fierce or dangerous animal. Rather, like St Francis of Assisi, St Petroc had a special way with wild animals and birds, and they were drawn to him. Creatures that

9. St Clether chapel and holy well – restored by Baring-Gould and admired by Betjeman.

were in nature predators or prey followed him peacefully and harmoniously as he moved about Cornwall and Devon proclaiming the Word of God. It was a tale that appealed to the pacifism in Betjeman's make-up. 'The Celtic Church tinkled in Cornwall with the bells of its saints expecting Christ at any moment', explained Betjeman, and 'the greatest of your number [was] Holy Petroc Abbot and Confessor'. 'Here on Bodmin Moor', he added, 'it would be no shock to see the bearded form of Petroc, with stags, poultry, and wolves following him; not bothering to eat one another, for devotion to the saint'.[63]

Baring-Gould's eccentricity also appealed to Betjeman. 'He enjoyed embroidering on stories and inventing others', he said: 'He researched into the past in the way he did, because he enjoyed doing it, not because he thought it was the scientifically correct way'.[64] Moreover, there was an audacious side to Baring-Gould that was especially attractive, a contempt for 'planners' and unimaginative authority. 'What local council', asked Betjeman more than half-admiringly, 'would allow a squire to-day to rebuild his house in Rhenish style as did Baring-Gould in his parish of Lew Trenchard, Devon. What vicar and Diocesan Advisory Committee would allow a squarson to remove tablets from other churches and put them up in his own, as Baring-Gould did at Lew?'.[65] Additionally, Betjeman was captivated by the story of Baring-Gould's marriage to Grace Taylor, the Yorkshire mill girl whom he had met and fallen in love with in 1864, when he was thirty years old and she a mere sixteen. Betjeman said that Baring-Gould had chosen her as the most comely and fecund-looking of all the local girls. At any rate, the marriage lasted for forty-eight years, until Grace's death, and she bore fifteen children, of whom all but one survived into adulthood. All the more remarkable was the fact that Baring-Gould, *Pygmalion*-like, had arranged for Grace to be taught good manners and to speak 'correctly' before the marriage was contracted. As Betjeman exclaimed in astonishment: 'What curate in an industrial parish in the North to-day would dare to single out a sturdy mill girl and have her sent to a place where she could learn to speak in educated manner and then marry her?'.[66]

In his day, before the sneering of 'hagiologists with a superior smile' and 'modern archaeologists with their horn-rimmed intensity'[67] (as Betjeman described them), Baring-Gould had been a popular figure in Cornwall. In 1897 he was elected President of the Royal Institution of Cornwall, serving for ten years, and in 1902 he was awarded the Institution's prestigious Henwood Medal for his two Presidential addresses, one about the 'Early History of Cornwall' and the other on 'Celtic Saints'.[68] It was this reputation that had first caught the attention of young Betjeman, drawing him towards *In the Roar of the Sea* and other works, and helping to mould his own imagined North Cornwall. As Simon Trezise put it: 'John Betjeman learned how to put Cornwall into verse and prose with the help of Sabine Baring-Gould'.[69] Yet this influence was not merely literary. There was also an equally important spiritual dimension. Here Baring-Gould's 'teaching of the Catholic Faith as practised in the Church in this country'[70] (as Betjeman expressed it), had offered a seductive blend of Anglo-Catholicism and Celtic Christianity, just as Hawker had done. It was, moreover, a faith rooted in Betjeman's own imagined North Cornwall.

Cruel Coppinger and 'the most terrible men on the Cornish coast'

Significantly, Baring-Gould, again like Hawker, had seen both 'good' and 'evil' in that North Cornwall landscape, and in his writings had played out the struggle between these two opposing forces in a manner that impressed Betjeman. It was Hawker who had first alerted Baring-Gould to the story of Cruel Coppinger, and Baring-Gould liked to imagine a wild north Cornish coast, populated until recent times by ruthless wreckers and smugglers, Godless characters who struck fear into the hearts of all the people thereabouts. In his novel *In the Roar of the Sea* he had, as Betjeman noted, relocated the story of Cruel Coppinger to the area around St Enodoc and the Camel estuary. In its original telling, which Baring-Gould repeated in *The Vicar of Morwenstow* and in *Cornwall*, Coppinger operated from his house further up the coast at Welcombe, near Morwenstow. He also had a base at Roscoff, in Brittany, it was said, from which he ran his cross-channel contraband business. A stranger from foreign parts, he had arrived by sea in North Cornwall in the midst of a raging storm, and had very soon become, said Baring-Gould, 'One of the most terrible men on the Cornish coast, remembered by his evil repute'.[71] Indeed, the 'terror linked with Coppinger's name throughout the coast was so extreme that the people themselves, wild and lawless as they were, submitted to his sway'.[72] There were still those alive, said Baring-Gould, who remembered Coppinger's poor ill-used wife, an heiress whom Coppinger had abused and degraded and 'thrashed with a rope till she consented to make over her little fortune to his exclusive use'.[73]

Coppinger was a semi-legendary figure, half story-book character and half real-life, who, in the oft-repeated tales of his outrageous behaviour, had come to epitomize the erstwhile smuggling, wrecking type. Baring-Gould claimed to have encountered others just like him in that vicinity, men larger than life who had spent their days operating largely beyond the law. 'I remember, as a boy', he said, 'an evil-faced old man, his complexion flaming red and his hair very white'. He 'kept a small tavern not in the best repute' and 'had been a smuggler in his day, and a wild one too'.[74] And then there were the wreckers. 'I remember an old fellow', wrote Baring-Gould, 'the last of the Cornish wreckers'.[75] Although he would never admit to having deliberately lured ships onto the rocks, this fellow confessed that wrecks were a welcome occurrence on the North Cornwall coast in his time, with the inhabitants from miles around gathering anxiously to plunder what they could from any vessel that had had the misfortune to come to grief on Cornish shores.

Ghosts, such as the infamous spectre at Botathen, near Launceston, manifestations of the Devil himself – as in his appearance at Bridgerule, where he attempted the abduction of a widow's beautiful daughter – and other tales of the mysterious and the occult, were sprinkled through Baring-Gould's work.[76] Fondly and romantically told, with an engaging style that absorbed the reader, there was nonetheless a lingering sense of evil, of menace and malevolence. And the landscape he described was itself sometimes malign: not only the all too obvious perils of sheer, precipitous cliffs but also the hidden dangers of the moors, where the unwary traveller might easily be ensnared. He recounted his own alarming experience at Redmire on Bodmin Moor, where he had become hopelessly lost one dark night and was almost sucked down into the bog, and he warned against the 'morass' of Trewartha Marsh, adding too that 'Crowdy [mire] is particularly ugly and dangerous'.[77]

Baring-Gould also shared Hawker's regret that the Methodists had become so entrenched in Cornwall. He mourned the passing of the old Cornish-language miracle plays, he said, such as that of 'St Meriadoc' (*Beunans Meriasek*, the 'Life of St Meriasek'), which had been performed in outdoor playing-places across Cornwall since medieval times. Forgetting that these plays had fallen victim of the Reformation and its aftermath in the sixteenth and early seventeenth centuries, Baring-Gould insisted that 'These dramatical performances were in full vigour when John Wesley preached in Cornwall'.[78] Alas, he said, 'The Cornish people became Methodists, and play-going became sinful', with *Beunans Meriasek* and the other dramas swiftly abandoned and soon forgotten thereafter, to the detriment of Cornwall's linguistic, literary and religious heritage.

'It was a welcome to Cornwall'

John Betjeman, for all his Anglo-Catholic enthusiasms and his eager embrace of Celtic Christianity, did not share these increasingly out-dated religious prejudices. On the contrary, he had more than a sneaking regard for 'Dissent' – evidenced, for example, in his temporary flirtation with Quakerism (and also, briefly, Lady Huntingdon's Connexion), and in his discerning admiration for at least some Nonconformist architecture. He was keen to see Methodism as complementary, even integral, to the fundamentally Christian landscape of North Cornwall, rather than in any way oppositional. But, he acknowledged, this was essentially a hidden, mysterious landscape, difficult to interpret and hard to understand. It was a landscape of varying mood, and, in Betjeman's own imagination, it was also by turns benign and light, dark and sinister. It was an estimation that reflected the powerful constructions of both Robert Stephen Hawker and Sabine Baring-Gould who, with their persuasive portrayals of the perpetual struggle between good and evil, had deeply impressed Betjeman. But it was too a dichotomy that undoubtedly reflected his own complex personality – light-hearted and optimistic one minute, gloomy and pessimistic the next – one that mirrored in the North Cornwall landscape his innermost struggles, especially those of religious faith and of his need to 'belong'.

In its smiling, welcoming guise, Betjeman believed, North Cornwall was a fastness of Christian goodness, with its 'little valleys where there are old churches and the wells of Celtic saints who lived 1,400 years ago ... the land is soaked in Christianity'.[79] But alongside those timeless Celtic saints – Morwenna, Petroc, and all the children of Brychan – who had filled the land with Christian blessings when southern England was still pagan, there were, as Betjeman was keen to acknowledge, the more recent adherents of John Wesley's faith. These, as Betjeman described in *Summoned by Bells*, were the local Cornish families, those who inhabited the scattered farms and hamlets of the locality. '[C]linging farms/ Hold Bible Christians',[80] he wrote approvingly, referring to the Methodist sect that had emerged in the North Cornwall-Devon border country in the early nineteenth century, just after the Napoleonic wars. Theirs was a simple piety, he thought, and the unquestioning, unshakeable faith of these good country folk also seemed to saturate the landscape with Christian benevolence. But alongside the recent, plain Nonconformist chapels of these Bible Christians were those ancient medieval churches, the real evidences of 'Celtic Cornwall' and the rootedness of Christianity in the countryside. For Betjeman, their foursquare Cornish towers were visible beacons of hope in the landscape. 'Lin-Lan-Lone' rang their cheery bells, said Betjeman, echoing Tennyson.[81] He knew them all, of course – St Mabyn, St Issey, St Kew, and the rest – but his favourite was St Endellion. 'St Endellion! St Endellion! The name is like a ring of bells',[82] he wrote, echoing the peals that rang so reassuringly across the North Cornwall landscape.

Late one summer evening, Betjeman explained, he had arrived in Cornwall by motor car, the road becoming increasingly familiar, with gaps in 'the high fern-stuffed hedges' now and again showing 'sudden glimpses of the sea ... Port Isaac Bay with its sweep of shadowy cliffs stretched all along to Tintagel'.[83] He passed the old 'granite manor house of Tresungers with its tower and battlements', and as he neared St Endellion church he heard the bells, with 'their sweet tone', being rung for practice. 'It was a welcome to Cornwall', he felt, and he remembered the benevolent words of the Ringer's rhyme painted on a board in the belltower:

> Let's all in love and Friendship hither come
> Whilst the shrill treble calls to thundering Tom
> And since bells are for modest recreation
> Let's rise and ring and fall to admiration.[84]

This was warm, safe, benign North Cornwall.

There were other places, too, in this imagined landscape, where Betjeman could feel equally secure. There was, for example, Port Isaac, only 'half a mile away'[85] from St Endellion, as he explained in a wireless broadcast in July 1949. 'I've walked between high Cornish hedges from St Endellion', he told his listeners, hiking down the lane from the church to this little fishing village hidden out of sight on the coast:

> The lane winds. The slate of the hedges is overgrown with grasses, bedstraw and milky-pink convolvulus, pale purple scabious and every so often valerian. From several places, standing on a hedge or looking through a gate, I can glimpse the sea. The sea is there all right – the great Atlantic, emerald green when I saw it, wrinkled, glimmering, sliding streaks of water, spotted dark blue here and there with reflections.[86]

It had been high-tide on that occasion, the ocean 'tamed and quiet for the moment, sliding round the inhospitable coast of North Cornwall', and 'From here on these high-up fields', he added, 'where blackthorn is sliced by the sea wind and leans inland, I can see all along the rocky cliffs to Rumps Point and Pentire'. And far below nestled Port Isaac itself. 'The final hill is very steep', he confessed, but it was worth it: suddenly 'you see it all – huddled in a steep valley, a cove at the end of a combe, roofs and roofs tumbling down either steep hillside in a race for shelter from the south-west gales'.

'Port Isaac is Polperro without the self-consciousness, St Ives without the artists', Betjeman reported approvingly, and he was relieved that modernity seemed to have passed it by, leaving the village a haven of tranquillity: 'There are no boulevards, no car stands or clinics; the dentist calls once a week and brings his instruments with him'. Thus far, the 'planners' – those faceless bureaucrats whose malevolent power Betjeman feared and loathed – had not penetrated Port Isaac, although 'it's the sort of place town planners hate'. For example, he said, 'The community centre is all wrong by town-planning standards. It's not the public house but the Liberal Club, for anyone who knows Cornish fishermen must know that most of them don't drink and many are chapel-goers'. And so, he explained, 'a Liberal club without an alcohol license is just the sort of place where you'd expect to find them'. These fishermen lived in cottages 'clinging by their eyelids to the cliffs', he added. 'Sparkling quartz known as Cornish Diamond is cemented into garden walls', he noted, 'figs and fuchsia bushes grow in tiny gardens; big shells from the Orient rest on window sills; brass and front-door paintwork shine; and every window that can looks out to sea so that even as they die the old fishermen of Port Isaac may watch the tides'. Betjeman feared that one day the planners would move the old people from these cottages 'to some very ugly council houses being built on the windy hilltop from those hideous grey cement things called "Cornish blocks"'.[87] But for now the chapel-goers were safe. Later, writing-up his talk for publication, Betjeman added that a 'simple Methodist chapel and Sunday school in the Georgian tradition hangs over the harbour and is the prettiest building in the town'.[88] And he had ended his broadcast by imagining Port Isaac at 'harvest-festival time', on an evening in late summer. 'Church is over but chapel is still on ... [and] Above the wail of the gulls and thunder of the sea beyond the headlands comes the final hymn from the Methodist Chapel across the green and gently lapping harbour water'.[89]

'St Protus and St Hyacinth, patron saints of Blisland church, pray for me!'

It was Methodism that gave Port Isaac its sense of benign tranquillity. At Blisland, on the edge of Bodmin Moor, it was Anglo-Catholicism and Celtic Christianity. 'Of all the country churches of the West I have seen, I think it is the most beautiful',[90] said Betjeman. 'I was a boy when I first saw it', he explained: 'I shall never forget that first visit – bicycling to the inland and unvisited parts of Cornwall from my home by the sea'. Leaving the Atlantic far behind, he had encountered huge hills and deep valleys, where 'the hedges became higher, the lanes ran down ravines, the plants seemed lusher, the thin Cornish elms seemed bigger and slate houses and slate hedges gave place to granite ones'. For here was 'the edge of Bodmin Moor, that sweet brown home of Celtic saints', and here too was Blisland village: 'It has not one ugly building in it', he wrote, 'and what is unusual in Cornwall, the houses are round a green'. The church itself, situated down a steep slope, was one of those that, in the manner Ninian Comper had described, would 'bring you to your knees when you first enter it'. It was a wonderful medley of styles, reflecting the preferences and practices of

10.   Blisland, a 'church whose beauty makes you gasp, whose silence brings you to your knees', its spectacular rood-screen of 1879 by F.C. Eden.

all the ages from the Norman to the contemporary. The magnificent rood screen, 'the glory of this church', together with 'the golden altars', stained glass, and the pulpit, were all designed by F.C. Eden in 1897. Eden, said Betjeman, 'had a vision of this old Cornish church as it was in mediaeval times … He centred everything on the altar, to which the screen is, as it were, a golden, red and green veil to the holiest mystery behind it'. The effect was extraordinary: 'it is a living church whose beauty makes you gasp, whose silence brings you to your knees, even if you kneel on the hard stone and slate of the floor, worn smooth by generations of worshippers'. It was a profound impression that never left Betjeman: 'St Protus and St Hyacinth, patron saints of Blisland church, pray for me! Often in a bus or train I call to mind your lovely church, the stillness of that Cornish valley and the first really beautiful work of man that my boyhood vividly remembers'.[91]

Blisland was a dramatic discovery. More familiar was Padstow, across the estuary from Trebetherick. It was, Betjeman said, 'an ancient unobvious place, hidden away from the south-west gales below a hill on the sandy estuary of the river Camel. It does not look at the open sea but across the tidal water to the sand dunes of Rock and the famous St Enodoc golf course'.[92] Today, he explained to his wireless listeners, 'Padstow is a fishing port and a shopping centre'. It was the only safe port of any size along this hazardous stretch of North Cornwall, and even then there was the Doom Bar on the estuary that had to be navigated carefully by mariners. 'There's not much grand architecture in Padstow', he added, 'It is all humble, unobtrusive houses, three storeys high'. But the 'main streets are, thank goodness, little altered ... Narrow public passages pass right through houses under stone arches and lead past high garden walls, down steps under other houses to further streets'. At one end of this intimate, friendly town was the parish church, dedicated, as Betjeman reminded his listeners, to St Petroc, and here was another opportunity to rehearse the many qualities of that holy man. 'Many miracles are recorded of him and tales of his kindness to animals', said Betjeman, remembering once more the stories told by Sabine Baring-Gould, 'and of his long prayers standing in a stream on Bodmin Moor ... He raised the dead, cured the sick and tamed a savage, serpent-eating monster'. He was a 'benign, bearded man', revered in Wales and Brittany as well as Cornwall and Devon. 'Blessed St Petroc!', said Betjeman: 'He was the chief of Cornish saints, a man of pervading gentleness that has never been forgotten'.[93]

Later, in a broadcast in February 1957, part of a series of church poems, Betjeman returned once more to St Petroc.[94] This time Betjeman imagined himself a timeless chronicler, reviewing the centuries in one broad sweep. He imagined too a fictional church of 'Stoke St Petroc', a name redolent of the Cornwall-Devon border country (Stoke Climsland is in Cornwall, Stoke Damarel in Devon), with echoes perhaps of both Hawker and Baring-Gould. Despite the passage of the ages, he said, and numerous interventions in the fabric of the church, reflecting the stylistic fads and fancies of different eras, the enduring significance and sanctity of the church itself had not altered. All was safe and holy, as it ever was. As Kevin Gardner has observed, 'Despite the alterations of time and man ... Betjeman insists that nothing that really matters has changed at all', and 'What Betjeman concludes about this little church suffices as his conclusion about this whole Church as well'[95]:

The church is there, restored it's true,
But still the same the ages through,
With sacraments and creed the same
As in the days when Petroc came.[96]

Here Betjeman was explicit in his treatment of location and context, placing the church firmly in 'our Western land' of 'Celtic Saints from Wales'.

Well yes, perhaps I am a ghost
With longer memory than most
And used our Western land to know
Just fifteen hundred years ago
And saw the corachs with their sails
Carrying Celtic Saints from Wales,
Among them Petroc, he who came
And gave this place its Christian name.
St Petroc, praise of God, his theme,
Waist deep in our brown moorland stream,
St Petroc with his staff and bell
And draughty, stone-built beehive cell,
St Petroc at his holy well
Baptising heathen, years before
Augustine reached the Kentish shore.
If Petroc's time you would recall,
Look in our ferny churchyard wall
And you will see, all black with moss,
The stone shaft of a Celtic cross.[97]

Moreover:

Stoke is a Saxon name for place
The prefix of that conquering race
Whose treatment of the Celts was shabby.
Years later when a Norman abbey
Built on St Petroc's sure foundation
Its little outpost mission station,
St Petroc's name was kept to show
Which Stoke we were, so strangers know

Stoke Petroc from Stoke Gabriel,
Stoke Climsland and Stoke Damarel.[98]

'a wailing tune half pagan'

For Betjeman, the unfailing, boundless goodness of St Petroc, etched
eternally in that landscape of churches, holy wells and ancient crosses,
personified warm, safe, benign North Cornwall. But there was another,
darker, pagan North Cornwall that lurked just beneath the surface, Betjeman
knew, just as Hawker and Baring-Gould had done, ready to reveal itself at
any moment. When he was a child, Betjeman had been taken by his parents
to the May Day festivities at Padstow. He had been impressed – perhaps even
terrified – by the 'Obby 'Oss, with its lurid mask and swaying dance, and
was mesmerised by the rhythmic beating of the drums and the haunting,
endlessly repetitive May Day tune. Here was something 'strange and secret',[99]
as Betjeman called it, intimations of another North Cornwall beyond the
Christian gaze. Years later, writing in the London *Evening Standard* (of all
places) in May 1936, he remembered the experience. 'It seems as though
the pagan gods are looking down on the town' on May Day, he wrote, and
the two 'Obby 'Osses – one 'red ribbon', the other 'blue' – were 'more
like Tibetan devil dancers' masks than horses'.[100] To follow the 'Osses as
they processed around the town, was to be drawn into a pagan ritual. 'The
song goes on and on', he said, 'sung by the children, the women and the
fishermen. The whole town sways to the tune'. And then, at 'every four
verses there is a religious hush, the hobby-horse bows down and the tune
changes to a wailing tune half pagan and half plainsong. Then up springs
the horse, up springs the teaser, up spring the dancers and the morning
song is resumed'.[101]

Later, in 1949, Betjeman told the story of a Padstow man in the trenches
in the Great War on eve of May Day. 'That night every man and woman in
Padstow is awake with excitement',[102] said Betjeman, and so it was on the
Western Front. 'On the night before May Day', Betjeman explained, 'the
Padstow man became so excited he couldn't keep still. The old 'obby 'oss
was mounting in his blood and his mates had to hold him back from jumping
over the top and dancing about in no man's land'. Back in Padstow itself,
the 'Oss – 'a man in a weird mask, painted red and black and white' with
'a huge hooped skirt made of black tarpaulin' – would be shortly processing
about the town, 'rushing at the ladies' in its time-honoured fertility ritual,
'a folk survival that is almost certainly of pagan origin', as Betjeman put it.

Such was its impact upon Betjeman, that when in 1954 he appeared on the wireless programme *Desert Island Discs* he chose the Padstow May Day song as one of his selected records.[103]

Padstow May Day was an extraordinary spectacle, performed just once a year. But that 'strange and secret' North Cornwall was also everyday and commonplace, said Betjeman, to be encountered down dark lanes, on windswept cliff-tops and exposed moorlands. Evening jaunts 'Past haunted woods and oil-lit farms' and 'Imagined ghosts on unfrequented roads'[104] hinted at this other North Cornwall, with 'remoter hamlets given over to magic, cruelty'.[105] He too, like Hawker and Baring-Gould, saw evil at large in the landscape, something he observed in his poem 'Trebetherick':

> From where the coastguard houses stood
> One used to see, below the hill,
> The lichened branches of a wood
> In summer silver-cool and still;
> And there the Shade of Evil could
> Stretch out at us from Shilla Mill.
> Thick with sloe and blackberry, uneven in the light,
> Lonely ran the hedge, the heavy meadow was remote,
> The oldest part of Cornwall was the wood as black as night,
> And the pheasant and the rabbit lay torn open at the throat.[106]

Some parts of Cornwall could 'feel intensely evil',[107] Betjeman thought, especially the border country out towards Baring-Gould's Lew Trenchard where even in recent times 'places really were remote: white witches, the evil eye, ghosts and strange customs'.[108] Figures from Cornish folklore peopled this threatening landscape. There was Coppinger, the notorious north-coast wrecker-smuggler made famous by Baring-Gould: 'Cruel Coppinger haunts me today',[109] Betjeman confessed. There was also 'the ghost of Jan Tregeagle and his hounds of hell'.[110] Tregeagle, the wicked steward of Lord Robartes, who behind his master's back had swindled the estate's poor tenant farmers, had, people said, sold his soul to the Devil.[111] At any rate, when he died his spirit would not rest. Tregeagle refused to go to Hell, where Satan was waiting for his part of the bargain, and the Devil and his hounds hunted for him across Bodmin Moor. At length, as punishment, Tregeagle was condemned to draining in perpetuity bottomless Dozmary Pool – in the bleak middle of the Moor – with a holed limpet shell as tool, an appalling task whose intimations of eternal damnation horrified Betjeman.

11. The 'Obby 'Oss: 'during May Day Padstow goes mad ... [one] realises that Cornwall is still a foreign country as remote from England as Ireland'.

This North Cornwall was hardly safe, and certainly not benign. Yet there was a 'happy terror' (as he put it) that Betjeman could enjoy when, safe indoors at night and protected from all that stalked outside, he could 'escape to a fire of driftwood' as 'the wind howls up the chimney'.[112] Ultimately, the sinister face of North Cornwall fascinated rather than repelled, complementing rather than negating the alternative landscape of warm embrace. Betjeman was alive to the perpetual struggle between good and evil – 'good and evil spirits are fighting here among us', he wrote, 'we are born into this struggle between good and evil'.[113] But, as in so many aspects of his life, he sought an accommodation, if not exactly a resolution, a recognition that this *frisson* of 'happy terror' was an integral, essential component of *his* North Cornwall. 'North Cornwall became part of him',[114] his daughter Candida Lycett Green would explain years later: its Janus-like character reflected his own fears and anxieties, as well as his hopes and aspirations, and was inextricably entwined in his life-long search for religious meaning, fulfilment and personal identity

For all its proximity to England, North Cornwall was in ambience almost impenetrably remote, thought Betjeman, more so even than other parts of Cornwall. 'Some think of the furthest-away places as Spitsbergen or Honolulu', he said, 'But give me Padstow, though I can reach it any day from Waterloo'.[115] Here, in this distant land, Christianity and paganism existed side by side, almost hand in hand. It was curious juxtaposition, he admitted. St Petroc might have viewed the 'Obby 'Oss with missionary 'displeasure',[116] said Betjeman, but the holy saint and pagan ritual were really two sides of

that same 'strange and secret' North Cornish coin. As he reflected: 'during
May Day Padstow goes mad' and one 'realises that Cornwall is still a foreign
country as remote from England as Ireland'.[117]

CHAPTER FOUR

'Caverns of light revealed the Holy Grail'

Betjeman and *The Secret Glory*

> Dear lanes of Cornwall! With a one-inch map,
> A bicycle and well-worn *Little Guide*,
> Those were the years I used to ride for miles
> To far-off churches. One of them that year
> So worked on me that, if my life was changed,
> I owe it to St Ervan and his priest
> In their small hollow deep in sycamores.[1]

Brought up, as we have seen, on a literary diet of Robert Stephen Hawker and Sabine Baring-Gould, with his head full of Celtic saints and ancient crosses and holy wells, the youthful John Betjeman was already a devotee of Celtic Cornwall and tales of King Arthur and his Knights of the Round Table. He had read and had been moved by Hawker's 'Quest of the Sangraal' – the Holy Grail – and, as he was to muse years later, the Quest somehow mirrored his own personal search for Cornwall. But, as Betjeman might also have agreed, the Quest was a wider reflection of other strivings in his life, not least his struggle for religious faith, and was a metaphor for the many anxieties, angsts and guilts with which he wrestled daily. And, as Betjeman revealed in his verse autobiography *Summoned by Bells*, this identification with the Holy Grail was given an unexpected dimension when, as an adolescent exploring inland North Cornwall in the early 1920s, he encountered the Rector of St Ervan.

'I found St Ervan's partly ruined church'

Still a schoolboy at Marlborough, Betjeman treasured his holidays in Cornwall. As so often in his life (see chapter six), Cornwall had become a

12. St Ervan church in its 'small hollow deep in sycamores'.

sanctuary, a place of freedom and escape, far from the regimen of austere and unforgiving public school existence. Years later he remembered those feelings of 'Doom! Shivering doom!' when, as at last the holidays drew to a close, he prepared for term time. 'Clutching a leather grip / Containing things for the first night of term – / House-slippers, sponge-bag, pyjams, Common Prayer, / My health certificate, photographs of home', he made his way gloomily from the railway station ('Marlborough was a lonely place') to boarding school and the 'sense of impending doom / Which goes with rows of desks and clanging bells'. Here, indeed, were the 'Inexorable bells / To early school, to chapel, to school again: / Compulsory constipation, hurried meals / Bulked out with Whipped Cream Walnuts from the town'. An then 'At first there was the dread of breaking rules – / "Betjeman, you know that new boys mustn't show / Their hair below the peak of college caps: / Stand still and have your face slapped." "Sorry, Jones" / The dread of beatings! / Dread of being late! / And, greatest dread of all, the dread of games!'.[2]

Worst of all was Upper School, said Betjeman, where bullying was disguised as time-honoured college ritual, the bullies themselves granted the deference and privileges befitting their status as senior pupils. 'Upper School captains had the power to beat', he said, 'Maximum six strokes, usually three'.[3] Alongside the perpetual fear was Betjeman's devotion to the college Chapel. Here he could be alone, immune for a moment from that world of punishment and bullying, and here too he could wonder whether there really was a God. 'Oh, who is God?', asked young Betjeman as he contemplated the hushed atmosphere of the Chapel, 'O tell me, who is God? / Perhaps

he hides behind the reredos .../Give me a God whom I can touch and see'.
An 'Old Marlburian bishop' told the pupils that the Chapel should be '"The
centre and the mainspring of your lives, / The inspiration for your work
and sport, / The corporate life of this great public school / Spring from
its glorious chapel. Day by day / You come to worship in its noble walls /
Hallowed by half a century of prayer"'. As Betjeman observed, 'The bishop
was more right than he could know', for 'Safe in the surge of undogmatic
hymns, / The Chapel *was* the centre of my life – / The only place where
I could be alone'.[4]

At last, the long summer holidays beckoned and, reunited with his family
again, Betjeman made his way down to welcoming Cornwall. Relations with
his parents were often fraught (see chapter six), so that sometimes there
were rows and arguments at Trebetherick. But Betjeman, with his bicycle,
Methuen Little Guide[5] and one-inch *Ordnance Survey* map, could escape into
the hinterland of North Cornwall on journeys that might take him as far
as Blisland on the edge of Bodmin Moor. One day, as he was to explain
in *Summoned by Bells*, he ventured to a new destination, St Ervan, a small
parish of no more than 3,000 acres to the south of the river Camel. Much
of St Ervan was high, windswept, almost treeless hill-country, typical of
that locality, but St Ervan churchtown itself – a tiny settlement of some
half-a-dozen dwellings, a rectory and the church – nestled in a valley 'deep
in sycamores',[6] as Betjeman put it.

When Betjeman visited St Ervan – in the summer of 1922, perhaps, or
possibly 1923, when he was about seventeen – the church building was in
something of a parlous state. The upper stage of the tower had become
ruinous many years before, and had been pulled down in 1883, never to
be rebuilt. Shortly after, in 1888, the rest of the church was injudiciously
'restored' (as were so many Cornish churches at that time), with the
truncated tower left in its state of decay. Two of the church bells rested,
out of commission, on the floor, while a third was mounted under a tripod
outside the church, where it could be tolled by the priest. It was here that
Betjeman first encountered the rector of St Ervan. As he explained:

> The time was tea-time, calm free-wheeling time,
> When from slashed tree-tops in the combe below
> I heard a bell-note floating to the sun;
> It gave significance to lichened stone
> And large red admirals with outspread wings
> Basking on buddleia. So, coasting down

> In the cool shade of interlacing boughs,
> I found St Ervan's partly ruined church.
> Its bearded Rector, holding in one hand a book,
> Struck, while he was reading, a heavy-sounding bell
> Hung from an elm bough by the churchyard gate.
> 'Better come in. It's time for Evensong'.[7]

Betjeman, to his adolescent embarrassment, found himself the sole member of the congregation that evening. 'There wasn't much to see' within the church, he said. It was 'Holy and small and heavily restored', and 'It held me for the length of Evensong, / Said rapidly among discoloured walls / Impatient of my diffident response'. After the service, the priest invited Betjeman for a cup of tea into the 'large, uncarpeted' Rectory with its 'waste of barely furnished rooms', where 'Clearly the Rector lived ... all alone'. The Rector 'talked of poetry and Cornish saints', and when Betjeman admitted that he thought of religion as 'mostly singing hymns / And feeling warm and comfortable inside', the kindly priest decided that he should 'Borrow this book and come to tea again'.[8] Betjeman took the volume, mumbled his farewells, and set out for home: 'up the hill' and

> On to St Merryn, down to Padstow Quay
> In time for the last ferry back to Rock,
> I bicycled – and found Trebetherick
> A worldly contrast with my afternoon.[9]

He began to read the book, as he had promised, and, to try to recapture something of the atmosphere of that late afternoon at St Ervan, he walked across the dunes from Trebetherick to the nearby church at St Enodoc:

> In quest of mystical experience
> I knelt in darkness at St Enodoc;
> I visited our local Holy Well,
> Whereto the native Cornish still resort
> For cures for whooping-cough, and drop bent pins
> Into its peaty water ... Not a sign:
> No mystical experience was vouchsafed:
> The maidenhair just trembled in the wind
> And everywhere looked as it always looked ...[10]

Revd Wilfred Ryan Johnson

Nonetheless, as he delved further into the book, the more he was enchanted by the intriguing volume he had been lent, and by the time he returned to Marlborough for the next term, he was so full of it that he could not put it down.[11] This volume that was already having such a profound effect upon young Betjeman was *The Secret Glory*, first published in 1922, a semi-autobiographical novel by Arthur Machen (1863–1947). Its impact, Betjeman always maintained, was truly life-altering. He said so in *Summoned by Bells* and he had said so before. In an interview, for example, later published in part in 1961, he had explained that he had been 'brought up C of E' but that, at Marlborough, he had refused to become confirmed, thinking 'that religion was [merely] hymn singing and feeling good and not being immoral'.[12] However, this was 'Until ... I remember one summer bicycling about in Cornwall and coming to a church, St Irvin [*sic*], in North Cornwall and meeting the vicar there who was a nice eccentric'. Then, he explained, telling the story shortly to be repeated so famously in *Summoned by Bells*, the priest guessed that for Betjeman religion was 'hymn singing in the chapel at Marlborough', and so decided that he should lend him *The Secret Glory*. This volume, said Betjeman, 'suddenly showed me there were the Sacraments, and then I became very interested in ritual and I was first, I suppose, brought to belief by my eyes and ears and nose. The smell of incense, and sight of candles, High Church services, they attracted me and I liked them'. Leaving Marlborough, Betjeman went on to university at Oxford, and once there he was 'confirmed and lived the full life of a Catholic in the Church of England'. There were times, he admitted, when his faith had faltered – 'the one fundamental thing is that Christ was God ... it's very hard to believe ... it's a very hard thing to swallow' – but 'if you can believe it, it gives some point to everything and really I don't think life would be worth living if it weren't true'.[13]

Unnamed in *Summoned by Bells*, the priest who had decided that young Betjeman must read *The Secret Glory* was Wilfred Ryan Johnson, Rector of St Ervan from 1915 until 1954. An insightful and affectionate pen-picture of the man and his ministry has appeared in Moira Tangey's *The Book of St Ervan*, published in 2006.[14] Here we learn that Johnson had first arrived in St Ervan in 1914 to assist the retirement of his predecessor, ninety-year old Revd Henry Barton, who had been incumbent since 1853. He moved swiftly to establish his authority in the parish, in 1914 arranging the consecration of a new churchyard, but soon found that 'the parish is practically entirely

Dissenting and rather hostile'.[15] He managed to fall out with the local schoolmistress and with members of the parish council, most of whom were also Methodists. Nonetheless, in time he won the affection of his parishioners, 'church' and 'chapel' alike. He was shy, rather old-fashioned and was remembered in St Ervan as somewhat eccentric, 'always dressed in a long black frock coat'.[16]

Like Robert Stephen Hawker, Wilfred Johnson was out of sympathy with the modern world, and he was 'bookish', insisting that a proper education should leave us 'eager to read, knowing what is worth reading, and able to read it'.[17] He was also a keen amateur historian, and during his long incumbency found solace in the history of the Church, especially in Cornwall. In the St Ervan parish magazine in 1949, for example, he noted that 30 January that year was the three-hundredth anniversary of the 'martyrdom of King Charles the First', who had 'died for high principles which greatly need assertion as against the tendencies of the modern world'.[18] Here indeed were echoes of Robert Stephen Hawker, not only the railing against modernity but also the implicit identification with the High Church values of Archbishop Laud (Charles I's erstwhile First Minister) and the Royalist cause in the Civil War. By 1949 Johnson had been in his parish for nigh on thirty-five years, and in that time he had learnt a great deal about the North Cornwall of which he was now so inextricably a part. He saw himself as part of the High Church tradition of that district, and integral to that tradition was remembrance of the Civil War and the cause of Cornish Royalism.[19]

In settling into his ministry in Cornwall, Wilfred Johnson had swiftly adjusted his natural High Church instincts to take account of Cornish Anglo-Catholicism and its intimate connection with the Cornish-Celtic Revival. Indeed, he was to become a leading member of the Anglo-Catholic movement in Cornwall in the first half of the twentieth century, and an enthusiastic Celtic revivalist. This reflected the Hawker and Baring-Gould inheritance. But there was also now the influence of a wider and growing group of activists from within the Anglican Church across Cornwall. There was, for example, the Revd Wlasdislaw Somerville Lach-Szyrma (1841–1915), vicar of Newlyn, who, among other things, was a Cornish-language enthusiast and had encouraged the flying of St Piran's banner as the national flag of Cornwall. There was Henry Jenner, of course, son of the vicar of St Columb Major and friend of Lach-Szyrma, and there was the Revd Thomas Taylor who had become vicar of St Just-in-Penwith in 1900, and whose book *The Celtic Christianity of Cornwall* was published in 1916 and dedicated to the

Breton Celticist, M. Joseph Loth. There was also Canon Gilbert Doble, later to be acknowledged by Betjeman as leading authority on Cornish and Celtic saints, and there was Edward White Benson, the first Bishop of the new Diocese of Truro, who had been enthroned on 1 May 1877. 'This Cornubia is a land of wonderment', he wrote, 'historical, physical, spiritual'.[20]

'the Ancient See of Cornwall'

Indeed, the creation of the Diocese and the building of the new Cathedral at Truro (whose foundation stone was laid in May 1880) had been encouraged by men such as Lach-Szyrma, who had demanded the restoration of what they saw as the 'Ancient See of Cornwall'. From the first, this Anglican renewal was linked explicitly to Anglo-Catholicism and the Celtic Revival, and the new diocese was seen as inherently 'Celtic'. As David Everett has concluded: 'The completion of Truro Cathedral represented the triumph of Anglican renewal in Cornwall, a movement that had successfully articulated Cornwall's Celtic identity as part of its drive to create a separate Cornish diocese and had claimed common cause with the Celtic Revival in reclaiming and celebrating the Celtic past'.[21] This spirit was given renewed impetus in 1923, about the time of Betjeman's encounter with Wilfred Johnson at St Ervan, when Walter Howard Frere (1863–1938) was appointed Bishop of Truro. A member of the Community of the Resurrection at Mirfield in Yorkshire – an Anglican monastic order 'now widely honoured but then viewed with protestant suspicion by the old-fashioned',[22] as Canon Miles Brown wrote in 1964 – Frere was a ritualist and liturgical scholar who fitted the Anglo-Catholic mould perfectly. He also took 'a keen interest in the relic of the Celtic past', said Miles Brown, and 'encouraged Cornish studies'.[23] He was, said his friend and colleague C.S. Phillips, 'fired by the romantic traditions of early Cornish Christianity',[24] and he had 'a great liking and admiration for the Cornish character, though in many ways it is so unlike his own very English one'.[25] Frere led the first diocesan pilgrimage to St Piran's Oratory, in the dunes near Perranporth, in 1924, and in 1927 he set up a committee – including Gilbert Doble, Thomas Taylor, and the antiquarian Charles Henderson – to complete a full 'Kalendar' of Cornish saints. The committee reported in 1933, paving the way for the formal liturgical observance in Cornwall of saints who 'should be honoured in a Celtic diocese'.[26]

Walter Frere acquired something of a reputation as 'an Anglo-Catholic socialist',[27] as A.L. Rowse put it, not least for his defence of two individualistic priests in the diocese: Jack Bucknall at Delabole and Bernard Walke at St Hilary, the first 'politically of the Thaxted type of Christian socialist', as Miles Brown explained, 'the other completely Latin in theology and practice'.[28] Bucknall, who was born in Camelford in 1888, arrived as the new curate at neighbouring Delabole in May 1925. Already known in Cornwall for his radical opinions – Rowse observed his notoriety as 'Christian Bolshevik, an Anglo-Catholic Socialist, a Mirfield monk'[29] during his earlier appointment at St Austell – Bucknell was a devotee of the Revd Conrad Noel, the 'Red' vicar of Thaxted in Essex. In 1918 Conrad Noel had founded his 'Catholic Crusade', which championed social justice and supported the international struggle of the workers against capitalism. Advocating such sentiments at Delabole, Bucknall soon became embroiled in controversy. On the one hand, he outraged the more staid and conservative of his parishioners, but on the other he exercised a magnetic appeal for those normally outside the realms of Anglicanism, especially younger people and 'Dissenters and riff-raff'[30] as one critic complained. The story of the subsequent battles between those determined to eject him and his equally stout defenders has been told in illuminating detail by Catherine Lorigan in her recent (2007) history of *Delabole*.[31] Frere intervened on Bucknall's behalf, insisting that he had not strayed from orthodoxy, as his opponents had claimed, and Bucknell remained at Delabole until he finally moved on in 1932.

At St Hilary, meanwhile, Bernard Walke had likewise generated controversy. He too was a fervent Anglo-Catholic with a developed social conscience. He acknowledged that in Cornwall 'the Oxford Movement had resulted in a quickening of the life of the Church' but even here, he said, there were still parishes where the chief act of Sunday worship was merely Morning Prayer, 'not the type of service to kindle the faith or stir the emotions of a Celtic people who have known Catholicism and have passed through the fire of [Methodist] revivalism'.[32] Walke believed that in such parishes there 'was nothing ... to kindle the faith that gave to Cornwall so many saints or to light again the fire that burnt so fiercely in the day of John Wesley. Only the worship of the Mass', he said, 'where time and space have ceased to be the supreme realities ... only the Mass could ever hope to win back man to the reality of God's love'.[33] Walke put this theology to the test at St Hilary, where he was vicar from 1912 until 1936, making the ritual of the Mass the centrepiece of Christian observance there. He also set about beautifying his church, introducing colour and a sense of splendour consistent with Catholic worship. There were paintings by his wife, Annie Walke, and candles and ornaments and statues. He acknowledged Cornwall's ancient Celtic-Catholic links with Ireland, and when 'Ireland lay under the terror of the Black and Tans ... we became involved in holding meetings for prayer in different parts of Cornwall on behalf of this distressed country'.[34] Likewise, he and like-minded colleagues attempted (albeit unsuccessfully) to launch a political and social movement to address the distress caused by unemployment among Cornish miners, at one stage even trying to reopen a defunct tin mine. Sympathy for Irish nationalists (and Catholics) was calculated to raise suspicions, as were activities of a 'socialist' nature, but it was the adornment of St Hilary church that stirred real anger. Hostility came to a head in 1932 when an extreme Protestant 'Kensitite' mob (followers of John Kensit's Protestant Truth Society, mainly from outside Cornwall but encouraged from within) raided St Hilary and laid waste to the church, smashing its candles and pictures and carrying off its statues. An exquisite reredos, designed by Ernest Proctor, was destroyed, and the fifteenth-century font was broken-up.

'Mirfield monks'

Although seemingly hermit-like in his remote living in St Ervan, Wilfred Johnson was immersed in the flowering of Anglo-Catholicism in Cornwall in this period, when he had first met John Betjeman, and was by no means immune from the Bucknell and Walke controversies. In 1946, and by now a senior Cornish churchman, Johnson was appointed a Prebendary of the Collegiate Church of St Endellion, a singular honour which reflected his standing in the diocese. The college of prebendaries at St Endellion had existed since medieval times but had fallen into disuse, although never abolished. In 1929 Bishop Frere announced his intention to rehabilitate this ancient college, and on 2 May that year, as Johnson himself explained, the 'new era was inaugurated in St Endellion church' with 'a solemn Eucharist ... at which the prebendal body assembled probably for the first time for centuries'. As Johnson added, 'Each prebend has an income, a modest income, and of late years they have all been held by priests whom it is desired to honour or whose income to augment'.[35]

Johnson was further honoured when he and Guy W. Hockley were asked to contribute a chapter to a volume on the life of Walter Frere, edited by C.S. Phillips and published in 1947, almost a decade after Frere's death. In this chapter, concentrating as it did on Frere's time at Truro, Johnson also revealed a great deal about himself and his own pre-occupations. He explained the symbolic and spiritual importance of the new cathedral, built

'by a generation of churchmen, who looked forward to a Church of the far
west, to … its special mission to the Cornish people', adding proudly that
'Truro has been from the beginning a diocese of definite churchmanship
of a high Prayer Book standard'.[36] He also acknowledged the former pre-
eminence of Methodism as 'almost the official Cornish religion', explaining
that in 'the eighteenth century the Celtic temperament of the Cornish
reacted with emotion to the preaching of John Wesley', adding that the
'Welsh, the other great branch of the Brythonic Celts, have exhibited a
similar effect'. Now, however, he said with a mixture of relief and regret,
Cornish Methodism 'has practically discarded revivalism' and 'is no longer
eccentric and racy'. Indeed, it had rather lost its 'intensity', although the
appeal, he thought, continued to be to 'feeling more than reason'.[37]

   Cornwall, then, had been ripe for the appointment of Walter Frere, said
Johnson, and was ready for the next stage of Anglican renewal. There were
critics who, wishing 'to raise prejudice against him', had dismissed Frere
as 'the Mirfield monk', just as they had done Jack Bucknall.[38] But Frere's
eight years at Truro, despite 'some misunderstanding, some prejudice,
much misrepresentation', had been a triumph, insisted Johnson, with the
bishop 'every year winning more and more of those who could admire the
scholar and the still greater number of those who learnt to love and revere
the saint'.[39] Like C.S Phillips, Johnson admired Frere's devotion to 'Celtic
Christianity', noting the creation of the 'Cornish Church Kalendar' and
the annual pilgrimage instituted by the bishop to 'some parish connected
with the work or name of a Cornish saint'.[40] Johnson had also observed
Frere's close friendship with Charles Henderson, Cornish antiquarian and
mentor of the young A.L. Rowse, and he understood how important Frere
had been in encouraging Henderson's work, especially the completion of
his *Cornish Church Guide* in 1928. As Johnson recorded, it was Frere himself
who had described with affection that 'very tall slim figure, of unusually
bright colouring and eyes, stooping slightly as if he was ashamed of being
so much taller than other people. Such was Charlie Henderson, for by that
name everybody in Cornwall knew him'. As Frere had admitted, 'I soon
found myself sitting at his feet and beginning to learn about the Duchy and
its history and its traditions'. This 'was not merely a matter of sitting in
chairs and listening and questioning', he said; 'it soon developed into plans
of exploration, or rather personally conducted tours'.[41] Henderson's influence
on the bishop had been equally profound, as Johnson realized, and when
Charles Henderson died suddenly on his honeymoon in Rome in September
1933, aged only thirty-three, Walter Frere was (like Rowse) devastated at a

promising life cut short, writing sadly that year of the loss of 'the greatest historian Cornwall has ever had'.[42]

Wilfred Johnson had also admired Walter Frere's handling of the Bucknall and Walke cases. At St Hilary, Johnson explained, in 'Walke's incumbency altar after altar, ornament after ornament were put into' the church. 'Some of the ornaments were extraordinary', Johnson admitted, 'but they all meant something in religion or love, and they were brought into an inner unity by that fact and into outer unity by artistic taste'. Frere agreed, although he did his best to find a compromise between Walke's supporters and detractors, on the one hand striving to bring St Hilary 'within the bounds of orderliness (a favourite word of his)', and on the other doing 'his best to protect him from bigoted attack'. Unfortunately, Walke's opponents were in no mood for compromise, said Johnson, and it proved impossible to prevent 'the wretched … Protestant attack, within and without the law, at St Hilary'.[43] At Delabole, meanwhile, Bucknall had attracted 'a large following. He like Walke, was a man of one piece', said Johnson, 'though the piece was different, and the gospel preached at Delabole was indistinguishably ecclesiastical and socialist'. In Johnson's opinion, the Bucknall affair had been a storm in a teacup, and left to its own devices the controversy would have fizzled out. However, 'the Protestant underworld took the opportunity to divert a little of the odium to the Bishop', and the affair was taken up 'with a seriousness which in retrospect seems almost unbelievable'. There were calls for 'disciplinary action', said Johnson, and some who 'wanted to starve out the priest', but Frere stood by his man, and 'was loyal, not only to priest, but to justice'. As Johnson concluded: 'It is true that a good deal had been said at Delabole which was unwise, but nothing which was unorthodox'.[44]

'an Episcopal fly in the ointment'

When Walter Frere retired from Truro in 1935, he was replaced by Bishop Joseph Wellington Hunkin, a native-born Cornishman and Low Church former Methodist, sent down (some said) to temper the Anglo-Catholic influence in the diocese.[45] Wilfred Johnson was one of those who eyed the appointment with suspicion. Certainly, Hunkin from time to time criticised the 'irregular practices' of High Church parishes. On one occasion at Torpoint, for example, he reminded the congregation that the Anglican Church was a Protestant Reformed church and that it was 'not Roman' and 'not mediaeval', and that he abhorred the use of 'Roman candles' and 'Roman slogans'.[46] To him, institutions such as the college of prebendaries seemed unnecessary and arcane. Edwin Stark, in his survey of the prebends of St Endellion in 1983, considered that since the rehabilitation of 1929, the 'only possible Episcopal fly in the ointment was perhaps the late Bishop J.W. Hunkin who, with the best of intentions, commented on pre-Reformation sinecures when he instituted a prebendary in 1949'. As Stark observed wryly: 'His sermon, on that occasion, evoked a gentle rebuke from the then Rector of St Ervan'.[47]

In April 1949 John Betjeman wrote to Wilfred Johnson, more than a quarter of a century since that all-important first encounter at St Ervan. He reminded Johnson that 'When I was a boy you lent me *The Secret Glory* by Arthur Machen which first opened my eyes to Catholicism as you did yourself when I came over on a bicycle from Trebetherick to tea with you'. He wanted now to 'thank you more than I can say for first showing me the Faith'. But Betjeman also wanted to thank Johnson for the 'humbling and unanswerable defence of dear old St Endellion and its prebends' that had appeared recently in the Wadebridge and Padstow edition of the *Cornish Guardian*. This was the 'gentle rebuke' to Hunkin that Stark was to recall years later. As Betjeman added, amplifying his support for the college, the 'Rector of St Endellion is worth visiting Cornwall to hear, and I have often recommended people to go to his sung Mass and they have never been disappointed. I am so glad you wrote in the *Guardian* as you did'.[48]

In the following year, 1950, Betjeman returned to the subject of St Endellion in a radio broadcast, prompted perhaps by the correspondence with Wilfred Johnson and the piece in the *Cornish Guardian*. He told listeners that St Endellion 'was a sixth-century Celtic saint, daughter of a Welsh king, who with her sisters Minver and Teath and many other holy relations came to North Cornwall with the Gospel'. Later, in the sixteenth century, the recusant writer Nicholas Roscarrock had lived in the parish, adding to its illustrious history. He 'loved the old religion and was imprisoned in the Tower and put on the rack', said Betjeman, but he also wrote a Life of St Endellion and composed a hymn in her praise. The church itself had a certain, indefinable mystery, he said, and seemed 'to go on praying when there is no one in it'. Moreover, as he explained, 'The Rector of St Endellion is also a Prebendary', which meant that the church was run by a college of priests, rather like St George's Chapel at Windsor. 'There are four prebends in the college', he added, they 'are the prebends of Marny, Trehaverock, Endellion and Bodmin'. There was a little income from each of these, he said, which was held by the priests or used for good causes. As Betjeman mused: 'How this heavenly medieval arrangement of a college of prebendary clergymen survived the Reformation and Commonwealth and Victorian interferers is another mystery of St Endellion for which we must thank God'. And, in a swipe at Hunkin, he added: 'Episcopal attacks have been made upon it; but long live St Endellion, Trehaverock, Marny and Bodmin! Hold fast. *Sancta Endelienta, ora pro nobis!*'.[49]

'two Protestant bigots'

When Wilfred Johnson died in 1954 he left money in his will for the restoration, at last, of the ruined church tower at St Ervan. The upper stage was not rebuilt, and instead the tower acquired a rather unusual, squat appearance. Nonetheless, it was, as Betjeman wrote in 1964, a fitting memorial to 'its famous rector, Prebendary W.R. Johnson'.[50] And, as Betjeman had said, Johnson was indeed 'famous' by the end of his life, at least in Cornwall and within the wider Anglo-Catholic tradition in the Anglican Communion. It was a fame that gave Betjeman great satisfaction, as he pondered both the flowering of Johnson's career as a Cornish High Churchman and his own maturing devotion to Cornish Anglo-Catholicism during the years that Johnson was at St Ervan. As Betjeman admitted, Johnson's influence had been profound. Intriguingly, for example, in 1933 Betjeman had written in support of Conrad Noel, the radical mentor of Jack Bucknall of Delabole, whom he thought the spiritual heir of William Morris.[51] 'In the village of Thaxted, in Essex,' said Betjeman, 'there has been an attempt, not unsuccessful, to centre the life of the place round the catholic service of the church'. Here, he added, the 'church has become a place of importance once more, not a seedy relic continually needing repairs to the chancel', with church social life no longer 'confined to tea parties'. At Thaxted, he said, 'the public-house is not looked upon as a place of sin'. And yet, he reflected, 'despite the religious atmosphere of Thaxted Church, and despite the communal life centring round it and the able and great character of Noel Conrad, the incumbent, one realises that it is only in remote agricultural districts that faith, as the mediaeval church knew it, stands any chance of surviving'.[52] Here, perhaps, Betjeman had St Ervan and its Rector particularly in mind.

Later, in 1964, Betjeman recorded his opinion of the St Hilary affair. He did not pull his punches, and he was prepared to name names. Although, he wrote, some of the 'bright paintings on the choir stalls of the legends of the Cornish saints' had survived, worked completed in the 1930s by St Ives artists such as Harold Knight, Dod Proctor and Annie Walke ('the

Farnborough,
Wantage,
Berkshire.

Tel. Chaddleworth 202.

XIV. IV. XLIX

Dear Rector Pulverdang,

there is no need to answer this
letter of thanks.

     When I was a boy you lent me
the Secret Glory by Arthur Machen which
first opened my eyes to Catholicism as
you did yourself when I came over on
a bicycle from Tubutciut to tea with
you. Then on visits I have never
forgotten though I was one of many
visitors, that must have been in
about 1917. So I must thank you
more than I can say for first shewing
me the Faith.

     Now I have to thank you for your

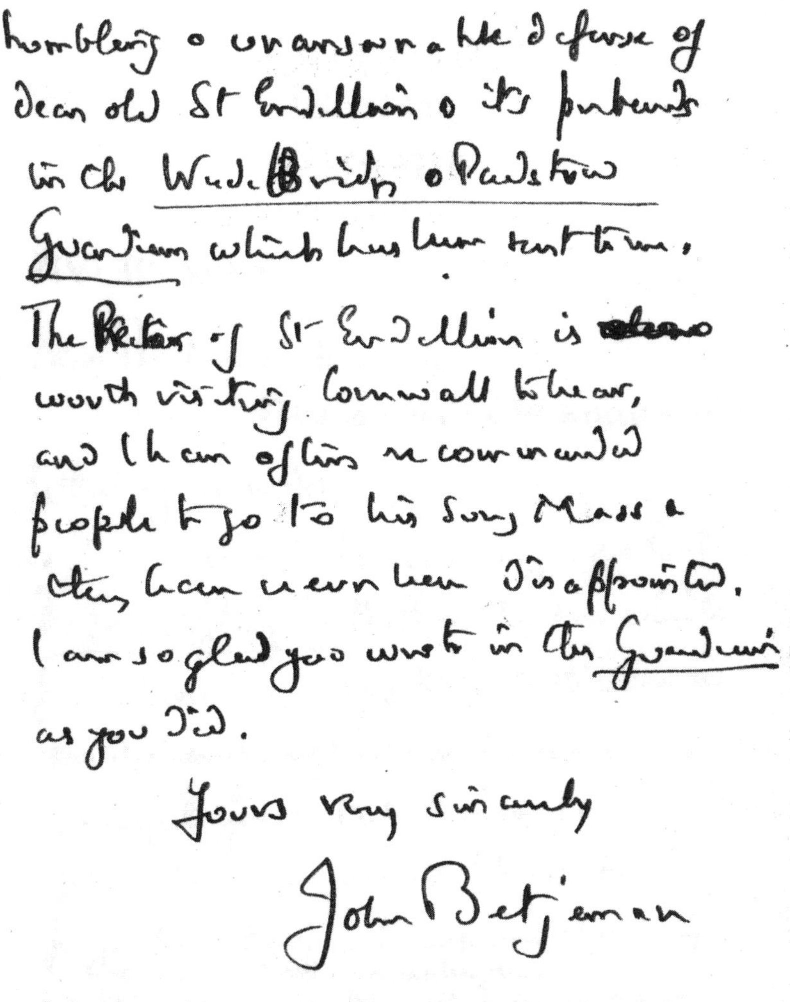

[handwritten letter]

humbling o unanswerable defence of
dear old St Endellion o its prebends
in the Wadebridge o Padstow
Guardian which has been sent to me.
The Rector of St Endellion is also
worth visiting. Cornwall to hear,
and I have oft/on recommended
people to go to his Sung Mass a
they have never been disappointed.
I am so glad you wrote in the Guardian
as you did.
        Yours very sincerely
            John Betjeman

13. John Betjeman's letter to Prebendary Wilfred Johnson, April 1949:
'thank you more than I can say for first showing me the Faith'.

wife of the famous vicar Bernard Walke'), much of the rest of the church was now a disappointment. As he explained: 'The church was despoiled of its decoration as the result of a scandalous persecution of its loved vicar by two Protestant bigots, a Miss King and a Mr Poynter Adams of St Minver'.[53] As he put it:

> In the name of legalism rather than love, they took civil action against him, hired maniacs to smash the font and other ornaments of the church and have left it a barren and sad place today, with few services, no guide to the remaining decorations and Bernard Walke in his grave and the home for crippled children he and his wife founded, dispersed.[54]

'a tolerant Anglican'

More generally, Betjeman's conversion – for that is what it was – to Anglo-Catholicism and to Celtic Christianity affected his whole life. As Kevin Gardner has observed in his study of *Faith and Doubt* in Betjeman's religious verse, it was 'the timeless permanence of Anglo-Catholicism'[55] that gave support to Betjeman's sometimes wavering belief. As Gardner has explained: 'As a tolerant Anglican, he [Betjeman] knows that no conversion experience can provide a formula for all believers'.[56] Yet most believers, Betjeman imagined, 'constantly experience Christ's "fitful glow"', as he himself did, 'a symbol of the ebb and flow of faith in the heart of the struggling believer'. This 'fitful glow' was likely to be experienced anywhere and at any time, and here, as Gardner has also observed, elements of Celtic Christianity – 'particularly the idea of the immanence of God in the natural world' – suffused Betjeman's belief.[57] The sudden and unexpected, but deeply moving, experience of God in a garden or in the countryside or in a seascape was central to his faith. And such experience was not confined to Cornwall, of course, although it was here that Betjeman had first encountered such feelings. Far beyond the Tamar and the traditional realms of 'Celtic Christianity', Betjeman was liable to find that sudden 'immanence of God' in the landscape. At Uffington, for example, deep in Alfred's Anglo-Saxon Wessex, there could still be that 'spontaneous and joyful outburst at the discovery of God not in a church but in nature'.[58] Yet even here, as Betjeman might have imagined, the omni-present Iron-Age 'White Horse' on the chalk downs above the village seemed to cast a perpetual 'Celtic' gaze across the ancient Vale, with its intimation, as S.P.B. Mais wrote, of a 'return to the west',[59] of the enduring influence beneath the English sub-strata of a deeper

Celtic past.[60] There was, as Betjeman always understood, a strongly mystical dimension to 'Celtic Christianity'.

Arthur Machen

Wilfred Johnson, then, had been a key figure in the life of John Betjeman, as Betjeman had himself insisted. On the occasion of that first meeting, he had shrewdly sized-up young Betjeman, getting the measure of the youth in those few words before Evensong and later over tea in the Rectory. In recommending *The Secret Glory*, Johnson had already detected the appeal that the volume would have for Betjeman – the withering satire in the book aimed at the English public school system (in which Betjeman had suffered more than most, as perhaps he had told Johnson) but also its full-blown advocacy of 'Celtic Christianity', and with it a bizarre plot enmeshed in a quest for the Holy Grail. Yet if Johnson deserved particular credit for guiding Betjeman, then so did the book itself, along with its author, Arthur Machen.

Arthur Machen (the pen-name of Arthur Llewellyn Jones) was born in 1863 at Caerleon-on-Usk in Gwent (as he always termed it, preferring the historic name to the more prosaic Monmouthshire) in South Wales. Long before *The Secret Glory* had appeared, Machen – whose adopted surname was supposed to rhyme with 'blacken' – had made a name for himself as a writer of supernatural horror. In novels such as *The Great God Pan* (1894), described in 2008 by popular author Stephen King as 'the most terrifying story ever written',[61] he had acquired a reputation as perhaps the most outstanding British writer of *fin de siècle* supernatural fiction, and had an enthusiastic following of readers and admirers to match. An occultist, Machen was a member of the Hermetic Order of the Golden Dawn, a secret magical order which practised theurgy and which, in the late nineteenth and early twentieth centuries, had a deep impact upon western occultism. Significantly, a number of Celtic revivalists was drawn to its ranks, notably William Butler Yeats, the Irish nationalist poet and purveyor of romantic 'Celtic Twilight' literature, and Aleister Crowley.[62] The latter, famously dubbed 'the most wicked man in England', was for a time active in Cornwall, as was his associate Philip Heseltine, who – in an echo of Llewellyn/Machen – changed his name to 'Peter Warlock' and (among other things) learned Cornish and set some of Henry Jenner's Cornish-language poems to music. Intriguingly, Heseltine had his own particular North Cornwall connections, he and his pregnant girlfriend 'Puma' (Minnie Lucy Channing) staying with D.H. Lawrence – who also found Cornwall 'pagan' and 'pre-Christian' — at Porthcothan, not far from St Ervan, during the Great War.[63]

Here was a fraternity of 'pagan' Celtic revivalism to which Machen was happy to belong, and he revelled in his Welsh origins in the pagan-Celtic land of Gwent. However, by the spring of 1922, when *The Secret Glory* first appeared, Machen had begun to alter his position. His *The Great Return* of 1915, about a return to the Wales of the Holy Grail, had presaged this change, and by the time his autobiographical *Far off Things* appeared in 1922, he had effectively recanted. Although he was to continue to write stories of horror and the supernatural, he recognized that hitherto he had mistaken 'awe' for 'evil', especially in his reading of the Celtic landscape. It was an important self-revelation that was, in its way, as significant as Betjeman's encounter with the Rector of St Ervan. As Machen put it:

> I have told, I think, how I was confronted suddenly and for the first time with the awe and solemnity and mystery of the valley of the Usk, and of the house called Bartholly hanging solitary between the deep forest and the winding esses of the river. This spectacle remained in my heart for years, and at last I transliterated it, clumsily enough, in the story of *The Great God Pan*, which, as a friendly critic once said, 'does at least make one believe in the devil, if it does nothing else'. Here, of course, was my real failure; I translated awe, at worst awfulness, into evil.[64]

As *The Secret Glory* made plain, this 'awe' was essentially Celtic-Christian, a position not unlike that later adopted by Betjeman himself where he reconciled as 'happy terror' the opposing but somehow complementary 'Christian' and 'pagan' dimensions of the Cornish landscape. In the book, the 'hero' — Machen's *alter ego*, Ambrose Meyrick, a schoolboy approaching manhood — struggles against the public school system which threatens to suppress his enthusiasms and creativity (which includes, like Betjeman, a passion for architecture), all the while nurturing a childhood vision of the Holy Grail hidden deep in his native Gwent. As Bevis Hillier, Betjeman's biographer, has commented, it is no surprise that the book made such an impression on the young Betjeman: 'It was suffused with a poetic romanticism, a passionate nostalgia for old saints, grail-quests, holy wells and holy bells of Celtic Wales, which chimed in perfectly with his interest in primitive Cornish saints'.[65]

As Hillier added, the book also chimed with Betjeman's own sense of a Welsh ancestry.[66] As we have seen (in chapter one), John Betjeman's great-grandfather had married one Mary Annie Merrick in 1830, and family tradition had insisted that they were descended from the Merricks – or Meyricks – of Bodorgan in Anglesey. It was a story told to Betjeman by his relation Rebecca Excelsior ('Celsie') Merrick, who more than anyone knew the Betjemann family history, and he clung to it firmly as evidence of his own Celticity. He might not be properly English but here was a Welshness that would allow him to claim affinity with his beloved Cornwall. That the hero of Machen's book was a Meyrick was an uncanny coincidence, and – as Betjeman knew already – many of the saints of North Cornwall were also those of Machen's Gwent, the off-spring of King Brychan who was said to have arrived from South Wales with his three wives and twenty-four or more saintly children. Their dedications, as we have seen, peppered North Cornwall. In the footsteps of Brychan and his many offspring, Betjeman felt able – as perhaps he imagined it – to plant his own latter-day 'Welshness' in North Cornwall.

At the very least, Betjeman felt an affinity with the fictional Ambrose Meyrick in *The Secret Glory*, and for Meyrick's (and Machen's) Gwent read his own North Cornwall:

> There were laughs
> At public schools, at chapel services,
> At masters who were still 'big boys at heart'–
> While all the time the author's hero knew
> A Secret Glory in the hills of Wales:
> Caverns of light revealed the Holy Grail
> Exhaling gold upon the mountain-tops;
> At 'Holy! Holy! Holy!' In the Mass
> King Brychan's sainted children crowded round,
> And past and present were enwrapped in one.[67]

Likewise, as Betjeman appreciated, there was a further echo of this important Welsh-Cornish connection in the cult of St Cadoc. There was a cluster of church dedications to the saint in the upper Usk valley in Arthur Machen's Gwent.[68] But there were also commemorations in North Cornwall – at St Cadoc's holy well, near the road from Padstow to Trevone along Harlyn Bay, and at neighbouring Cadoc Farm.[69] St Cadoc, Betjeman knew, was a grandson of Brychan and reputedly a leading monastic figure in early sixth-century South Wales. His principal Welsh dedication was at Llangattock-nigh-Usk but among others in Gwent was Caerleon; birthplace, of course, of Arthur Machen. Here was another uncanny coincidence or, as Betjeman imagined it, another mystical revelation of affinity. He searched for the ruined well-chapel near Trevone, picking his way across the boggy ground, with its tangled mass of brambles and bracken. And suddenly there was:

> A flame of rushlight in the cell
> On holy walls and holy well
> And to the west the thundering bay
> With soaking seaweed, sand, and spray,
> > Oh good St Cadoc pray for me
> > Here in your cell beside the sea.
>
> St Cadoc, when the wind was high,
> Saw angels in the Cornish sky
> As ocean rollers curled and poured
> Their loud Hosannas to the Lord,
> > His little cell was not too small
> > For that great Lord who made them all.
>
> Here where St Cadoc sheltered God
> The archaeologist has trod,
> Yet death is now the gentle shore
> With Land upon the cliffs before
> > And in his cell beside the sea
> > The Celtic saint has prayed for me.[70]

'eternal conflict between England and Wales'

We should not underestimate the extent to which Betjeman took seriously the 'Celtic' identity lent by his presumed Merrick/Meyrick descent. When, as an undergraduate at Oxford, he insisted on taking a Welsh-language option he was not merely, as others have suggested, being difficult and perverse in the face of authority, but was also expressing his sense of ancient kinship.[71] When L.T.C. Rolt, the railway historian and preservationist, urged Betjeman to join the Talyllyn Railway preservation society he did not hesitate, on several occasions making the journey to West (Welsh-speaking) Wales to travel on the little narrow-gauge trains.[72] Rolt had written to Betjeman in July 1950, explaining that the Talyllyn was now 'the only

independent statutory railway company in Britain'. He and a few friends
had 'been trying to devise ways and means of ensuring the survival of this
unique line, but the recent death of the owner, old Sir Haydn Jones, now
makes it a "now" or "never" matter'.[73]

Rolt proved spectacularly successful in his bid to save and revitalize the
railway, and a little over three years later, Betjeman – as railway enthusiast but
also Welshman-by-descent – was penning a glowing Foreword to Rolt's book
Railway Adventure, which described the preservation project.[74] Intriguingly, in
an echo of Betjeman's own sense of being 'part of the problem' in Cornwall,
Rolt also felt that the re-launching of the Talyllyn as a tourist attraction
would add to the numbers of English in-migrants and to the summer influx
of English visitors that were already putting pressure on local Welsh-speaking
communities. Moreover, just as Betjeman's 'Meyrick' identity had lent him
Celtic credentials, so Rolt felt that he too had some tenuous right to 'belong'.
As he put it: 'That the Welsh language should survive as strongly as it does
in this part of mid-Wales is a tribute to the strength and vigour of the native
tradition, but the price of invasion is patently apparent in sprawling coastal
towns ... [and] the loud, harsh accents of London, Lancashire, Birmingham
or the Black Country'. And yet, as he added, 'Though I have come over the
mountains myself as an invader, I felt that a childhood spent at Welsh Hay
[-on-Wye] gave me some sort of passport, and before long I found myself
looking at the summer invasion from the Welshman's point of view'.[75] It
was a position that Betjeman understood perfectly.

Similarly, Betjeman sympathized with and understood the predicament
of the Revd R.S. Thomas, the Welsh Anglican priest whose poetry he much
admired. A paradoxical individual, Thomas was in many ways an apparently
'English' figure – in his embrace of Anglicanism, for instance, instead of
Welsh Nonconformity, and in his speech, which was decidedly BBC-style
received pronunciation, even public school in sound. He was born in Cardiff,
into an English-speaking environment, but it was on a visit as a child to
Holyhead on Holy Island off Anglesey – not far from the Meyrick home
at Bodorgan, as Betjeman no doubt recognized – that he became aware of
another Wales, Welsh-speaking and decidedly un-English, with a past steeped
in Celtic Christianity. The Welsh name for Holyhead was Caergybi, named
after the Cornish saint St Cybi, and, as Byron Rogers argues in his biography,
for R.S. Thomas Holy Island became 'a model of Wales', just as 'his own
life was a model for the distant past of his race'.[76] It launched Thomas into
a quest for Welshness that led him to learn the Welsh language (although
he could never write poetry in it, and spoke it with an English accent) and

to move ever westwards to a succession of increasingly remote parishes as
he sought constantly to locate himself in the 'real Wales'. He became an
ardent Welsh nationalist, refusing even to condemn those arsonist extremists
who burnt down English second-homes. Yet he remained an 'outsider', and
even as a child he felt that he did not really 'belong' anywhere, a conviction
that stayed with him until old age. Again, it was a position that Betjeman
understood perfectly. When he wrote his Introduction to R.S. Thomas'
poetry collection *Song at the Year's Turning*, published in 1955, he saw how
Thomas had tried to reach out to his Nonconformist countrymen – 'no
doubt sometimes suspicious' – hoping that he might draw them across to
the Church. 'By talking to his parishioners in their own language about the
things they knew', said Betjeman approvingly, 'he would win the souls to the
[Anglican] Christian faith and the sacraments'.[77] Three years later, in 1958,
an appreciative Thomas dedicated his latest collection, *Poetry for Supper*, to
John Betjeman, along with Rupert Hart-Davis the publisher.[78]

Betjeman empathized instinctively with L.T.C. Rolt and R.S. Thomas
in their quests, seeing in their experiences a mirror of his own. He also
felt about Wales much as he did about Cornwall, although he visited it
less often and wrote about it only occasionally. But when he did write,
it was glowing prose, full of wonder and enthusiasm. He insisted that
the best-loved hymn tune remembered from his childhood was the Welsh
'Hyfrydol',[79] and even now, he said, to hear the tune evoked images of
lonely Welsh hill farms, Nonconformist chapels, Celtic saints and Celtic
crosses. Even Herefordshire, he said, with a hint of proprietorial pride, was
a 'secret, partly Welsh, county', where in the southern areas 'the Welsh
were never driven out by the Saxons and they assimilated the Normans in
their own way', so that Kilpeck and neighbouring churches seemed 'Celtic
and unlike any other Norman work in England'.[80] Moreover, he said, 'in
the Welsh districts the old parish church is, Celtic fashion, some way
off from the village'.[81] Likewise, he was fascinated by the ambiguity of
Shrewsbury, jewel of the Welsh marches, with its English bridge and its
Welsh bridge. 'The bridges', he explained, served to 'symbolise the eternal
conflict between England and Wales', especially in this border country of
Shropshire where 'you will find someone called Edwards calling himself
English and someone called Smith calling himself Welsh'.[82] Further south
was Breconshire, or 'Brecknock', as Betjeman preferred (shades of King
Brychan), a 'remote Welsh county' and 'a kingdom in itself, of richly
wooded valleys surrounded by mountains, and with the cathedral town of
Brecon as its capital'.[83] Further south still was Cardiff, with its intriguing

castle. 'Caernarvon and Windsor have richer associations', said Betjeman, and 'Kenilworth is more famous, but for quaintness, learned ingenuity, gorgeousness of colour, jokes, excitement and splendour, Cardiff Castle has them all beaten'.[84] And beyond Cardiff and its castle was the hinterland of Glamorgan and the Black Mountains, explored by Betjeman in the summer of 1956. He saw Llanthony Abbey in the beauty of the evening light, and made his way to 'the top of the mountains beyond on the lonely road to Hay, [when] a storm broke out and I saw patches of light and flashes of fork lightning over miles of mountain to the Brecon Beacons and Mynydd Epynt'. As he concluded: 'Why go abroad? Wales is abroad and wonderful enough'.[85] For Betjeman, Wales was 'abroad', and yet in a very important sense it was *not* 'abroad' – it was his.

The Secret Glory had allowed Betjeman to make sense of his complex 'Celtic' identity – 'Cornish', perhaps, by affinity; 'Welsh', certainly, by descent – and to see Wales and Cornwall as 'abroad' but 'not abroad'; 'other' places where, nonetheless, he might strive legitimately to belong. It had also introduced him, as we have seen, to the sacramental fabric of 'Celtic Christianity' as it was understood and practised in contemporary Cornwall, moving him beyond the enthusiasms of Robert Stephen Hawker and Sabine Baring-Gould that he had absorbed as a child to embrace now the Anglo-Catholic world of Wilfred Ryan Johnson and his clerical colleagues in the diocese of Truro. But there was yet more to this extraordinary book, as Betjeman realized.

'a sentimental philanderer ... Red Martyrdom'

In *Summoned by Bells*, published in 1960, nearly forty years since that meeting at St Ervan, Betjeman observed curiously that 'I would not care to read that book [*The Secret Glory*] again'. His explanation was that he might be disappointed. After the passage of all those years, he said, it might not ring so true: 'It so exactly mingled with the mood / Of those impressionable years, that now / I might be disillusioned'.[86] However, there were perhaps other reasons for Betjeman's discomfort, and for his growing ambiguity towards the book over time.

In the second of his autobiographical volumes, *Things Near and Far*, published in 1923, Machen had quoted at length from a review of *The Secret Glory* that had appeared in *The Nation and the Athenaeum*, penned by J. Middleton Murry. It is a review that Betjeman must have seen. He had continued to read Machen's work, and after Machen retired to Old

Amersham in Buckinghamshire, Betjeman (then living nearby in Berkshire) was an occasional visitor as well as correspondent. In September 1943, for example, Machen wrote from his home in the High Street to invite Betjeman to come across one Saturday evening.[87] Later, Machen moved to Beaconsfield, not a million miles away, where he died in December 1947. Inevitably, the two men compared notes, and Betjeman must have been reminded of Middleton Murry's scathing words. Murry thought Machen's 'onslaught' on the public school system unconvincing. But far worse, said Murry, was the character of Ambrose Meyrick:

> Ambrose Meyrick, if he could be jerked for a moment by his creator into a semblance of real existence, would justify the worst outrages wrought upon him by his equally incredible *alma mater*. He is a sentimental philanderer with aesthetic Catholicism, a mystical Celtic dreamer, a Soho Bohemian (before Soho was ruined, of course); but these crimes are nothing compared to his incorrigible penchant for 'poetic prose'. Mr Machen has encouraged him in it. He will have a great deal more to answer for in the day of judgement than the schoolmaster who tried to beat him out of it.[88]

Betjeman, in his religious anxieties, had always fretted that he would himself have a great deal to answer for on judgement day, and, having identified so closely with Ambrose Meyrick, here in Murry's review was a critique that (he might have thought) could apply equally to him. To suggest that Betjeman was a 'sentimental philanderer' in any sense is perhaps going too far, although it is true that he had a (usually platonic) weakness for beautiful and intelligent women, forever experiencing 'crushes' on those interesting young ladies that he met in the course of his work. More seriously, there was the never-to-be-resolved tension in his life between his love for his (increasingly estranged) wife Penelope and his constant lover-companion, Lady Elizabeth Cavendish (see chapter six). Nor was Betjeman a 'sentimental philanderer' in Murry's sense that he dallied uncritically with 'aesthetic Catholicism', although his wife Penelope, much to his regret, did go over to Rome. Yet, as we know, he *was* drawn to the aesthetic 'Celtic church' (those Cornish saints waist-deep in cold streams), and to the Anglo-Catholic church in Cornwall which he held to be its direct inheritor. To that extent the accusation levelled against Ambrose Meyrick by Murry also applied abundantly to Betjeman. Moreover, as we have seen, he was certainly 'a mystical Celtic dreamer', and possibly also a 'Soho Bohemian' in the sense that Murry meant it. But most of all, Betjeman had an overwhelming penchant for 'poetic prose' – which was, as it happens, perhaps the best description of his blank verse *Summoned by Bells*, that literary place where he had publicly confessed the influence of *The Secret Glory* and his conversion to Celtic Christianity and Anglo-Catholicism.

To the discomforting observations posed by Middleton Murry was added the fate of Ambrose Meyrick himself. Put simply, in the pages of *The Secret Glory* Meyrick found salvation – and martyrdom – through his embrace of Celtic Christianity and pursuit of the Holy Grail. He was driven by the twin imperatives of kicking at his public school in dullest England and hankering after the secrets of the Grail locked in deepest Wales. At his 'hideous school', set amid 'the weary waves of dun Midland scenery bounded by the dim, hopeless horizon', his 'soul revisited the faery hills and valleys of the West'. He longed for 'the whole company of the Blessed Saints of the Isle of Britain', for the 'deep apple-garths in Avalon', and 'all the dear land of Gwent'.[89] He watched trains 'vanishing into the west ... away towards the haven of his desire', and celebrated in his heart 'the Ancient Mass of the Britons ... the religion that led me and drew me and compelled me was that wonderful and doubtful mythos of the Celtic Church'.[90]

Thus far, Betjeman's identification with Ambrose Meyrick was complete. He too, when weighed down by the daily routine of London suburbia, knew that 'west of westward, somewhere, Cornwall lay', and that 'Somewhere among the cairns or in the caves / The Celtic saints would come to me'.[91] Likewise, at mundane Harrow-on-the-Hill, his subconscious would sometimes allow him to imagine that Cornwall was really near at hand. 'Then Harrow-on-the-Hill's a rocky island', he explained, and 'There's a storm cloud to the westward over Kenton, / There's a line of harbour lights at Perivale'. Then he saw the 'little fleet of trawlers under sail ... rounding rough Pentire in a flood of sunset fire'. But, he mused, 'Can those boats be only roof tops / As they stream along the skyline / In a race for port and Padstow / With the gale?'.[92]

Thereafter, however, there was much to discomfort Betjeman. First of all, as Ambrose Meyrick was initiated into the secrets of the Holy Grail, so it became clear that this rare privilege also carried a terrible responsibility and an inevitable, terrifying destiny. To pursue the Holy Grail was to condemn oneself to a life of perpetual search, perpetual yearning. But to come close to the Grail was to earn a dreadful fate, that of martyrdom. And then, in his journeying, Ambrose Meyrick strayed and stumbled, as did so many of those who allowed themselves to be distracted in their lifetime's quest. Still rebelling against his school, he took up with one of its domestic servants, Nelly Foran, absconding with her. He could not quite believe it: 'I cannot feel she is really Nelly Foran who opens the door and waits at table, for she is a miracle ... [a] wonderful, beautiful body shining through the darkness':

> I saw golden Myfanwy, as she bathed in the brook Tarogi.
>   Her hair flowed about her. Arthur's crown had dissolved into a
>   Shining mist.
>   I gazed into her blue eyes as it were into twin heavens. All the
> parts
>   Of her body were adornments and miracles.
>   O gift of the everlasting!
>   O wonderful hidden mystery!
>   When I embraced Myfanwy a moment became immortality.[93]

Yet this Myfanwy *was* Nelly Foran. Posing as Mr & Mrs Lupton (named ironically after Ambrose's school), they find lodgings in London. Soon Ambrose has taught Nelly how to smoke, and together they sit up in bed puffing at their cigarettes. At breakfast, 'They laughed so loud and so merrily over their morning tea ... that the landlady doubted gravely as to their marriage lines'. However, 'She cared nothing; they had paid what she had asked, money down in advance, and, she said: "Young gentlemen *will* have their fun with the young ladies – so what's the good of talking?"'.[94] But suddenly it all began to seem a bit sordid, and Ambrose knew it had to end. As he broke the news to Nelly, she looked at him 'with the most piteous longing ... I shall never forget the sad enchantment of her face ... the tears were wet on her cheek'.[95] But it had to be done. Thereafter, Ambrose led a life of relative obscurity until, on the death of its Keeper, the Holy Grail was placed in his charge: 'he received it with the condition that it was to be taken to a certain concealed shrine in Asia and there deposited in hands that would know how to hide its glories forever from the evil world'. He did as he was bid but as he neared his destination he was captured by 'the Turks or the Kurds – it does not matter which'. They insisted that he spit upon the image of Christ Crucified but he refused: 'So they bore him to a tree outside the village and crucified him there'. And thus 'It was in this manner that Ambrose Meyrick gained Red Martyrdom and achieved the most glorious Quest and Adventure of the Sangraal'.[96]

We know that Betjeman was fascinated by Ambrose Meyrick's progress

– evidenced, for example, in his poems 'Myfanwy' ('Golden the lights on the locks of Myfanwy') and 'Myfanwy at Oxford' ('Gold Myfanwy blesses us all')[97] – but Meyrick's experience was one from which he inevitably shrank. The metaphor of martyrdom was all too powerful, and Betjeman knew that in his own life, with its numerous distractions and his great love of fun and frivolity, he too would stray one way or another from the straight and narrow. Guilt, angst and a wavering, doubtful faith would, perhaps, be his 'martyrdom'. But he was to keep up his personal quest for the Holy Grail, both in the sense of rooting himself ever more deeply in Cornwall – especially North Cornwall – and in pursuing a religious vision which owed much to Hawker, Baring-Gould and, most especially, to Wilfred Johnson, the Rector of St Ervan.

For Betjeman, *The Secret Glory* had been a revelation and an inspiration, even if its portents were profoundly unsettling. The volume had encouraged awareness of a his own 'Celtic' identity, an identity that had led him to Wales as well as Cornwall and which would, in time, as we shall see, take him to Ireland and as far as Australia. Likewise, the book had also strengthened his growing commitment to Anglo-Catholicism and its links in Cornwall, as in Wales, with a mystical Celtic Christianity. Ultimately, for Betjeman, this was a faith that might even bear the dread of Red Martyrdom:

> St Cadoc blest the woods of ash
> Bent backwards by the Western lash,
> He loved the veinéd threshold stones
> Where sun might sometime bleach his bones
>   He had no cowering fear of death
>   For breath of God was Cadoc's breath.[98]

CHAPTER FIVE

'A Longing for Ireland'

Séan O'Betjemán
and the 'Anglo-Celtic Muse'

One day in the 1970s, soon after he had been appointed Poet Laureate, John Betjeman was visited in his London home by a television crew from *RTE*, the Irish state broadcasting service. As they entered the cramped quarters of his living room with their cameras, sound recording equipment and all the other paraphernalia of programme making, the journalists and technicians were astonished when Betjeman welcomed them in Irish. 'Go mbeannai dia dhibh' ('hello', or literally 'may God bless you') he said breezily, speaking with apparently effortless recall that more-than-a smattering of Gaelic that he had learned long before, in the 1940s.[1] For the *RTE* team, and for viewers in Ireland, here was another, unexpected side to John Betjeman. Already familiar as England's favourite poet, Betjeman had now revealed an Irish dimension to his already complex make-up.

But perhaps the *RTE* people ought not to have been so surprised. If they had done their homework, they would have discovered Betjeman's deep and distinguished links with Ireland. There were literary connections, as might be expected, reflecting Betjeman's intimate knowledge of Ireland – its people, places, landscapes, architecture – and his enduring affection for that country. But Betjeman had also lived in Ireland for a time during the Second World War. Here he had played a significant role in mediating the uneasy relationship between the then still newly independent and determinedly neutral Irish Free State (or 'Eire', as it had by then become) and a beleaguered United Kingdom living in constant fear of German bombs. To that extent, he had found for himself a modest place in the making of modern Ireland, and in so doing had carved out an important Irish niche in his kaleidoscopic personal identity, adding 'Irish' to a composite 'Celtic' identity that already encompassed 'Cornish' (by affinity) and 'Welsh' (by descent). Likewise, Ireland was to find itself inextricably entwined in the complex story of John Betjeman and Cornwall, as would, in time, Scotland, the Isle of Man, and even Australia.

'Irish peers, Irish architecture ... Irish poetry'

Even before the dark days of the war, Betjeman had cultivated his Irish enthusiasms. In 1939, for example, he had been asked to contribute to an anthology of young writers edited by Michael Harrison. Here he listed his chief interests as 'Irish peers and Irish architecture and pre-Celtic-Twilight Irish poetry, written in English'.[2] Later, as he learned Irish, so he came to appreciate Gaelic poetry and culture, facility with the language opening-up vistas unavailable to monoglot English-speakers, except in translation. His knowledge of Irish may never have been extensive but he worked hard to master its essentials when living in Dublin during the war. His daughter Candida Lycett Green, who was born in Ireland, recounts how Frank Gallagher, Director of the Irish Government Information Service, found for Betjeman a good teacher of Irish. As Candida explains, her father 'used to practise expressions from the phrase book out loud on top of the bus going to and from work'. Inevitably, 'fellow travellers would help him out and by the time he left Dublin he could write whole letters in Gaelic, and later taught my brother to count in it before he could in English'.[3]

Betjeman had also developed a taste for Celtic Twilight poetry, despite his later protestations, and his poetic form as it developed came to owe much to William Butler Yeats. Yeats was the 'driving force of the Irish literary revival', according to Robert Welch, 'who virtually invented modern Irish literature in English'.[4] In both prose and poem Yeats deployed Celtic themes drawn from traditional Irish folklore, culminating in the publication in 1893 of *The Celtic Twilight* – a collection of dreamy, melancholic, wistful poetry that exemplified the 'twilight' movement. As early as 1926 Betjeman had met Yeats, travelling with him on a long train journey to Galway, and in 1931, as he pondered the global economic downturn and troubled international situation, he dreamed of fleeing with Camilla Russell (his then girlfriend) to that remote island sanctuary, the 'Lake Isle of Innisfree' of Yeats' romantic-nationalist poetry.[5]

But, as Betjeman was to insist in Harrison's anthology in 1939, his first love was indeed the Anglo-Irish poetry of the eighteenth and nineteenth centuries. Betjeman especially admired the work of William Allingham, for example, born in County Donegal in 1824, a poet who befriended Tennyson and Rossetti and the pre-Raphaelite circle. It was Allingham who wrote the popular *The Fairies* ('Up the airy mountain ...'), his poetry exhibiting a style distinctly Irish (with a number of rhythms that do not usually occur in English writing) which he shared with other Anglo-Irish poets of the time.[6] It was a style, as Derek Stanford has observed, that may also be detected in Betjeman's own work, an 'imitation which is one third game of skill, one third humour, one third homage'. As Stanford put it, somewhat patronizingly, in studying poets such as Allingham, Betjeman 'became acquainted with the minor felicities of the Anglo-Celtic muse'.[7] Yet this assessment, important as it is, managed to underestimate both the stature of such Irish poets and the depth of their influence upon Betjeman and his work.

Oliver Goldsmith, for example, born in County Longford in 1724, one of those Anglo-Irish writers admired by Betjeman, was hardly minor. A friend of Samuel Johnson, this was the Goldsmith (of *She Stoops to Conquer* fame) who wrote *The Deserted Village*, a poem which first appeared in 1770. It is a work that has entered the canon of both Irish and English literature, and is one of two Goldsmith poems included in *The New Oxford Book of English Verse*.[8] Based, it is said, on Goldsmith's childhood experiences at Lissoy in County Westmeath, it describes the clearance of an imaginary village ('sweet Auburn') by a rapacious landlord anxious to 'improve' his estate. It is, according to Robert Welch, a poem that 'recreates an idealized picture of the contented community of the past', while expressing 'indignation against the luxury and materialism of modern civilization' and 'disapproval at the trespass of aristocratic self-indulgence on the simple virtues of the villagers'.[9] It is a hymn to a disappearing way of life:

> Sweet Auburn, loveliest village of the plain,
> Where health and plenty cheered the labouring swain,
> Where smiling spring its earliest visit paid,
> And parting summer's lingering blooms delayed,
> Dear lovely bowers of innocence and ease,
> Seats of my youth, when every sport could please,
> How often have I loitered o'er thy green,
> Where humble happiness endeared each scene![10]

Here, said Goldsmith, were 'sports beneath the spreading tree', with 'young contending as the old surveyed', and 'slights of art and feats of strength'. Here too were 'bashful virgin's side-long look of love' and 'matron's glance that would those looks reprove'. Such 'were thy charms, sweet village; sports like these, / With sweet succession taught even toil to please'. But, alas, 'these charms are fled', for 'the tyrant's hand is seen / And desolation saddens all thy green: / One only master grasps the whole domain'.

Sometimes read as a Tory idealization of a vanished 'Golden Age', the poem can also be seen as a precursor of Yeats' Celtic Twilight themes and, indeed, of the romantic-nationalist ideology of Eamon de Valera, architect of Irish independence and Prime Minister of Ireland during Betjeman's wartime sojourn in Dublin.[11] The 'Ireland which we dreamed of', said de Valera, 'would be the home of a people who valued material wealth only as a basis of right living'. These were people 'who were satisfied with frugal comfort and devoted their leisure to things of the spirit; a land whose countryside would be bright and cosy homesteads'. Here the 'fields and villages would be joyous', he said, with 'the romping of sturdy children, the contests of athletic youths, the laughter of comely maidens', with cottage firesides 'forums of the wisdom of serene old age'.[12] It was a vision of Ireland more than reminiscent of Oliver Goldsmith's. It was also John Betjeman's.

'that passion for Ireland'

As a small child Betjeman had first fallen under the spell of Goldsmith's verse. It had been a nursery-room favourite, the mainstay of bedtime reading. In 1978, writing to his wife Penelope, Betjeman explained that 'I have just re-read Goldsmith's *Deserted Village* which', he claimed, 'influenced me more than any other English poem'. He recalled that 'Ernie', his father, 'used to read it to me almost daily when I was six or seven'. Betjeman still thought it one of the best poems in the English language, and, he confessed, it 'gave me a longing for Ireland from which I have never really recovered'. Reflecting on his estrangement from his father in later years, he added ruefully: 'I am most surprised at that passion for Ireland induced by Ernie of all people'.[13]

Betjeman began to give expression to this 'passion for Ireland' when, in the summer of 1926, while still a student at Oxford, he was invited by his friend Pierce ('Piers') Synnott to visit his seat in County Kildare. As Candida Lycett Green has put it: 'this was the beginning of JB's [Betjeman's] never-ending love affair with Ireland'.[14] Synnott had inherited the house – Furness, near Naas – from his father on the latter's death in 1920, and it was everything that Betjeman had imagined an Irish country residence to be. There was a ruined monastic church, reputedly haunted, in the grounds, together with yew trees from which (it was said) rebels were hanged in the

great Irish rising of 1798. It was at Furness that Betjeman first met Katharine
Tynan, the Irish poet and friend of W.B. Yeats, who promised to introduce
him to other Irish literary figures. From Furness, Betjeman was invited
to visit 'Cracky' William Clonmore at Shelton Abbey in Arklow, County
Wicklow, a visit he repeated twice again in the following year, and in 1928
he was a guest of Basil Dufferin at Clandeboye in County Down. By 1930,
as Candida Lycett Green remarked, 'Ireland had already become a regular
place of pilgrimage for JB each summer'.[15] In that year he was invited to
Pakenham Hall in County Westmeath (shades of William Goldsmith) by his
new friend Frank Pakenham, later to become the celebrated Lord Longford
of political and literary fame. At the time of Betjeman's visit, Pakenham Hall
was owned by Frank's elder brother Edward, who had inherited it when he
was thirteen on their father's death at Gallipoli. Like Furness, Pakenham
Hall was for Betjeman everything that an Irish seat should be. There were
high spirits too, which suited Betjeman, including the lusty rendering of
Irish nationalist ballads such as 'Bold Fenian Men', 'Boys of Wexford' and
'Paddies Evermore', tempered by loyalist songs like 'Derry's Walls', 'The
Old Orange Flute' and 'The Orange Lily-O'.[16] According to Candida Lycett
Green, Pakenham Hall became Betjeman's 'spiritual home in Ireland'.[17] In
July 1939 he wrote to Edward Pakenham and his wife Christine: 'Many,
many thanks for Ireland', he said.[18]

It was in the great houses of Ireland in these years that John Betjeman
acquired his undying affection for the Anglo-Irish peerage. In October
1938 he wrote to Elizabeth Bowen, exclaiming that 'the Anglo-Irish are
the greatest race in Western Europe' (she, indeed, was a member).[19] It was
a view he was never afraid to repeat, as late as August 1977 insisting in a
letter to television producer Ken Savidge (with whom he was collaborating
on a programme on Dublin) on his unflagging support for the Church of
Ireland and 'the great and neglected race, the Anglo-Irish'.[20] In 1967, in
frivolous mood, he had written to his friend Patsy Zeppel, complaining
about life in general: 'I would rather be a very obscure drunk Irish Peer of
the Act of Union in 1800', he said, 'but we can't have everything we want,
can we?'.[21] In fact, Betjeman had become an associate member of the Irish
Peers Association in 1955, partly out of nostalgic sentiment, partly to foster
his own self-identification with Ireland, and partly as a serious endeavour
to enhance the influence of the Irish peerage in Britain. In 1961 the last
of the twenty-eight Irish Representative Peers at Westminster (created at
the independence of the Irish Free State) died. In consequence, the Irish
Peers Association reformulated itself in 1963, campaigning now for the

appointment of a new set of Representative Peers. As its membership card explained, the Association considered that 'In view of the community of interests obtaining between the United Kingdom and the Republic of Ireland, it would doubtless be to the public advantage for Ireland to have 28 more friends in the House of Lords'.[22] In 1965 the Association boasted John Betjeman CBE as a leading member, in the company of such worthies as The Lord and Lady Dunboyne, The Earl of Westmeath, and Lt-Col The Marquis of Ormond CVO, MC, DL.

There was also here a hint of hob-knobbing with the gentry (something Betjeman was sometimes accused of in England), of social climbing and romantic affectation. But Betjeman was also deadly serious. At length, as we know, his search for the 'Celtic other', in which to locate his personal identity and to put down permanent roots, settled on Cornwall. But, despite his childhood days at Trebetherick and the life-altering experience of St Ervan and *The Secret Glory* (see chapter four), in the period before the Second World War it was often Ireland rather than Cornwall that was at the forefront of his imagination and aspirations. In 1931, as noted above, Betjeman had feared that economic depression might be a prelude to a general collapse of the international system. He said so to Camilla Russell. 'I shall whisk you off to Ireland when the collapse comes', he promised.[23] A fortnight later he repeated the intention, writing to Camilla in 'the twelve a.m. express (all stations) Belfast to Cavan change for Great Southern Railway to Float'. He longed, he said, to 'take you away to a large and comfortable house in the Irish Free State where we would live in happy madness and sin until we died'. But for the moment he had to make do with describing the Irish countryside through which the train was passing. It was 'a delightfully obscure journey right through the North of Ireland over the border and into the dear old Free State which is far better'. He explained that 'I am now in a very decayed first-class carriage', immersing himself in the atmosphere of rustic antiquity, with the train 'jolting through Irish landscape with a glimpse now and then through beech trees of an imposing eighteenth-century house with cracked stable and broken windows doubtless the residence of some insane and obscure peer'.[24]

As the train neared Cavan, Betjeman remembered that County Cavan was one of those Ulster counties not included in the new statelet of Northern Ireland. Protestants there felt marooned in the hostile theocracy they imagined the Free State to be, while their Catholic neighbours eyed them with suspicion, considering them representatives on the wrong side of the border of the oppressive regime they thought to operate in the North. The result of this mutual incomprehension was communal strife, and Betjeman reported to Camilla that 'Cavan where I have forty minutes to wait is the scene of the Protestant v. Catholic riots'. Mischievously, he added: 'I hope I shall see some'.[25] But this was not so much gleeful irresponsibility as enjoyment of the *frisson* of exotic danger that he sometimes imagined to lurk in the Irish countryside, a feeling not unlike that 'happy terror' that he had already discerned in the landscape of North Cornwall. It also reflected Betjeman's understanding of the political nuances of contemporary Ireland, something that would stand him in good stead when he worked there for the British government in the war. There was, for example, a fight at the Dublin Horse Show when some of the punters sang 'God Save the King', an incident he was also careful to report to Camilla.[26]

For all its apparent intensity and passion, the engagement of John Betjeman and Camilla Russell did not last. Provocative as always, Betjeman had sent Camilla an allegedly pornographic book, and when her father got to hear of it he demanded that she end the relationship. By then Betjeman had already met Penelope Chetwode, his future wife, and she swiftly replaced Camilla in his fanciful imaginings of running away to Ireland to live happily ever after. By the late 1930s these fantasies had become more solid, and Betjeman began to consider seriously the possibility of making Ireland his home. He told T.S. Eliot that he would move there 'If I had any [financial] competence of my own',[27] and he outlined his plans to his mother, Bess. Ernie, his father, had died in 1934, and by 1938 Bess had decided that their smart Arts & Crafts house at Trebetherick was too large for her. 'Undertown', the holiday-home that Ernie had had built in 1929, close by St Enodoc golf course, was sold and Bess acquired instead a more modest, practical property at Rock on the estuary opposite Padstow.

'Ireland is what Cornwall *was*'

For Betjeman, it seemed like the end of an era. Although his relationship with his father had been often stormy, with Trebetherick the scene of rows and confrontations, he now felt a sense of loss as the family association with the place was severed. 'I am very sorry you're now saddled with a Rock Bungalow', he wrote to his mother, 'it's sad to think of poor Undertown no longer ours and that we will no longer sit on that slate terrace and look across to Bray Hill'. As he admitted: 'I feel as though I had lost an important part of me ... I suppose I feel unhappy now that it is gone because of childhood memories and all the Cornish saints and tufts of grass and rocks and pools that I shall always remember'. He was mourning a lost childhood but it was also a farewell to Cornwall, or so it seemed. He already feared 'the ruination of the place', he wrote, rationalizing in his mind the decision to quit Trebetherick, making the pill less bitter to swallow, and he complained of local road-widening schemes and the destructive presence of new developments. Cornwall was being spoiled, he said, and it was time now to turn from one Celtic country to another: 'Goodbye St Enodoc ... Ireland is what Cornwall *was*'.[28]

'I stand by my original idea of going to Ireland and buying a small property there', he wrote to Bess in October 1938: 'I can get a decent sized house and demesne for about twelve hundred pounds'. He would have to borrow the money, he said. The Chetwodes had disapproved of their daughter's marriage to Betjeman in 1933, and he was careful now not to antagonize them further. 'Won't want to do it with P[enelope]'s money', he explained, 'because the Chetwodes would kick up a fuss', especially 'as they hate Ireland and the Irish'. And as for the future: 'How I am going to afford to live in Ireland, I neither know nor care. All I do know is that away from aeroplanes and motor cars I at once expand'. Ireland was his muse, he said: 'I have written all that I have written that is worth writing in Ireland, and I regard it as a salvation'. Ireland was his personal salvation but the country might soon become the saviour of European civilization as a whole, he thought, just as it was after the fall of the Roman Empire. Then pagans and barbarians had run amok in Europe (including the Anglo-Saxon invasion of Britain), leaving Ireland to stand alone as the shining beacon of Christianity. Returning to the fears he had expressed to Camilla Russell at the beginning of the decade, he foresaw the collapse of Europe, now seemingly imminent as Nazi Germany flexed its muscles with ever increasing menace. War was likely, perhaps even inevitable, and Betjeman hoped that Ireland would be able to stand apart from it. 'I think it possible that should Europe collapse', he explained to his mother, 'Ireland will become what it was in the seventh century, the last home of civilization in the Dark Ages'.[29]

War did indeed break out. It put paid to any genuine plans that Betjeman might have had for settling permanently in Ireland. But, paradoxically, it led directly to his two-and-three-quarter years sojourn in Dublin, working for the British government. Early in the war, Betjeman had been employed at the Ministry of Information, where his experience in journalism and broadcasting lent itself to the propaganda war effort. This doubtless qualified him for his future role in Dublin. But so too did his widespread knowledge of Ireland and Irish culture, his established network of friendships with Irish notables and opinion-formers, and his understanding of the intricacies (and dangers) of Irish politics. Indeed, he had not been above dabbling in politics himself. He was, for example, a friend of Dermott MacManus, the Irish writer and activist, who had been introduced to him by the Pakenhams.

Army Comrades Association

MacManus had been a member of both the British and Free State armies, and was now involved in a political movement called the Army Comrades Association. The ACA, as it was known, had emerged in Ireland after the 1932 election. Formed principally of former Free State soldiers, those who had fought the IRA in the Civil War after independence, the ACA acted as a paramilitary police force for Cumann na nGaedheal, the 'pro-Treaty' government party that had sanctioned the partition of Ireland as part of the deal to create the Free State. The ACA provided protection at Cumann na nGaedheal meetings and rallies, deterring attacks from the IRA and other potentially violent opponents. Among other things, the movement won the approval of W.B. Yeats, together with those alarmed by the rising power of Eamon de Valera (whose Fianna Fail party had narrowly won the 1932 election) and his alleged continuing links with the IRA. In an atmosphere where, to some observers at least, a renewal of the Civil War seemed possible, the security offered by the ACA was welcomed by Cumann na nGaedheal and its leader William Cosgrave. In fact, the ACA shortly began to develop a life of its own. Marching under the red saltire of St Patrick, rather than the orange-and-green tricolour, the ACA adopted a blue-shirt uniform, giving rise to the name by which the movement is best known – the Blue Shirts. Increasingly identified with fascist movements elsewhere in Europe, the Blue Shirts paraded and drilled, as did Mosley's Black Shirts in England, and de Valera took steps to have them banned. In the event, the Blue Shirts soon found themselves out of step with the developing pace of Irish politics, and were largely overtaken by events. First of all, Cumann na nGaedheal merged with the smaller Centre Party and elements of the ACA to found the new 'United Ireland' party or Fine Gael. The remnants of the now discredited Blue Shirts soldiered on for a time (some of their number went to fight for Franco in Spain) but to all intents and purposes the Army Comrades Association was already dead, no longer a force in Irish political life.[30]

Although Betjeman, as a result of his wartime experiences, would come to view the partition of Ireland as a tragedy, and likewise grew to like and admire de Valera, he was in 1933 sympathetic to the ACA. Taking his cue, perhaps, from those Anglo-Irish friends fearful of the militant republicanism they saw in de Valera, Betjeman flirted briefly with the movement. In April 1933 he wrote to his friend Michael Rosse (The Earl of Rosse) in his 'Gothick Castle' in Ireland. 'Please excuse this rather unexpected letter on what will be, from me, an unexpected subject', Betjeman said. 'I have a friend [Dermott MacManus?] whose card is enclosed', he explained, 'who is one of the Big Three in the new White Army in Ireland. As you are an Irish Citizen and I expect have opinions about Dev's [de Valera's] actions and politics at the moment, I thought you might be interested in the enclosed pamphlets about the ACA – the White Army'. He went on to offer his own analysis of the present Irish situation, concluding that the 'only hope lies in the ACA. Cosgrave's party is full of corruption, though Cosgrave himself is all right and I shouldn't think the Cuman na Gaedheal (sic) will ever get in again. The Centre party doesn't count and the IRA is communist, as we all know'. Outlining the political relationship between Cumann na nGaedheal and the ACA, he explained that the movement 'will support Cuman na Gaedheal where it can and put up its own members when it can't'. He urged Rosse to take an interest in the movement, adding that 'If you can let the Captain [MacManus?] (card enclosed) see you either when you are in Dublin or else let him come and see you for half an hour in your Gothick Castle, he could tell you all about it, what it has done and what it wants to do'. In case Rosse was not convinced, Betjeman offered an afterthought: 'The Captain is a nice man. Do see him. He is interested in Hindu eroticism as well as the ACA'.[31]

Rosse replied from his home at Birr Castle, County Offaly, on 20 April. His possibly tongue-in-cheek response was no doubt designed to warn Betjeman off from potentially dangerous political dabblings. 'I am very angry indeed', Rosse wrote, 'that you should have got as far as Dublin and not come to pay me a visit. The least you could have done, it seems to me, was to have brought the gallant Captain down yourself and introduced him to me'.[32] In another note, Rosse added that 'the President [of the ACA], I think, O'Higgins, called on my agent the other day and was only with difficulty prevented from coming and laying his suit before me!'. To ensure that Betjeman was left in no doubt about the difficulties of the situation, he added that 'I have no political views myself and though I understand the aims of the ACA are excellent, one is better not involved in any organisation at present'.[33] Between 1911 and 1926, the twenty-six counties of what became the Free State had lost thirty-four percent of its Protestant population, much

of it Anglo-Irish, some killed in 'the Troubles' and many more driven away
or deciding that it was time to leave.[34] Those who remained, like Michael
Rosse, knew that they had to play their cards sensibly and well. It was an
important political lesson for John Betjeman, and would stand him in good
stead for what was to come.

United Kingdom Representative to Eire

In 1937 de Valera had introduced a new Constitution, and with it Ireland
became a republic in all but name. The country was no longer the 'Irish Free
State' but 'Eire'. The British monarchy was recognized only as 'a symbol
of co-operation' between Ireland, Great Britain, Australia, Canada, New
Zealand and South Africa. There was no mention of a British 'Empire' or
even 'Commonwealth', let alone membership of it, and the role of Governor-
General was reduced to that of near irrelevance. The new Constitution
also made claim to the whole island of Ireland, effectively abrogating the
Treaty of 1921, and it recognized the special place of the Roman Catholic
Church in the life of the nation. As Ireland thus edged inexorably towards
the Republic that it became eventually in 1948, so the British government
firmly maintained its legal fiction that Ireland was a Dominion of the British
Commonwealth, just like Australia and the others. But while Australia and
the other Dominions declared war on Germany in 1939 as a matter of course,
following where Britain led, Ireland instead declared its neutrality. The
ambiguity, even absurdity, of Eire's constitutional relationship with Britain
was made plain by the continuing presence of German diplomats and other
interests in Dublin. Yet Britain never formally recognized Irish neutrality, a
policy that Betjeman would later see as folly and a barrier to good relations
between the two countries.

In 1938 Betjeman had expressed the hope that, if Europe was consumed
by war, Ireland might be spared, becoming perhaps the last bastion of
European civilization. Little did he recognize then that he was soon to
play a distinctive role in the story of Irish neutrality. On the declaration
of war on 3 September 1939, Britain found itself in the uncomfortable
position of having no diplomat accredited to the Irish government. In the
atmosphere of constitutional ambiguity, it had not been possible to appoint
a 'high commissioner' to Ireland – de Valera considered the term too
redolent of imperial representation, as in Britain's 'high commissioner' to
Australia or Canada – while the appointment of an 'ambassador', with its
implied recognition of Irish independence outside the Commonwealth, was

equally unpalatable for the British. A compromise was struck, with both governments agreeing to a 'United Kingdom Representative to Eire'. This diplomat was to be Sir John Maffey, a former head of the Colonial Office, a career civil servant later described by Lord Longford (Betjeman's old friend, Frank Pakenham) as 'a man of commanding stature and personality, a public servant of the highest distinction'.[35] As Longford observed, the position of the UK Representative was potentially fraught with difficulty: 'A new West Briton court in the centre of Dublin would not win the respect of the majority of the Irish people'. But 'Sir John Maffey was to prove an admirable choice, tactful, discreet and discerning'. Moreover, he 'won de Valera's confidence, the respect of all who met him and the friendship of many of the people of Ireland … He was a key figure in the testing years of neutrality'.[36]

Maffey set about appointing his staff, and John Betjeman was recommended (possibly by Brendan Bracken, then Minister of Information in Churchill's government) as Press Attaché to the UK Representative.[37] He took up the post formally in Dublin in January 1941 but had been sent on a preliminary visit the year before, partly to allow him to test the water in Ireland but also no doubt to show his own mettle. One of his several tasks, apparently, was to float before his Irish opposite numbers a suggestion that, should a German invasion of Ireland seem likely (a not entirely implausible fear in 1940, especially in Northern Ireland), then Eire and UK forces in the island of Ireland should be placed jointly under American or French command to resist the attack. This could be, it was insinuated, part of a 'symbolic union'[38] of North and South, something that Churchill spelt out in a memorandum to de Valera in June 1940 when the conditions for considering a 'Union of Ireland' were discussed. However, with the United States at this point determined to remain out of Europe's war, and with France itself collapsing, it was hardly a viable suggestion. More useful was the intelligence that Betjeman was able to feed back to London. As well as noting that the IRA was and always would be impervious to any attempts at persuasion, and that Irish opinion would remain suspicious of Britain until the partition question had been resolved, he also urged that the British government should support de Valera, not least because he commanded widespread respect throughout nationalist Ireland. He concluded too that, whatever the circumstances, there should be no further discussion of a possible German invasion of Ireland, a contentious subject in which the Irish did not appreciate British gratuitous advice. Betjeman was learning fast, and he received a congratulatory letter from E. Rawdon Smith at the

Ministry of Information. 'You seem to have reconnoitred the position so thoroughly', wrote Rawdon Smith admiringly, adding that he looked forward to Betjeman's return to England so that he could 'give us an "appreciation of the position", with recommendations'.[39]

Following his formal appointment, Betjeman launched something of a charm offensive. He made friends with the Irish poet Jack Taylor (they shortly collaborated on a book, *English, Scottish and Welsh Landscape*) and with the artist Jack Yeats, younger brother of W.B. Yeats. He even struck up a friendship with Senator Sean MacEntee, one of the more notoriously anti-British members of de Valera's government, and became a firm favourite of the MacEntee family, as did Betjeman's wife Penelope.[40] But, as he reported to his friend John Lehmann, 'They are all very fearful of British propaganda here', adding 'I don't blame them'.[41] Hitherto, Betjeman had enjoyed excellent relationships with the Anglo-Irish, some still nostalgically unionist in their political sympathies, others displaying a nationalist pride in their new Irish citizenship, while still maintaining bonds of affection and kinship with Britain. Now he was routinely encountering a more hardened enmity which was shocking, a deep-seated hatred of Britain – or rather, England – which he found difficult to accept. As he explained to his dear friends, John and Myfanwy Piper, writing in March 1941, 'All able-bodied pro-British have left Ireland for the English services and we are at the mercy of people who are either anti-British, anti-German and pro-Irish (a faint majority) ... [or] are pro-Irish and pro-German (about forty-eight per cent) ... [or] two per cent pro-German above everything'. It was a far cry from his romantic dreams of Ireland in those suddenly distant pre-war days. 'I am beginning to hate Ireland and the Irish', he told the Pipers: 'God bless England. God Save the King. Up the British Empire. The C of E (High) for Ever!'.[42]

A few days later, on St Patrick's Day, he wrote again to John Piper, complaining that 'A woman who is pro-Nazi and thinks she is a spy has made a pass at me and I have been through embarrassing scenes in motor cars'.[43] He was now aware that the time-honoured tactics deployed by enemy agents everywhere to compromise and discredit diplomats were being tried on him. It was a deeply unsettling revelation. Nonetheless, the charm offensive went on, and he was now busily learning Irish. But, as he admitted to his friend Oliver Stonor, 'I have to go about saying "Britain will win in the end" and I have to be charming to everyone ... The strain is far greater than was that of living in London during the blitz'. Still, he was happy enough to sign himself 'Séan O'Betjemán', and concluded his letter with 'Is mise le meas mór' ('I am, with great respect').[44] Later, in May 1941, he confided to John and Myfanwy Piper the difficulties caused for him by the belligerent and often insensitive attitude of the British government towards Ireland. The government steadfastly refused to understand Irish neutrality and failed to realise that de Valera considered a British victory would be in Ireland's best interests. Betjeman fumed: 'if conscription is introduced into the Six Counties [Northern Ireland], which it probably will be, I shall resign this job with a clear conscience'. He added, 'believe me, if it is done and if it means that our government is so damn silly over Ireland, then God help its tactics in the rest of the world'.⁴⁵ By now his perspectives were becoming more Irish; more appreciative of Irish anxieties and more critical of his own government. Often, he found himself having to explain and defend Ireland's diplomacy. And as well as his learning to speak Irish, his terminology was also acquiring an Irish flavour – 'Six Counties' was an exclusively nationalist description of Northern Ireland.

'a bloody British spy'

Fortunately, letters such as those to the Pipers which, in other circumstances, would be deeply embarrassing if they had fallen into the wrong hands, went out of Ireland in diplomatic bags and avoided the prying eyes of the official censor. Usually, when asked what his job as Press Attaché entailed, Betjeman replied on the lines of 'One friend gained for England, is one enemy for Germany and that is my job'.⁴⁶ But occasionally he let his guard down, such as when he wrote to Frank O'Connor, an Irish journalist, that he was just 'a bloody British spy'.⁴⁷ What O'Connor did with this potentially dangerous information is not clear but the word that Betjeman was a spy got out. This, perhaps, accounted for Betjeman's appearance on an IRA hit list. The IRA was now convinced that a German victory over Britain was inevitable and, heeding German promises that Northern Ireland would be handed over to Eire, it decided to redouble its efforts by hitting British targets in Ireland as well as the UK. These targets included Betjeman. Apparently, an IRA gunman loitered outside the UK Representative's office, waiting for Betjeman to emerge. Luckily, Betjeman was away at the time, and later – so the story goes – one of the IRA leadership read Betjeman's poems and decided that he would make a very unlikely spy.⁴⁸

Indeed, it does seem unlikely that Betjeman engaged in 'spying' as such. However, in the role of Press Attaché, Betjeman would have strayed routinely from straightforward public relations and media handling into the darker realms of propaganda and what is called today 'information warfare'.

Although Betjeman protested at the time that he did not do 'propaganda', there is evidence that he was involved in some elaborate information warfare activities. For example, a Ministry of Information memorandum dated 2 April 1943 (and tellingly entitled 'Counter Propaganda for Eire') detailed Betjeman's part in a plan to 'counteract the Gaelic broadcasts given by Dr Hartmann', an Irish-speaking Nazi propagandist whose radio programmes were beamed into homes across Ireland. It had been suggested that a speaker of Scots Gaelic might be recruited to broadcast British propaganda in Ireland but Betjeman, with his knowledge of Irish and his wider appreciation of the nuances of Celtic cultures, advised that Scots Gaelic was not sufficiently close to Irish for the plan to work. He also advised that 'there are no Irish Gaelic speakers in Northern Ireland' on whom the British government might draw, and even if there were, they would doubtless be of nationalist disposition and so unco-operative. Instead, Betjeman intimated confidently that he 'could find a speaker for these [proposed broadcasts] who would be a strong British partisan and, at the same time, be thoroughly understood by all Gaelic listeners in Eire'. The compiler of the memorandum, G.L. Marshall, also noted that 'Betjeman told me that the Eire Government could not possibly object to the BBC broadcasting a bulletin in Gaelic calculated to publicise the methods which the Nazis are adopting in Europe to put difficulties in the way of the R[oman] C[atholic] Church'. Moreover, Betjeman had advised, the Irish government could hardly complain about 'any propaganda on the subject of religious persecution generally including Jewish atrocities'.[49]

As the war drew on, and the scales of the conflict began to shift, so the atmosphere in Ireland started to change. The entrance of America on the side of Britain had a strong impact on Irish opinion, as did the growing likelihood of a German defeat. Moreover, and thanks in part to Betjeman's efforts, the Irish public had become more aware of the real nature of the Nazi regime and was now less susceptible to German propaganda. All this combined to make Betjeman's life easier. His public relations task seemed less formidable, and the enmity he encountered less raw. Moreover, in early 1943 he and Penelope had moved to Collinstown Park, a country house at Clondalkin, outside Dublin. As he remarked to Oliver Stonor, it was exactly the kind of retreat he had imagined in the 1930s, although here he was embroiled in diplomatic activity rather than living his imagined life of a reclusive Anglo-Irish writer. As he put it, Collinstown Park 'is what one would dream of as the ideal existence – if it weren't for Irish politics – and what I often longed for'.[50]

Work became more congenial. Betjeman wrote reviews for the *Dublin Magazine*, opened arts exhibitions, helped the tourist board with a survey of local architecture (he had been a founding member of the Irish Architectural Records Association in 1940), and entertained visiting VIPs at Collinstown Park. His popularity soared – so much so that, when it was time for him to relinquish his post and return to England in 1943, the *Irish Times* treated his departure as front-page news.[51] Betjeman himself paid glowing tribute to the people of Ireland. 'After more than two years' residency here', he said, 'I shall return to England with the profoundest gratitude to Ireland ... where everyone – Roman, Anglican, Nonconformist – believes in another world and everyone goes to church'.[52] It was a consummate piece of diplomacy – an inclusivity which recognized the equally valid contributions of different traditions to Irish life, and which hinted at the religious and moral superiority of Ireland over England. But this was not just another piece of good public relations. He believed what he said, and in private Betjeman expressed similar sentiments. As he prepared to leave, he wrote to Frank Gallagher. 'I am very depressed to be going', he admitted: 'So many friends made, so much kindness'.[53]

Back in England, there were lingering feelings of loss. Working now for the Admiralty at the requisitioned Empire Hotel in Bath, Betjeman wrote to his Irish friend Mabel Fitzgerald in August 1944, confessing that 'We miss Dublin a lot. More than words can express'.[54] He also retained his sophisticated appreciation of Irish politics. It was a tribute to his diplomatic skills that he had made friends among the more hard-line Republican Left, convincing them that he understood if not necessarily shared their convictions and aspirations. One of their number, Brian O'Neill, had written to Betjeman at the time of his departure. 'You've seen from the newspaper tributes what is thought in official and unofficial circles of your work,' he said, 'and now the West Britons have been effusive ... [a] word from the Left may not be superfluous'. He went on: 'In a way, it is the fact that you have made so many friends among the Left which only a few years ago had hostility to Britain as its common plank that best measures the success of your personality and understanding'. O'Neill looked forward to the creation of a united, socialist Republic of Ireland, outside the Commonwealth and with all links with Britain and the monarchy shorn for ever. He hoped that, when that great day arrived, Betjeman might return as British ambassador. 'May you come back', he wrote, 'as Britain's first Minister Plenipotentiary to the democratic Irish Republic'.[55]

'all this division and misery'

Certainly, Betjeman continued to work to promote understanding of Ireland in England. On the same day in February 1946, for example, he wrote to his old friends Frank Pakenham and Frank Gallagher. To the former, he complained about the mutual misapprehensions that still existed between the two countries. 'Popular misconceptions about Ireland in England', he said, were 'a) Paddies' and 'b) Celtic Twilight'. Likewise, 'Popular misconceptions in Ireland about England' were 'a) that English people know Irish history' and 'b) that English people despise Ireland'.[56] He wrote to Gallagher in similar vein, adding that it was vitally important for the English to be taught 'how to appreciate the ancient nation Ireland is'.[57]

Betjeman also retained his sense of Irish self-identification. In October 1952, for example, he concluded a letter to P. Morton Shand as 'Séan O' Betjeméan (sic), The well known Oirish Nationalist'.[58] Partly tongue-in-cheek, as ever, the signature was meant seriously as well as in jest. In the years before the war, and especially during his spell as Press Attaché, Betjeman had been exposed to the complexity of Irish nationalism (and unionism). As he explained to James Mitchell in June 1974, his considered position was that the Act of Union between Britain and Ireland in 1801 had been a mistake. It had led to the increasingly exclusive identification of Irish nationalism with Roman Catholicism, and this had marginalized the Anglo-Irish and alienated the Presbyterians and Nonconformists. And this, in turn, had led inexorably to the partition of Ireland. If only, he said, the parliamentary compact won by Henry Grattan and his 'Patriot' party in 1782 had endured. Here the British government had acknowledged the legislative independence of the Irish parliament in Dublin, with Ireland and Britain recognized as sovereign nations linked only by the Crown and common membership of the Empire. All this was undone in 1801, when the Irish parliament was abolished, an appalling folly in Betjeman's estimation. 'If Grattan's parliament had survived there would never have been all this division and misery', he said.[59]

Grattan's parliament had been as 'unreformed' as that of Britain's before 1832, and shared the same deleterious features. But Betjeman felt that it would gradually have become more democratic and more inclusive, just as that in Britain had. Moreover, its continued existence would have ensured a central role for the Anglo-Irish in guiding the fortunes of the modern Irish nation. It was, said Betjeman, the Anglo-Irish and the Church of Ireland that 'had bred all the most effective revolutionaries in Ireland e.g. Robert Emmett, Swift, Parnell, Lord Edward Fitzgerald, Wolf Tone, Henry Grattan'.[60] Yet Irish nationalism had been usurped by Roman Catholicism, leading to sectarian bitterness, partition, and estrangement from Britain. He had seen a glimmer of light at the end of the war, when anti-British hostility had abated in Eire and relations between the communities in Northern Ireland had seemed to become more friendly. But the problems of partition had not gone away, and by the late 1960s they had again come to the fore. As Betjeman explained to James Mitchell: 'before the Civil Rights campaign in Northern Ireland ... the Protestant (i.e. Presbyterian) demonstrations in Derry were becoming light-hearted folklore and you would find harmony and laughter on both sides'. Now, he added with regret, 'all the amity after the War has gone'.[61]

As Betjeman confessed to James Mitchell, 'I am in an invidious position with regard to Ireland'.[62] By 1974 his yearning for the old 'Patriot' parliament of Henry Grattan would have seemed quaintly anachronistic to most observers, more redolent of the curious Anglo-Irish unionist-nationalism of the Gaelic-speaking Pan Celticist, Lord Castletown, who had helped found the romantic Pan Celtic Association in 1899, than of any political position relevant to the current situation.[63] Nonetheless, privately he was in agreement with the idea that there should be a timescale for the withdrawal of British troops from Northern Ireland, although fearing that the problems there might now be insoluble, and condemning 'the bloody IRA'[64] for again stoking the fires of violence and hatred. Additionally, that sense of latent threat that he had experienced at Cavan all those years before had never really left him, and during the war he may well have recognized the personal danger posed by the IRA. In the mid-1950s, as the IRA re-emerged in Northern Ireland and old hit lists were dusted off, he wrote reassuringly to Penelope (then staying at Clandeboye in County Down) that 'I don't think you'll be involved in the IRA activities'.[65] Later, when increasingly incapacitated by the early onset of Parkinson's disease, he developed an irrational fear of 'Irish drunks' who might accost him the street, causing him to falter and stumble as he sought to defend his Irish record. Even in 1972, when he wrote his *London's Historic Railway Stations*, he had worried about 'the Irish drunks who have always haunted Euston'.[66]

Ireland with Emily

The effects upon Betjeman of his Irish experiences were many and varied, and long lasting. Most significant, perhaps, was his estimation of Eamon de Valera. Before the war, as we have seen, he shared Anglo-Irish suspicions of de Valera's republican agenda. But as he came to learn more about Irish politics, so he swiftly reversed his opinion, deciding that de Valera was on Britain's side and deserving of British support. Betjeman expressed this view through diplomatic channels but he was also prepared to air it in public. In the *Daily Herald* newspaper in 1945, for example, he wrote of de Valera's 'greatness'. He insisted that 'de Valera is no Nazi, no sympathizer with Germany, no bomb-thrower and', he went on, 'I suspect he regrets the old hatred of England which once made doubly difficult our negotiations for a working basis with Ireland – a basis which de Valera, on his terms, still earnestly desires'. But, as Betjeman acknowledged, the 'history of the English in Ireland does not make elevating reading ... There is reason for this hate. Irish history is full of "If only England had ..."'.[67]

In developing this opinion of de Valera, Betjeman may well have been guided and supported by Frank Pakenham, who later as Lord Longford was to collaborate with Thomas P. O'Neill to produce the authoritative biography *Eamon de Valera*, first published in 1970. In this admirable volume Longford repeated Betjeman's view, writing that de Valera had 'expressed sympathy for Britain throughout the war when few British people were able to feel much sympathy for him'. He also saw the 'greatness' that Betjeman had glimpsed, and he described, as Betjeman had done, de Valera's 'extraordinary degree of perseverance and ability to command public confidence'. As Longford and O'Neill concluded, reviewing de Valera's long and distinguished career, and his extraordinary tenacity and single-mindedness: 'It is true of him, if it is true of any man of our time, that he has been fashioned of the stuff that endures'.[68]

This was a summing-up with which Betjeman would surely have concurred. But he might also have recognized the perhaps surprising congruity between his own romantic imaginings of Ireland – derived, as we have seen, from those early Anglo-Irish writers such as Allingham and (especially) Goldsmith – and the nationalist ideology of Eamon de Valera. As Betjeman admitted, his early enthusiasm for Ireland had grown from his appreciation of those writers, especially Oliver Goldsmith and his *The Deserted Village*, the captivating poem that Betjeman as a small child had demanded again and again as bed-time reading. De Valera, meanwhile, had exhibited more than a hint of Goldsmith's influence when he had articulated that happy, muscular rural idyll that was for him Ireland idealized. Betjeman and de Valera had had much more in common than either of them could possibly have realized before Betjeman's appointment to Ireland in 1941. Betjeman, perhaps, was even more of an 'Irish nationalist' than he had at first suspected.

Betjeman's own poem that forever ties him to Ireland is his *Ireland with Emily*, first published in 1945. As Patrick Taylor-Martin has described it, '"Ireland with Emily" is Betjeman's most beautiful tribute to the Irish landscape and its people who, at the time that he wrote it, seemed to live in an age of faith, uncorrupted by consumerism and the shallow sophistication it confers'. It was, Taylor-Martin agreed, 'one of his finest poems'.[69] There is a strong sense of place – Kildare, Roscommon, Westmeath, Leix – and of people ('Julias, Maeves and Maureens'), together with an intimate entwinement of religion and landscape that is characteristic of Betjeman:

> Bells are booming down the bohreens,
>   White the mist along the grass.
> Now the Julias, Maeves and Maureens
>   Move between the fields to Mass.
> Twisted trees of small green apple
> Guard the decent whitewashed chapel,
> Gilded gates and doorway grained
> Pointed windows richly stained
>   With many-coloured Munich glass.
>
> See the black-shawled congregations
>   On the broidered vestment gaze
> Murmur past the painted stations
>   As Thy Sacred Heart displays
> Lush Kildare of scented meadows,
> Roscommon, thin in ash-tree shadows,
> And Westmeath the lake-reflected,
> Spreading Leix the hill-protected,
>   Kneeling all in silver haze?[70]

There is also a melancholy tinge to the poem, with its evocation of a forgotten landscape 'far and foreign' and the 'last of Europe's stone age race'. There is additionally a sense of impending loss, reflecting perhaps Betjeman's own farewell to Ireland but suggesting too that Ireland may not remain forever that last unsullied bastion of European Christian civilization:

> In yews and woodbine, walls and guelder,
>   Nettle-deep the faithful rest,
> Winding leagues of flowering elder,
>   Sycamore with ivy dressed,

Ruins in demesnes deserted,
Bog-surrounded bramble-skirted —
Townlands rich or townlands mean as
These, oh, counties of them screen us
        In the Kingdom of the West.

Stony seaboard, far and foreign,
        Stony hills poured over place,
Stony outcrop of the Burren,
        Stones in every fertile place,
Little fields with boulders dotted,
Grey-stone shoulders saffron-spotted,
Stone-walled cabins thatched with reeds,
Where a Stone Age people breeds
        The last of Europe's stone age race.[71]

These last lines have often been criticized. Patrick Galvin, the Irish poet, thought that Betjeman's preferred Ireland was exclusively that of the Anglo-Irish, country houses, and the old Protestant Ascendancy, and that he had had only contempt for 'the native Celtic literature and way of living', a prejudice reflected in these lines in 'Ireland with Emily'.[72] G.S Fraser, the Scottish poet and critic, thought likewise, considering Betjeman's portrayal of the Irish peasantry as 'a Stone Age people' a 'harsh' judgement which mirrored his estimation of them as (it was alleged) 'primitive savages'.[73] It was an assessment repeated uncritically by Taylor-Martin, who in Betjeman's defence could only protest that the reader's 'lack of sympathy with his social attitudes should not blind one to his artistry'.[74] But that surely is to miss the point. Not only, as we know, had Betjeman's enthusiasm for Ireland widened considerably (he had even learned Irish), but his description of the people of the far west as the 'last of Europe's stone age race' was designed to be complimentary, even reverential. In his humility, Betjeman saw them as the last remnants of that ancient Celtic society that had once encompassed all Europe. That old civilization had been over-run, in ancient times by the Vandals, Visigoths and others who had sacked Rome, and again more recently by the Nazis and their allies who had laid waste to much of Europe. Yet in farthest Ireland European civilization had endured, as Betjeman had hoped it would, although now, ironically, its simplicity and purity were under threat — from modern consumerist mass culture.

'remote inland counties'

'Ireland with Emily' presented an idealized Ireland which Goldsmith and de Valera would have recognized, and of which they would have approved. Writing to his mother in 1938, Betjeman had observed that, with the increasing ruination of Cornwall at the hands of mass tourism, Ireland now was what Cornwall was – and he was transferring his affections accordingly. He had also felt much the same about England, writing to T.S. Eliot from Pakenham Hall in July 1938 to explain that Ireland 'is what England was like in the time of Rowlandson with Roman Catholicism thrown in. I can't think why we don't live here'.[75] Earlier, in 1933, Betjeman had complained that 'No part of England is today so remote that one can sit in it for half an hour without hearing somewhere the hoot of a train or the roar of car and motor bicycle'. Yet in Ireland, he explained, 'it is certainly possible sometimes to find silence among those remote inland counties, where the colour-washed towns will be full of jennet-, donkey- and horse-drawn carts of a market day, and when on every other day of the week houses and fields are as still as the bare hills'. Moreover, he added, 'today in Ireland something of the faith of the Middle Ages prevails. To people who live in small cabins among wastes of bog and water, closed in by hills and only approached by uneven lonely roads, the silence brings a faith'. Ironically, he concluded, tongue-in-cheek, that it 'is not for me or for anyone to say that the old way of life [in Ireland] is "better" than the present [in England], or that a community which lived in stone dwellings, clustered firmly round an ancient church, is more permanent than the community which lives in motor cars and small flats and houses taken on a short lease'.[76]

Betjeman's imaginings of Ireland, as well as reflecting nationalist yearnings for that Celtic rural idyll, also mirrored the wider anti-industrialism to which he had been susceptible in England, his search for that 'other' Ireland matching his quest for that 'other' England – and, indeed, for that 'other' Cornwall. Intriguingly, here again there was a close, almost uncanny correlation between Betjeman's approach and the work of H.V. Morton. Just as Morton's *In Search of England* had anticipated so much of Betjeman's own writing on England – and Cornwall – so in his *In Search of Ireland* (first published in 1930) Morton expressed attitudes and opinions that would shortly be Betjeman's too. Morton had also written companion volumes on Scotland and Wales, complementing that on Ireland, and, as Michael Bartholomew, Morton's biographer, has observed, he 'recognised that Scotland, Ireland and Wales each had a unique history, culture and landscape

... they were not to be tacked on to England as mere Celtic appendages'.[77] This too was Betjeman's view. Like Betjeman, Morton approved of Irish independence, also regretting partition (although believing that Northern Ireland was unlikely to remain long outside the Free State).

Moreover, H.V. Morton elaborated a view of modern Ireland, again just as Betjeman had, where (as Bartholomew has put it) the country has 'somehow managed to reach the twentieth century without having to sever its links with its medieval, horse-drawn, anti-mechanical, spiritual past'.[78] As Morton himself wrote, 'Ireland may be poor, but at least her flesh and blood are not humiliated by the tyranny of mechanical things'.[79] Ireland was still the land of Celtic saints, and there was a 'Hogarthian robustness', such as had existed in England in the eighteenth and nineteenth centuries before the onset of standardization. Morton dined, as Betjeman had done, in the grand houses of the Anglo-Irish but he also visited the simple earth-floored cabins of Connemara, finding there a people still steeped in Gaelic tradition. The 'manner in which these Irish peasants have kept alive the traditional literature of the Gael is one of the wonders of the world', he exclaimed in admiration, and 'there was a fineness ... characteristic of all the Connemara peasants, and a queer smothered nobility' as they wrung a living from their stony fields and remained true to their ancient Celtic past.[80] There was more than a hint here of 'Ireland with Emily', and reverence for that 'last of Europe's stone age race'.

Betjeman continued to write about Ireland. In a thoughtful article on 'Irish Towns' in the *Daily Telegraph* in 1963, for example, he admitted that it was sometimes difficult to reconcile Celtic Ireland with the Anglo-Irish legacy. 'On the political side', he said, 'the Irish of an older generation prefer the ruined remnants of the Celtic civilization, the crosses and round towers of days before the long and sad history of the English invasions'. This meant, sometimes, that they felt unable to empathize with or embrace other forms of 'Irishness'. 'Though the Irish Georgian Society is doing a great work in awakening public appreciation of the eighteenth- and early nineteenth-century architecture in Ireland', he said, 'people there still find it hard to forget that the ruined wall on the outskirts of the [typical Irish] town may once have sheltered the park and demesne of a landlord who was absent in England, and whose agent oppressed his tenants'. This was despite the fact that 'some of the finest architecture of this Georgian Ireland is by native Irish architects', and that part of the melancholy appeal of the Irish landscape today was 'the shell of an Adam-style mansion burnt down in "The Troubles"', where 'the gates are rusty, and the winding avenue is grass-grown', and all that remains is the crumbling 'distant house' and the 'weedy, walled garden and reed-choked lake'. And yet the Celtic and the Anglo-Irish could somehow coalesce to forge that 'other' Ireland which Betjeman, and others like him, including Morton, found so irresistibly appealing, and with which he continued to identify. 'Here as yet are no chain stores and diesel fumes. This is an Ireland', said Betjeman, 'that may still be seen'.[81]

Later still, in the 1970s, he made television programmes about *Betjeman's Dublin* and *Betjeman's Belfast*. The warm sense of self-identification still ran strong, and Betjeman busied himself with various Irish interests. He was, for example, active in the Irish Railway Record Society, writing affectionately of obscure lines such as 'the Sligo, Leitrim and Northern Counties' and 'the County Donegal Joint'.[82] And he was, of course, a stalwart of the Irish Peers Association. Yet the reality was that, after the intense wartime spell in Dublin, Betjeman's Irish dream had quietly faded. He never lost his enthusiasm for Ireland. But that young man's passion of the 1930s – that he must at all cost escape England and seek refuge in a rambling house deep in the Irish countryside, preferably with an adoring lover in tow, where he might write grand works – had been replaced by new, perhaps more practical ambitions.

'I am a Scottish nationalist'

To begin with, England was not that easily abandoned, and in the years before and after the war Betjeman had found himself writing and broadcasting for a largely English audience, for which he was richly rewarded. Moreover, the Cornwall that he had said a sad but almost scornful farewell to back in 1938 was swiftly rehabilitated after his return from Ireland. He continued, as we know, to fret over 'development' and the growing intrusion of mass tourism – not least his discomforting complicity in the process, as he saw it – but he came back to Cornwall with a fresh eye. Cornwall became again what it had been in childhood and early youth, a place of liberation and fulfilment (see chapter six), and he asserted once more the proprietorial sense of 'his' North Cornwall, although increasingly willing now to lift his gaze to other parts of the 'Duchy', as he termed it. Cornwall was, of course, more accessible than Ireland – it was far simpler to arrange a contingent existence that allowed Betjeman to commute between London and Trebetherick, than it would have been to continually criss-cross the Irish Sea – and, for a time at least, he could find there an anonymity that had been impossible in Dublin.

Much of the Celticity that Betjeman had imbibed in Ireland was transferred seamlessly to Cornwall. Ireland the land of saints gave way to Cornwall the land of saints, as Betjeman remembered again those Cornish holy men and women whom he thought he had abandoned when 'Undertown' was sold in 1938. Shortly after his return from Ireland, he began to date letters according to the 'Cornish calendar' (as he described it). On 2 October 1944, for example, he wrote to Lady Mander (the Cornish writer Rosalie Glyn Grylls), noting that this was the anniversary of the 'Translation of St Petroc'.[83] A fortnight later, he was writing to Mabel Fitzgerald on 16 October, the saint's day of 'St Austell (Cornish Calendar)', and in the following month he wrote to Geoffrey Taylor, observing that the 24th was the feast of St Minver.[84] Trebetherick itself was part of this rapprochement with Cornwall. Betjeman began to visit again, staying now with friends, and he did so repeatedly until at last he bought a house there in December 1959. Indeed, it was at Trebetherick in February 1960 that he finished his 'epic'[85] (as he called it), his autobiographical blank-verse prose-poem *Summoned by Bells* which, with its lengthy Cornish sections, forever tied Betjeman to Cornwall in the public mind.

Nonetheless, despite this vigorous re-engagement with Cornwall, Betjeman's sojourn in Ireland, like his discovery of *The Secret Glory* and his own Welsh connections, had had the effect of deepening both his appreciation of Pan-Celtic sentiment and culture *and* his own composite 'Celtic' identity. It led him to Scotland, which he had visited only briefly in the past, and to the Isle of Man. It also took him to Australia, where a surprising (not least for him) extension of this 'Celtic' embrace was his exposure to this remarkable country. Here, in two memorable visits, he encountered a new English-speaking culture that was plainly 'not England' but reminded him strongly of his own alternative identities, especially in the many comparisons and connections between Australia and Cornwall that he discovered. Betjeman took to Australia immediately; it was, in a sense, part of his alternative Celtic world.

When in Scotland he became, inevitably, 'Iain MacBetjeman', and sometimes he was also 'The well-known Scottish Nationalist'.[86] On his return from Ireland, as well as restoring links with Cornwall, he made a determined effort to get to know Scotland. Writing to Anthony Barnes and Jonathan Guinness in June 1947, Betjeman insisted, only slightly tongue-in-cheek, that 'I am Scottish *Nationalist* not Scottish Unionist. I deplore the Union'.[87] Six months later, he was writing to Patrick Kinross in similar vein, explaining that 'I am fast going Scottish-Nationalist. I hope you are too'. Indeed, he

added, 'I prefer Scotland now to any country on earth'.[88] There was a note
of sincerity, even seriousness, within this typically frivolous correspondence.
It was, after all, the period of agitation and debate leading up to the Scottish
Covenant movement of 1949, when over two million signatures in favour
of a Scottish parliament were collected and presented to the government in
London.[89] Home Rule for Scotland was back on the agenda, albeit somewhat
briefly, and it was a political atmosphere which Betjeman, with his recent
experiences of Ireland, could not have failed to notice. It is not clear if he
regarded the Act of Union of 1707 between England and Scotland in the
same negative way that he saw the union between England and Ireland. But,
as he told Patrick Kinross, he did consider that 'Edinburgh is the loveliest
city in the world',[90] with all the attributes of a great capital city. It was,
he wrote to his friend Stuart Piggot in 1946, 'more beautiful than Rome,
even. The capital of capitals, the Modern Athens'.[91]

In the autumn of 1956 Betjeman joined a three-week tour of the Scottish
isles, organized by the National Trust of Scotland, taking his young daughter
Candida with him. Years later, she recalled that 'He loved the Scottish islands
more than I can express'.[92] Fair Isle, Rona, St Kilda, Rum, Iona, Staffa and
the Orkneys were all visited in turn, and Betjeman was deeply impressed.
A year or so later he was in Edinburgh, giving a talk at the university, and
staying at Gosford House at Longniddry, East Lothian. From there he wrote
to Candida. 'I like being in Scotland so much I wished I lived here', he
exclaimed, adding that 'It is as foreign a country as France but with baps
and bannocks instead of omelettes and strong tea instead of wine'.[93] He had
written fondly of Aberdeen, as he had of Edinburgh, and when he visited
Glasgow in 1959 he found much to praise there too. He remembered St
Mungo, 'the seventh-century Celtic saint who is buried under the Cathedral',
as he put it, and he recalled too Mungo's saintly exhortation to 'Let Glasgow
flourish'. He admired the Glasgow School of Art, designed by Charles Rennie
Mackintosh, considering it 'one of the most original buildings in Britain',
and he enthused generally about this 'great city'.[94]

Yet Betjeman did not let his Scotophilia blind him to the social problems
that existed in Glasgow, striking an almost political note when he complained
that out of a population of over a million, 'about 400,000 are not satisfactorily
housed'. He had visited in Glasgow the worst slums he had ever seen, he
said, where 'Small children with no park or green space for miles play in
rubbish bins with dead cats and mutilated artificial flowers for toys'. He
had seen tenement blocks with one lavatory for every four families, and in
one tenement he found five children with their parents: 'The coal and the

14. John Betjeman as family man – with wife Penelope, son Paul, and daughter
Candida.

marmalade and bread were in the same cupboard. There was one sink with a
single cold tap'. The politicians, no doubt, were at fault for not tackling slum
clearance adequately, Betjeman fumed, 'But Christian charity must overrule
political expediency'.[95] The anger was palpable, as he wondered how such
poverty could exist in this extravagantly beautiful country, and perhaps we
do see here a glimmer of John Betjeman, the Scottish nationalist.

'whitewashed Celtic cottages, where people still speak Manx'

Betjeman made a similar attempt to get to know the Isle of Man. He visited
in the summer of 1949 and was enchanted by what he found, a microcosm of

all he loved in Ireland and Cornwall. 'I must say I think it all blends together beautifully', he observed in a letter to H.S. Goodhart-Rendel, 'and what with narrow gauge railways, electric trams, horse trams, the glens, the fairy lights and the wild mountains and unexplored lanes among whitewashed Celtic cottages, where people still speak Manx, the island is all an old sensualist like me could desire'. He explained how 'one day I was able to get lost among blueberries on a mountainside looking for a Celtic chapel and then, after a long downhill walk ... took a bus and then a train to Douglas where I drank champagne at two shillings a glass and ate shrimps and mussels'.[96] He could not quite get over the Isle of Man, and soon took to using Manx postage stamps (as opposed to English ones), insisting that they were 'legal' in the United Kingdom and proudly sticking them on envelopes as a badge of his newfound Manx enthusiasms and his own separate identity.

Two years later, in 1951, in a contribution to a book entitled *Portrait of Islands*, edited by Eileen Malony, Betjeman explained to his readers that the Isle of Man 'is a bit of Ulster set down in the sea, a bit of England, Scotland, Wales and Cornwall too, a place as ancient as them all, a separate country, Norse and Celtic at once'. There were small fields with 'Cornish-looking hedges', he said, along with 'brown moorlands', mountains, 'wooded glens', and 'whitewashed cottages thatched with straw and drowned in fuchsia bushes'. The Manx people themselves spoke their own language – 'half Scottish, half Northern-Irish Gaelic', he explained with the authority of an Irish speaker – and Manx surnames, such as Quayle, Kermode, Kelly and Cregeen, 'seem almost all to begin with C, K or Q'. They were a shy and poetic people, he added, and 'The look of their country is Celtic. There are

15. A preference for Manx postage stamps, rather than English ones – John Betjeman writes to his friend Jonathan Stedall, then resident in Sussex.

smallholdings and plenty of *antiquities* … The island looks like Cornwall, Wales and Ireland mixed'. He provided a thumbnail sketch of Manx history, revealing how the island had managed to preserve its independence. He also described the working of Tynwald, the Manx parliament, explaining that 'He who has not seen Tynwald on Tynwald Day does not know how ancient and independent Man is'. He admitted that 'Of course the feeling of another country is in the air as soon as one lands … it has its own flag of three armoured legs on a red background, its own language …, its own customs in both senses of the word'. But 'the full Manxness shines on 5 July, the annual holiday of Tynwald Day'. Here the Manx government in all its pomp progressed to the top of Tynwald Hill at St John's, in the middle of the island, where new laws were read out in English and then in Manx. Here, said Betjeman, 'in this ancient circle of the hills time seems nothing. As the old Manx language is read out, the sun shines down on us, although the peaks of every mountain around us are hidden in clouds. It is always fine, I am told, at St John's on Tynwald Day'.[97]

Like Cornwall, the Isle of Man attracted more than its fair share of English tourists. But, said Betjeman, somehow the island seemed to cope. Between June and September some half a million people crossed over from the coast of neighbouring Lancashire, 'whole towns at a time', and on summer evenings the front at Douglas would be thronged with holidaymakers, while others enjoyed variety shows at the Palace, and 'a thousand couples dance in one of the big halls'. Yet despite this influx, it was still possible to find peace and solitude. 'Each time I have visited the Isle of Man', said Betjeman, 'it has been at the height of the season and each time I have been able to lose myself in the country'. The secret, perhaps, he said, was that in this twin population – 'the Manx and the visitors' – 'the Manx come first'. When 'the last boat of holidaymakers has steamed out of Douglas harbour back to Lancashire, about fifty thousand Manx are left behind', and they quietly regained their island and their independence, much to Betjeman's satisfaction.[98] 'Oh Ellan Vannin', Betjeman sighed, 'ancient kingdom of Man: I like to wander down your late-September lanes when dew-hung cobwebs glisten in the gorse and blackberries shine, waiting to be picked. Oh Ellan Vannin'.[99]

Betjeman was also aware, however, of an incipient Manx nationalism, one which had developed after the war as the islanders became nervous of the British government's increasing tendency to try to prescribe policy for the Isle of Man in areas as diverse as international trading agreements and the licensing of radio station frequencies. This led to the foundation in 1961 of Mec Vannin (Sons of Man), a political party designed to resist British interference and assert Manx independence. Its leader was Wing Commander Roy MacDonald, member for Peel in the House of Keys (the lower house of Tynwald), an unlikely figure who would have appealed to Betjeman. MacDonald 'would never be taken for a Celtic nationalist visionary', wrote William Greenberg in his 1960s survey of Celtic nationalism. Instead, he was a 'bluff, tweedy, middle-aged extroverted ex-officer, [and] it is easier to imagine him on a golf course in the Home Counties than in mystic conclaves of Celtic blood-brothers and the like'.[100] Yet he represented a polite, slightly quirky Manx nationalism of the type Betjeman found attractive, and although there is no evidence that he and MacDonald ever met, he warmed to the Manx nationalists, just as he had warmed to the pomp of Tynwald and the shy modesty of Manx-speaking cottagers. Indeed, Betjeman sometimes imagined himself as Lieutenant-Governor of the Isle of Man and said, only slightly tongue-in-cheek that, in the unlikely event of him being offered the job, he 'would change my name to Ewan Quetjeman and work for Manx Independence'. Gravely, he observed that 'Whenever an English monarch visits the Isle of Man, a mist hangs over the island'.[101]

Betjeman's fascination with the legal trappings of Manx self-government – the ceremonies on Tynwald Day, the reading of new legislation in Manx, the three-legged flag, the Lieutenant-Governorship – was reflected in his interest in (and affection for) other constitutional eccentricities, as he saw them. For example, he insisted in a *Spectator* article – again only half in jest, and with echoes of Arthur Machen and the Holy Grail – that 'I have not been able to sleep lately for thinking of Monmouth. Is it Welsh or English?'. After much inquiry, he said, he had been told by the *South Wales Echo* 'that culturally it is Welsh, but that the Men of Gwent [Monmouthshire] regarded themselves as neither Welsh nor English'. Absurdly, Betjeman concluded that 'As a keen Manx Nationalist I am in favour of total independence for Monmouth, Berwick-upon-Tweed and the Soke of Peterborough'.[102] But this was less a reduction to make Celtic nationalists look quaint; more an example of Betjeman making fun of himself, laughing at his own pre-occupations and enthusiasms, of taking himself none too seriously. Moreover, he genuinely did delight in the diversity of these islands, as we have seen. It was a diversity and 'independent spirit', he wrote in July 1953, which 'refuses to be crushed by the money-worshippers, centralizers and unimaginative theorists who are doing their best to kill it'.[103] Besides, the precise constitutional status of Monmouthshire and Berwick-upon-Tweed was a question that could still worry political scientists as late as the 1990s, while the Soke of

Peterborough was very much a live issue when Betjeman was writing.[104] In the 1950s the Soke was still an administrative county in its own right but increasingly under the spotlight of Whitehall policymakers who considered it 'too small', leading to its amalgamation in 1965 with the adjoining small county of Huntingdonshire, much to Betjeman's regret.

'Australia where one meets Cornwall at every turn'

Betjeman never made any secret of his dislike of 'abroad'. As early as April 1930 he had written from Bonn to his friend Patrick Balfour, admitting that 'It is useless to pretend I enjoy myself abroad'.[105] Subsequently, further continental trips and holidays were endured rather than enjoyed, and when he and Penelope visited Cincinnati in the 1950s (where he was briefly Visiting Professor), they both found America stifling and claustrophobic – the all-pervasive warmth of the central heating but also America's materialist culture.[106] By contrast, Cornwall, Wales, Ireland, Scotland and the Isle of Man, although indisputably 'foreign' when viewed by Betjeman's English persona, were never 'abroad'. A visit to each of these was a form of Celtic 'coming home', where Betjeman deployed his Celtic credentials to claim common cause, or at least affinity, and sought refuge from his life in England.

Significantly, Betjeman felt much the same about Australia. Unlike his Cornish friend A.L. Rowse, who fell in love with America and spent several decades moving constantly between the United States, Oxford and Cornwall, Betjeman made only two trips 'down under'. Yet he came to identify with Australia almost as strongly as Rowse did with America, and he discovered important Cornish connections there, just as Rowse had done in the States, with Australia added to those 'other' places that were not 'abroad'. Nevil Shute, a childhood friend from early Trebetherick days, had moved to Australia and found fame with his novel, *A Town Like Alice*. He had been encouraging Betjeman to come out for some time, and in 1961 Betjeman took the plunge, accepting a British Council invitation to visit Australia. He arrived on 1 November and stayed for over a month. He travelled widely, visiting every state and the national capital, Canberra. He instantly made friends with the Australians. He told his daughter Candida that he 'had *never* met an Aussie he didn't like', and he 'marvelled at the beauty of Australian girls ... with their healthy skins and athletic figures'.[107] Years later, in an obituary article in May 1984, the *Daily Telegraph* still thought it important to record that 'Sir John loved New Zealanders and Australians',[108] according to his secretary.

On arrival in the great city of Sydney he was surprised to find that it reminded him of Cornwall. It was full of 'Trebetherick bungalows', he wrote to Penelope, 'in gardens full of flowers, jacaranda trees, and tamarisks'.[109] A few days later he could report definitely that 'I'm *loving* Aussieland'. He had travelled out now into the countryside of New South Wales, visiting the historic goldrush towns around Orange and Bathurst. Here again there were Cornish comparisons. Orange itself was 'like Polzeath laid out on a grid system', with 'charming old colonial houses with ironwork verandahs on two floors', buildings that were thought to date from 'when they first found gold'. Moreover, he told Penelope, 'there were derelict mines, hawthorn hedges and a varied farm or two in the style of old Cornwall – this is because the Cornish were pioneers in the gold fields in about 1840'.[110] In fact, it had been copper that had been discovered in the locality in the 1840s, first at Copper Hill in 1846, and then in 1849 at a place called Cornish Settlement, a village that had already attracted a clutch of emigrants from Cornwall.

William Tom, from Blisland, near Bodmin, had been one of the first to arrive in the district, and shortly he was joined by scores of his countrymen and their families – John Lane (also from Blisland), George Hawke from St Eval, Richard Grenfell from St Just-in-Penwith, Robert Smith from St Keverne, Edmund Harvey from Camelford, and many more. They carved out farms with Cornish names such as 'Pendarves', 'Rosemerrin' and 'Tremearne', and, in this heavily mineralized country, it was only a matter of time before they stumbled across tell-tale mineral specimens that they recognized from home. Experienced Cornish copper miners were brought in from South Australia to work the new discoveries at these 'Cornish Mines', as they were dubbed, and in January 1851 the first dray-full of copper for export left Cornish Settlement 'surmounted', it was reported at the time, 'with a small banner bearing the Cornish coat of arms, and with the motto "One and All" inscribed'.[111] Later in the year, it was William Tom's son, also called William, who at neighbouring Ophir helped make the gold discoveries that Betjeman noted, precipitating the great Australian goldrushes of 1851, first in New South Wales and then in Victoria.[112]

As Betjeman realized, the Cornish (including the Tom family, from his beloved Blisland) had made a significant impact on Australian history. As he wrote excitedly to A.L. Rowse on his return to England, 'I've just come back from Australia where Cornwall meets one at every turn in place names and mining ... I am dotty about Australia'.[113] He was also right about the hawthorn hedges. Remarkably, those early settlers at Cornish Settlement and environs had brought a variety of plants, bushes and saplings from Cornwall,

and began to create a mixed farming-mining community that, as Patricia Lay
has explained, 'physically ... looked as much like Cornwall as was possible in
the Australian landscape'. There were 'narrow lanes ... edged with hawthorn
hedges', as there were in Cornwall, together with 'avenues of oak, ash and
other imported trees'. These had all the appearance of 'Cornish lanes', just
as Betjeman had observed.[114]

In South Australia, there were more encounters with the Cornish past,
although Betjeman was not able to venture as far as the old Cornish mining
districts of Burra Burra in the mid-North and Moonta-Wallaroo-Kadina
('Australia's Little Cornwall') on northern Yorke Peninsula. But he did visit
the wine-producing Barossa Valley which, along with its extensive vineyards,
could boast a smattering of Cornish place names, such as Truro and Penrice,
together with the remains of old Cornish mines like Wheal Barton and the
Crinnis.[115] He also delivered a lecture to a packed audience in the Bonython
Hall at the University of Adelaide, a gothic Oxbridge-style building named
in honour of Sir John Langdon Bonython, the South Australian newspaper
magnate and Vice-President of the Cornish Association of South Australia at
its foundation in 1890. Like Sabine Baring-Gould, Bonython had also been
a President of the Royal Institution of Cornwall, and, as Betjeman knew,
there was a gallery named in Bonython's honour in the museum in Truro in
Cornwall. In a whirlwind visit to Adelaide, Betjeman was introduced to the
people and places that mattered. He was interviewed on the ABC by Geoffrey
Dutton, a lecturer at the University and descendent of Francis Dutton, co-
discoverer of the Kapunda copper mine in the mid 1840s, one of the first
workings in Australia to employ Cornish miners and the very first to import
a Cornish beam engine from Cornwall.[116] He dined at the Adelaide Club
and had lunch at St Peter's College, a leading boy's school, whose principal,
the Revd J.S. Corfield Miller, had been chaplain at Marlborough College,
Betjeman's old school. He also visited St Michael's Retreat at Crafers, in
the Adelaide Hills, staying there for two or three days, travelling up by the
old road that took him past the ruins of Wheal Gawler, a silver-lead mine
discovered in 1841 by two Cornish miners, the very first metaliferous mine
in Australia.[117]

The visit to Australia had been a tremendous success, and in his report
to the British Council Betjeman confessed that 'I feel ten years younger ...
I have not enjoyed myself so much since I was an undergraduate at Oxford
in 1925'. He also knew enough of Australia now to write that 'I had been
to the Mid West of America as a professor of poetry for a month and can
assure you that the experience was as depressing as Australia and Tasmania

were exhilarating'. Moreover, he said, the 'resemblance of Australia to the Mid West is only superficial and its outward manifestations is (*sic*) in petrol stations, sky signs and point blocks put up by insurance companies in the capitals'. Indeed, he concluded, 'I had no sense that Australia was a copy of America nor, except in the Melbourne and Adelaide clubs, that it was a copy of Britain'.[118] Betjeman remembered his Australian sojourn vividly and with affection. More than a year after his return to England, he wrote nostalgically to friends in Australia:

> Think not, old cobbers, you are out of mind
> Though out of sight. Day after day I long
> For sun girt, sunkissed, surfing Aussie land.
>
> "Oh come back!"
> The wattle and the wallabies cry out.
> And soon, please God, I will.[119]

'a country I could live and die in'

In fact, Betjeman did not return to Australia until August 1971, when he made four half-hour television programmes, encompassing Tasmania, Queensland, Melbourne, New South Wales and Canberra. Older now, and suffering the first effects of Parkinson's disease, the visit was perhaps not quite as successful or as exhilarating as that first trip. Nonetheless, he was determined to enjoy himself, writing to Candida from Sydney that he was happy 'because Aust. Wine is so good. So is Australian architecture'. He talked breezily of 'Tazzie' and 'Brizzie' (Tasmania and Brisbane, in Australian parlance), and was delighted to 'Have seen a lot of Barry [Humphries] and his two wives'.[120] One of the many outcomes of Betjeman's Australian work was the close relationship that he developed with the performer Barry Humphries. In many ways, Humphries, a complicated man of various personae, was Betjeman's Australian *alter ego*, as both men realized, and among the many things that they had in common was a love of fine art and a love of Cornwall.[121]

There were echoes of Cornwall in the old Tasmanian tin-mining town of Zeehan, which Betjeman thought 'too beautiful for words ... Australians take it for granted and we don't know about it'.[122] He also visited northern Queensland, with its 'palms and sand and coloured fish and snakes and wallabies and kookaburras and koala bears and endless beer and Aussie wine

– fatal at midday'. Again, there were Cornish comparisons, he told Candida, 'the houses are like Trebetherick if it had tin roofs and every garden is bright with jacaranda, bougainvillaea, camellia, magnolia, pear and eucalyptus'. More introspective and thoughtful than on his first visit, Betjeman was also aware now of the Aboriginal population. 'The abo[rigine]s are silent, dignified and quite numerous', he reported to Candida, 'but they see with their ears and they are alert to sounds but not to sights'.[123] Betjeman had been reading Alan Moorhead's famous book about Captain Cook in the Pacific, *The Fatal Impact*, and in one of his periodic depressed moods, reflected gloomily that 'The Whites should never have come here'. As he surveyed the damage done to Aboriginal society by European intrusion, he returned sadly to his old theme, the one he had rehearsed so often in Ireland and in Cornwall: 'There's not such a thing as progress'.[124]

Writing to his friend Mary Wilson, wife of the former British Prime Minister, from Port Arthur in Tasmania, he explained that in 'an odd way this terrifying Tasman Peninsula is like Cornwall – gorse, lilies, and the difference is the glorious gum trees brown in the rich greenness'. But, once more, there was a gloomy note. Here, he said, was evidence of the 'latent sadism in the human race: Port Arthur is the Belsen and Buchenwald of the 1830s – the English this time, but most unusually, the Irish doing the floggings and torture'. Today, he added, 'Tourism has contributed its little offering – where once men were flogged to death, and others turned cannibal, you can buy little model prisons as keyrings. It is horrible'.[125]

Nonetheless, in more cheerful moments, Betjeman decided that, so fond was he now of Australia, it was 'a country I could live and die in'.[126] He told Mary Wilson that 'If I were young, I *think* I would settle out there. People are all so nice to each other. I can't get over it'.[127] But when it was time to leave Australia, he contemplated the strange juxtaposition of his twin loyalties, Cornwall and Australia, of these two so very different but, to him, profoundly similar places that were tied together now in his own sense of personal identity, two components of his 'Anglo-Celtic muse'. In saying farewell to Australia, just as he had said farewell to Ireland many years before, he knew that Cornwall would be waiting for him on the other side of the world:

> Cocooned in Time, at this inhuman height,
>> The packaged food tastes neutrally of clay.
>> We never seem to catch the running day
> But travel on in everlasting night

With all the chic accoutrements of flight:
    Lotions and essences in neat array
    And yet another plastic cup and tray.
'Thank you *so* much. Oh no, I'm quite all right'.

At home in Cornwall hurrying autumn skies
    Leave Bray Hill barren, Stepper jutting bare
        And hold the moon above the sea-wet sand.
The very last of late September dies
    In frosty silence and the hills declare
        How vast is the sky, looked at from the land.[128]

CHAPTER SIX

'I'm Free! I'm Free!'

Cornwall as Liberation

Blesséd be St Enodoc, blessed be the wave,
Blesséd be the springy turf, we pray, pray to thee,
Ask for our children all the happy days you gave
To Ralph, Vasey, Alastair, Biddy, John and me.[1]

These lines, from one of John Betjeman's best known and best loved poems, 'Trebetherick', appeared in his collection *Old Lights for New Chancels* in 1940, in the darkest days of the war and on the eve of Betjeman's diplomatic appointment to Eire.[2] His Shell guide to Cornwall had come out in June 1934,[3] evidence of the depth of his Cornish commitment, but by the time he penned 'Trebetherick' in 1939 there was already a sense of loss, of saying farewell to Cornwall. His father dead and 'Undertown', the family home at Trebetherick, already sold, it seemed to Betjeman that ties with Cornwall were loosening. Moreover, he feared that Cornwall was being ruined by development and mass tourism, and he had already turned his attentions to Ireland, which he thought to be still 'unspoilt', and perhaps even the final outpost of European civilization, should war consume all else. There was a note of heavy nostalgia in these lines, a sense that those 'happy days' spent with childhood friends were already slipping from view. But in the hope, expressed in his prayer to St Enodoc, that his own children might one day also savour the delights of that Cornish coast, there was a hint that Betjeman's farewell to Cornwall was not as final as he had sometimes insisted, that there was room for rapprochement and return.

In fact, as we know, this rapprochement came sooner rather than later, and on his return from Ireland in the autumn of 1943, Betjeman was quick to restore his energies and affections to Cornwall. His time in Ireland, like the earlier discovery of his Welsh descent, had bolstered his sense of multiple Celtic identity and allegiance. But it was Cornwall, his first love

in early childhood, and readily accessible from London where perforce
he had now to spend much of his time, that was in the decades ahead to
become the principal focus of his 'Celtic' enthusiasms. In early childhood,
Cornwall had offered 'liberation' of a sort, with young Betjeman making
friends with local boys and girls – some Cornish, some holidaymakers
– and enjoying adventures on the cliffs and sea-shore. Cornwall was, says
A.N. Wilson, 'his childhood refuge'.[4] Then, in adolescence, youthful forays
on his bicycle to places such as Blisland and St Ervan had afforded another
kind of 'liberation', an opportunity to escape into another world beyond
the tight parental control that was exercised in his alternative existence in
London. These forays had also allowed liberation from the constraints of
public school life at Marlborough, and at St Ervan had introduced him to
the mysteries of Celtic Christianity and Anglo-Catholicism. Here, indeed,
was the first hint of that escape from urban England (see chapter one) and
the quest for the Celtic 'other', his personal 'Holy Grail'. 'Escape', he could
exclaim with still-fresh enthusiasm as late as 1969, 'over the Saltash Bridge
by Isambard Kingdom Brunel, 1859: the first railway link between Cornwall
and England. Not another county, another country'.[5]

As John Hurst has observed, Betjeman's 'devotion to Cornwall' reflected
his 'need to escape from ever encroaching pressures of the twentieth century's
erosion of community'.[6] As an only child in London, Betjeman had often felt
alone, overwhelmed by the bustling anonymity of the great city, whereas in
Cornwall there was always welcoming companionship, a powerful emotional
contrast that stayed with him for the rest of his days, evoked in his verse
autobiography *Summoned by Bells*. Likewise, says Hurst, Betjeman was moved
by that 'spiritual quality in the Cornish tradition that provides an antidote to
the corrosive secularism … that is the norm in the modern Western World'.[7]
Cornwall offered a refuge from unthinking irreligion but it was also, as we
have seen, a bedrock of Christian faith, whose Celtic hues appealed directly
and overwhelmingly to Betjeman. To this search for community and belief
was added other 'liberations'. As an adult, Betjeman constantly sought solace
in Cornwall. First, he took annual family holidays at Trebetherick, a release
from the 'hack journalism' of the metropolis that he found oppressive. Soon
too, he forged a close if sometimes volatile relationship with A.L. Rowse,
the Cornish historian and poet. It was Rowse who encouraged Betjeman in
his Cornish writings, and it was he who introduced Betjeman to the wider
Cornwall that lay beyond the confines of North Cornwall. Later, as Betjeman
formed an intimate personal relationship with Lady Elizabeth Cavendish, so
Cornwall offered a new kind of 'liberation'. Retreat to Cornwall gave him

space to develop his friendship with Elizabeth, for them to be alone together beyond the public gaze, and allowed him to escape the constraints (as he saw them) of his marriage to Penelope Chetwode. Increasingly, these Cornish sojourns with Elizabeth were part of a pattern that enabled him to balance the conflicting demands of his constant companion (as she had become) and his (increasingly estranged) wife. And at the end of his life, Cornwall provided the peace, solitude and time for reflection that Betjeman needed to cope with the disabilities of encroaching illness. The final 'liberation' was death; at Trebetherick in May 1984.

'Cornwall ... the healer of all wounds'

Betjeman 'had had a personal "love affair" with Cornwall since he was a child', reported the West Hartlepool *Mail* shortly after his death.[8] This, of course, was the consensus view, readily agreed to and echoed by other commentators, with many observing how fitting it was that he should have passed away in his beloved Cornwall. But Candida Lycett Green, his daughter, added a yet more subtle insight when she wrote later that 'Cornwall ... was usually the healer of all wounds and continued to be throughout J[ohn] B[etjeman]'s life'.[9] And so it was; these healing powers were an essential part of the liberation he found in Cornwall. Although, as Patrick Taylor-Martin noted, Betjeman had had 'an essentially normal childhood', the healing qualities of Cornwall had been apparent since those early boyhood days. As Taylor-Martin added, his 'parents loved him deeply' but with that sometimes claustrophobic 'possessive affection of which the parents of an only child alone are capable'.[10] Holidays in Cornwall, then, were an antidote to this sometimes constricting environment. Travelling westwards by train to North Cornwall, young Betjeman anticipated the freedoms that lay ahead:

> Oh what a host of questions in me rose:
> Were spring tides here or neap? And who was down?
> Had Mr Rosevear built himself a house?
> Was there another wreck upon Doom Bar?[11]

Safely tucked-up in bed at night at Trebetherick, Betjeman listened to the sea outside – 'through the open window came the roar / Of full Atlantic rollers on the beach' – and in the morning ventured out before others had even stirred:

Then before breakfast down toward the sea
I ran alone, monarch of miles of sand,
Its shining stretches satin-smoothed and vein'd.
I felt beneath bare feet the lugworm casts
And walked where only gulls and oyster-catchers
Had stepped before me to the water's edge.
The morning tide flowed in to welcome me,
The fan-shaped scallop shells, the backs of crabs,
The bits of driftwood worn to reptile shapes,
The heaps of bladder-wrack the tide had left
(Which, lifted up, sent sandhoppers to leap
In hundreds round me) answered 'Welcome Back'.[12]

However, as Greg Morse has observed,[13] there was a sense that this liberation was conditional – fleeting or momentary – that even in healing Cornwall new anxieties could come crowding in. 'Even his breezy Cornish poems ambush us with tides of anxiety', agrees Hugo Williams:[14]

Bright as the morning sea those early days!
Though there were tears, and sand thrown in my eyes,
And punishments and smells of mackintosh,
Long barefoot climbs to fetch the morning milk,
Terrors from hissing geese and angry shouts,
Slammed doors and waitings and a sense of dread,
Still warm as shallow sea-pools in the sun
And welcoming to me the girls and boys.[15]

Likewise, there were social anxieties. For all his desire for companionship, here was a sometimes awkward little boy, an only child who often found it difficult to be like other boys and girls. Betjeman would refuse to take part in organized sports (he always hated games) and was sent home to bed in disgrace. He was 'a common little boy' in the estimation of one of the adult organizers who had come down to Cornwall to help with the children during the holidays, a perception that was somehow confirmed when he won a treasure-hunt whose questions had been devised by his mother: 'an unfortunate affair: / My mother set the clues and I, the host / Knew well the likely workings of her mind'.[16]

Yet Betjeman took the rough with the smooth, even at that tender age finding exhilaration in all the experiences – good and bad – that made

Cornwall feel 'different'. Here too were early intimations of that 'happy terror' that he came to savour when in Cornwall:

> Paralysis when climbing up the cliff –
> Too steep to reach the top, too far to fall,
> Tumbling to death in seething surf below,
> A ledge just wide enough to lodge one's foot,
> A sea-pink clump the only thing to clutch,
> Cold wave-worn slate so mercilessly smooth
> And no one near and evening coming on –
> Till Ralph arrived: 'Now put your left foot here.
> Give us your hand' ... and back across the years
> I swing to safety with old friends again.[17]

'before the dark of reason grows'

'Childhood', as Betjeman observed, 'is measured out by sounds and smells / And sight, before the dark of reason grows'. In Cornwall, there was any number of new sounds, smells and sights to delight the senses, so different to those of everyday London. Here one could 'Hear again the wild sou'westers whine!' and catch the 'coconut smell of gorse' and 'Sweet scent of drying cowdung'. Here too one could see Stepper Point where 'On its Atlantic face the cliffs fall sheer', and across the estuary at Padstow one could gaze anew in the windows of unfamiliar shops: 'The Misses Quintrell, fancy stationers, / Had most to show me – dialect tales in verse / Published in Truro (Netherton and Worth) / And model lighthouses of serpentine'. And, at the end of each such sensual day, there was the cosy intimacy of quiet evenings indoors:

> What pleasure, as the oil-lamp sparkled gold
> On cut-glass tumblers and the flip of cards,
> To feel protected from the night outside:
> Safe Cornish holidays before the storm! [18]

What was the storm? There was the return to London, of course, although (as A.N. Wilson has noted), this was ameliorated to some degree by Betjeman's attendance at the Dragon School in Oxford. Bullied at Highgate Junior school, not least because of his German-sounding surname, Betjeman was moved by his parents to the Dragon in 1917. At Trebetherick, his parents, Ernie and Bess, had met A.E. 'Hum' Lynam, whose brother Charles – 'Skipper' – was headmaster at the Dragon. Later, Hum replaced Skipper as head, bringing still closer for Betjeman that sense of connection between school and distant Cornwall.[19] It was here, indeed, as Jon Stallworthy has written, that Betjeman first acquired his lasting reputation as an 'ebullient exhibitionist with a love of Cornwall'.[20] But these were also the years of the Great War; a momentous storm which affected the Dragon School as it did all else:

> Before the hymn the Skipper would announce
> > The latest names of those who'd lost their lives
> > For King and Country and the Dragon School.
> > Sometimes his gruff old voice was full of tears
> > When a particular favourite had been killed.
> > Then we would hear the nickname of the boy,
> > 'Pongo' or 'Podge', and how he'd played 3Q
> > For Oxford and, if only he had lived,
> > He might have played for England – which he did,
> > But in a grimmer game against the Hun.[21]

Neighbours of the Betjemanns in London had sons who had become casualties in Flanders, and young John had already suffered for his 'German' name. The latter experience left an enduring scar but, as he admitted, for the schoolboys at the Dragon the war seemed far away and unreal: 'the trenches and the guns / Meant less to us than bicycles and gangs / And marzipan and what there was for prep'.[22] The real storm, perhaps, was the encroaching 'dark of reason' and its sly ally, Marlborough College, Betjeman's next school, where strict formal learning and institutionalized sport heralded the arrival of adolescent angst and quickened the end of childhood innocence. Yet here again the healing power of Cornwall offered respite and a renewed taste of freedom. There was, as we have seen, the life-altering encounter with the Rector of St Ervan (see chapter three). But there was also adolescent awakening, played out far beyond the rigid masculine bounds of Marlborough, the carefree atmosphere of sunny summer holidays in exotic Cornwall encouraging a certain eroticism – or at least amorous thoughts and fantasies; the prospect of sexual adventure.

'all the nuts go to the toe'

Although, as Bevis Hillier has remarked, Trebetherick and neighbouring North Cornwall was not then considered 'smart', compared to other Cornish localities,[23] it nonetheless attracted its fair share of well-heeled 'up-country' devotees – who stayed regularly at local boarding houses or summer lets, or acquired second homes, or even moved down permanently. There were, as Betjeman remembered, the inevitable colonels and commanders, retired from the army and navy, and home from India or the China Station. Likewise, there were retired colonial administrators, back from Borneo or Bahamas, along with schoolmasters, professors, and various types of businessmen, many of these not yet retired but eagerly awaiting each year the recharging of their batteries in Cornwall. Additionally, there was a smattering of the of 'the artistic and discriminating, who', Betjeman explained, 'sketched, etched and painted the scenes we know so well, finding in Cornwall and North Devon a second Brittany'. They were to be found especially at 'St Ives, Polperro and Looe, Boscastle and Clovelly', he added, lending these places a certain bohemianism, enhancing the sense of the exotic already encountered there.[24] There were also the various literary figures attracted to the 'unending mystery of Cornwall', as Denys Val Baker has called it, those drawn to then fashionable imaginings of Cornwall as 'a land drenched in legends, impregnated with memories of barbaric and druidical rituals ... [and] an underlying current of occult power'. Here writers, like artists, with 'their more highly developed imaginations and intuitive powers', as Val Baker put it, could respond to the 'creative spirit' of the 'timeless land'.[25]

By the eve of the Great War, Cornwall's reputation as an apt destination for such 'creative' types, with their often outlandish ways and radical moralities, was already established. As Brenda Maddox has observed: 'The Cornish were accustomed to having bohemians ... in their midst; their long tapering county was, according to a local joke, "a stocking in which all the nuts go to the toe"'.[26] D.H. Lawrence, briefly at Porthcothan and then at Zennor, had during the war attempted the creation of his *Rananim*, his proposed community of like-minded souls, attracting creative individualists such as the composers Cecil Gray and Philip Heseltine, and the writers Jack Middleton Murry and Katherine Mansfield.[27] At St Buryan, near Penzance, Colonel W.H. Paynter, owner of the Boskenna estate, set out deliberately to encourage such bohemianism. Lamorna Birch, the Newlyn School painter, was a frequent visitor at Boskenna. Another visitor was the occultist Aleister Crowley, rumoured to have held a satanic ritual in nearby Trevellow woods, and other guests included D.H. Lawrence and the artist Augustus John. As Jim Hosking has observed, the Colonel's 'most endearing characteristic was his ever-youthful capacity for enjoyment'.[28]

He had the knack, for example, or so it was said, of persuading attractive young ladies to dance naked for him on the lawns, and enjoyed the habit of inviting Windmill Theatre girls down to Cornwall for intimate weekends.[29] Before and during the Second World War one of his houseguests was Mary Farmar, the future novelist Mary Wesley. 'Wild Mary', as she was known then, warmed to the Boskenna household, with its unconventional manners and cosmopolitan atmosphere, befriending the Colonel's liberated daughter Betty and adopting the Paynter's uninhibited lifestyle. She decided, for example, 'that perhaps the most amusing thing a woman could do was to have several children by different fathers', an amusement that she went on to experience herself.[30]

It would be wrong to imagine that all such communities in Cornwall were pulsing hotbeds of 'alternative' behaviour, with their unlikely but potentially explosive blends of moneyed, creative and bohemian refugees from metropolitan life. But even at staid Trebetherick the youthful Betjeman sensed a certain air of 'liberation'. He was drawn, for example, to Anne Channel, a woman in her late thirties or early forties, who exercised an irresitable attraction for men far younger than herself. As Joan Kunzer told Bevis Hillier in 1977, 'She was very daring ... John [Betjeman] always liked her very much. She was about forty and used to run after all the young men. She had a bungalow on the way to Polzeath, they used to sit there surrounding her like a male harem – these *boys*'.[31] Betjeman found Anne charming and rather amusing, and in his poem 'Old Friends', written years later and published in *High and Low* in 1966, remembered her with affection. 'Where is Anne Channel who loved this place the best', he asked, 'With her tense blue eyes and her shopping-bag falling apart, / And her racy gossip and nineteen-twenty zest, / And that warmth of heart?'.[32]

In another of his Cornish poems, 'North Coast Recollections' (published in *Selected Poems* in 1948), Betjeman recalled the pangs of adolescent love experienced during those seaside sojourns. There were the temptations of tennis girls at play – 'Demon Sex, / That tulip figure in white cotton dress, / Bare legs, wide eyes and so tip-tilted nose'[33] – and the frustrated, unrequited longings of poor 'John Lambourn' for his secret love:

> First love so deep, John Lambourn cannot speak,
> So deep, he feels a tightening in his throat,
> So tender, he could brush away the sand
> Dried up in patches on her freckled legs,
> Could hold her gently till the stars went down[34]

In *Summoned by Bells*, Betjeman also related his 'tender, humble, unrequited love' for Biddy Walsham, the 'Biddy' of his earlier poem 'Trebetherick', but grown now from childhood playmate to the shapely object of his desires. He invited Biddy to a dance, and asked her Aunt Elsie if he might borrow her car for the occasion. He imagined the motor 'with its leather seats / And Biddy in beside me! I could show / Double-declutching to perfection now'. And as he demonstrated his driving prowess, 'Biddy would scream with laughter as I'd charge / Up the steep corner of Coolgrena drive' and 'If my hand / By accident should touch her hand, perhaps / The love in me would race along to her / On the electron principle, perhaps ...?'. But Aunt Elsie wisely said 'no', sensing the dangers and explaining that he was really still a boy: '"So surely, John, it's sensible to walk"'.[35]

Although his amorous stratagems were thus thwarted, there was at Trebetherick on long, sultry summer days an ambience that could be intoxicating. This in itself was part of the liberation that Betjeman craved, and the tingling bitter-sweet experience of unfulfilled desire was not always an unpleasant sensation. Later, as an undergraduate at Oxford, Betjeman affected the homosexual tendencies so fashionable at that time and place. In August 1929, a year or so after being famously sent down from university for failing his Divinity examination, he wrote from Trebetherick to his (homosexual) friend Patrick Balfour to explain that 'I have discovered a rather beautiful girl here aged thirteen and like a Shepperson drawing and my sex becomes rampant'. As he mused, 'I think I must be a bit heter[osexual]'.[36] Trebetherick had worked its magic once more.

'I feared my father, loved my mother more'

By now, as Candida Lycett Green has observed, 'JB trekked religiously to Trebetherick ... each year'.[37] In 1929 his father, Ernie, had built the family holiday home there; 'Undertown', a stylish 'Arts & Crafts' house of which John Betjeman – not yet worried about being 'part of the problem' in Cornwall – greatly approved. But by then Betjeman's relationship with his parents, especially Ernie, had already begun to deteriorate. No longer the doting parents who took him lovingly on his longed-for Cornish holidays, for youthful Betjeman they had become now inconvenient encumbrances, an impediment to the independence he now sought in Cornwall. In earlier years, father and son had enjoyed a certain closeness. Taylor-Martin has argued that Ernie was then 'a kind and affectionate man and, in the early days at least, his son loved him'.[38] As Betjeman himself admitted: 'My dear deaf father, how I loved him then / Before the years of our estrangement came'.[39] Part of that love was a mutual enthusiasm for Cornwall, which Betjeman had inherited from his father. Ernie was a keen golfer, enjoying the rounds of golf at St Enodoc with those retired colonels and businessmen down for the season, but he had also a more sensitive appreciation of Cornwall, which he passed on to his son. He was a rather good amateur artist, as Betjeman recalled:

> He liked the rain-washed Cornish air
> And smell of ploughed-up soil,
> He like a landscape big and bare
> And painted it in oil.[40]

Ernie admired the Newlyn School of painters, especially Stanhope Forbes and Frank Bramley. At a visit to the Tate Gallery on one occasion, Ernie pointed out to young John the famous painting 'A Hopeless Dawn', by Bramley. It was, said Betjeman, the 'picture first to move me'.[41] The guttering candle, the hopelessness and grief of the young wife and her aged mother, and the unspoken story of the Cornish fisherman lost in the raging seas depicted beyond the cottage window, combined to make a deep and lasting impression upon him. Yet, despite this capacity for mutual enthusiasm, there were already signs of emerging incompatibility between father and son. Young Betjeman was hopeless at carpentry, no good at sports, and could not handle a shotgun – all to his father's great irritation. Moreover, Betjeman showed no inclination to take over his father's Pentonville firm, dedicated to the making of expensive drinks cabinets, coffee-room trolleys, and numerous other luxury items, including the patented 'Tantalus' (a secured decanter, designed to prevent the servants pilfering the contents), to meet the demands of middle-class, middle-brow London. 'Fourth generation – yes, this is the boy', Ernie would explain, assuming automatically that his son would inherit the business.[42] But even as a youngster, Betjeman found the products dull and uninteresting, even ugly:

> Where is beauty?
> Here, where I write [Trebetherick], the green Atlantic bursts
> In cannonades of white along Pentire.
> There's beauty here. There's beauty in the slate
> And granite smoothed by centuries of sea,
> And washed to life as rain and spray bring out

Contrasting strata higher up the cliff,
But none to me in polished wood and stone
Tortured by Father's craftsmen into shapes
To shine in Asprey's showrooms under glass,
A Maharajah's eyeful.[43]

Moreover, Betjeman soon recognized the social stigma of being 'in trade',
and this reinforced his already implacable opposition to taking on the firm.
It also fuelled a growing resentment against his father. Ernie, for his part,
detected his son's disdain. At Marlborough, Betjeman had begun to cultivate
his 'aesthete' persona, a posture that did not appeal to no-nonsense Ernie.
His son, he decided, was now unfortunately devoted to 'laziness, affectation
and snobbery'.[44] Such mutual suspicion and misunderstanding would boil
over in the close confines of Trebetherick:

'Don't fidget boy. Attention when I speak!
As I was saying – now I look at you –
Bone-lazy, like my eldest brother Jack,
A rotten, low deceitful little snob.
Yes, I'm in trade and proud of it, I am!'
Black waves of hate went racing round the room
My gorge was stuck with undigested toast.

'My boy, it's no use sulking. Listen here.
You'll go to Bates and order for the car,
You'll caddy for me on the morning round,
This afternoon you'll help me dig for bait,
You'll weed the lawn and, when you've finished that,
I'll find another job for you to do.
I'll keep you at it as I've kept myself –
I'll have obedience! Yes, by God, I will!'[45]

'You damn well won't!', was Betjeman's retort, 'I'm going out today!'. He
made a dash for the door, outflanking his father, and, ignoring his mother's
plaintive cries – 'Come Back! ... He *is* your father, John' – slammed it in
his father's face. He 'ran like mad and ran like mad and ran ...':

'I'm free! I'm free!' The open air was warm
And heavy with the scent of flowering mint,

And beetles waved on bending leagues of grass,
And all the baking countryside was kind.[46]

John's mother, Bess, found herself caught between the two opposing wills
of her son and husband. Betjeman confessed that 'I feared my father, loved
my mother more'. But, for all their closeness, he kept his love in check, he
said, and 'here in Cornwall I would run away / And leave her as we let the
tension mount'. Ernie was perpetually angry, and Bess bore the brunt of
his wrath if there was no water in his dressing-room jug, or if the potatoes
were hard, or the bacon cold, or the whiskey not decanted. Perhaps this
contributed to her hypochondria; her body 'one huge toothache', as Betjeman
described it. But Bess had little choice in siding with her husband. 'We've
sent you to a most expensive school', she explained, 'And John, oh John,
you've disappointed us./ Your father said to me the other day / How much
he wished you were like other boys'.[47]

Ernie hoped that his son might join him on angling trips, going to out
sea with local fishermen to try their luck, as other fathers and sons did.
But for Betjeman these expeditions were to be avoided at all cost, deploying
whatever ruse might come to hand. In August 1929, for instance, writing
from the safety of Bodmin Moor, where he was picnicking, he told Patrick
Balfour that 'I have been very busy this morning avoiding a ghastly day
of fishing'. As he explained, the 'arrival of a letter for me ... gave me an
excuse to stay for a long time in the lavatory and so avoid going'.[48] Even in
Ireland, Betjeman was not always beyond his father's reach. In June 1926
he complained to his Irish friend Pierce Synott that he had met Ernie at
Ballynahinch, 'where I was obviously not wanted'.[49] Quite what Ernie was
doing in Ireland is not clear. But it was rumoured that he kept a mistress
there, and this might account for his coolness and irritation in having to
deal with his son. At any rate, he took John on one of his dreaded fishing
trips, where Betjeman endured a day of flies and heat, and had to listen to
his father's constant carping about having been swindled in Dublin.

Next year, in September 1927, Betjeman was again complaining to Pierce
Synott, this time about his father's recent illness and his mother's long list
of ailments, real and imagined. 'Ernie is getting better', he wrote, 'but is
exceedingly sorry for himself. Bess is dying of misery and martyrdom'.[50] A
month later, and he reported gloomily to Synott that on 'Saturday I go to
spend a ghastly few days in Cornwall with my parents'. Ernie, he explained,
had been diagnosed with heart trouble: 'This means he will die in about
five years – just enough for him to ruin my life'.[51] In April 1932, a little less

LANTEGLOS-BY-FOWEY

but

MOTORISTS BUY SHELL

YOU   CAN   BE   SURE   OF   SHELL

16. 'Lanteglos-by-Fowey – Motorists buy Shell': Ernest Betjemann's jolly line-drawing, first published in John Betjeman's 1934 Guide to Cornwall and reproduced in the 1964 version.

than five years later, and now working for the *Architectural Review*, Betjeman wrote to Patrick Balfour, saying that he was down in Cornwall with the distinguished photographer, E.O. Hoppé, to take pictures of the Georgian houses of mid-Cornwall (for an article on Glynn and Boconnoc, as it turned out): 'Advantages are that no Ernie or Bess will be there'.[52] And so it went on. In fact, Ernie lasted until June1934 when he died suddenly at his works in Pentonville Road. His death was met by Betjeman with a mixture of relief and remorse, for while there was never to be a meeting of minds, there had been an eleventh-hour rapprochement of sorts, prompted by Betjeman's emerging feelings of guilt.

That very month Betjeman had published his Shell Guide to Cornwall. In an olive-branch gesture, he had invited Ernie to contribute an article to the book on (of all things) 'Fishing'. Here, in plain matter-of-fact language, Ernie explained to his readers that 'Sea fishing around the Cornish coast

is in most places very good'. It was advisable, he said, if hiring a boat for
the day, that 'local fishermen' should accompany amateur anglers, 'for
the currents are strong and the wind springs up unexpectedly'. Here, as
Betjeman must have mused, was the 'in trade' businessman, used to buying
his way in the world. 'At all the seaside towns and villages fishermen and
boats can be hired', reported Ernie, 'and the majority of men are only too
anxious to give their patrons a good day's sport. Rates vary, according to
the type and class of boat'.[53] Here too was the 'exploitation' of the locals
– and their ready collusion – that Betjeman had already come to loathe (see
p. 22–3). But he had the good grace to leave such observations unedited,
and his father also contributed a jolly line-drawing of two fishermen at a
Cornish harbour-side, along with a couple of mermaids and two donkeys.
There was a humorous strap line: 'Lanteglos-by-Fowey, but Motorists Buy
Shell' – no doubt Betjeman's own creation. Here was a lightness of touch
that hinted at a last minute thawing of the relationship between father and
son. Betjeman, it seems, had tried to make amends before it was too late.
As he wrote touchingly in his introduction to the guide: 'the Editor would
like to thank his father for the article on fishing in Cornwall. If an Editor
is allowed to dedicate a book, he would like to dedicate this one to him.
His father first taught him to love Cornwall'.[54]

'a man of genius'

Betjeman had spent part of January and February of 1934 at Trebetherick,
and such was the success of his Cornwall guide that a second edition was
before long going to print. But, as we know, Betjeman's Cornish interests
were now fading, his gaze having turned increasingly to Ireland. His father's
death, the sale of 'Undertown', and growing concerns about 'development',
quickened what seemed to be Betjeman's disillusion with Cornwall. Indeed,
he appears to have visited Cornwall hardly at all between that winter of 1934
and the immediate post-war period. These were his 'Uffington years' – he
and Penelope had moved to Garrard's Farm at Uffington in Berkshire in the
February, and it remained their English home until 1945 – and also his war
years, some of which he spent in Ireland. His peacetime work as a journalist
kept him in London's orbit (Uffington was on the Great Western mainline
to Paddington), and the birth of his son, Paul, in 1937 had brought the new
responsibilities of fatherhood. In all this, despite the continuing popularity
of his Shell guide, Cornwall gradually disappeared from view.

However, the wartime years in Ireland served to rekindle Betjeman's

'Celtic' enthusiasms. He learned Irish, embraced Irish culture, and was sympathetic to Irish nationalism, developing a more than sneaking admiration for Eamon de Valera, and explaining Eire's neutrality to an often hostile British press. Returning to Britain in 1943, he brought this rekindled enthusiasm with him, remembering once more his Welsh credentials, developing new interests in Scotland and (especially) the Isle of Man, and, most significant of all, renewing his intimate connections with Cornwall. He spent a week at Trebetherick in March 1946, for example, returning again during the May, setting a pattern of journeying to and fro that would continue up until the eve of his death.[55]

An important component of this renewed intimacy with Cornwall was his emerging friendship with A.L. Rowse, the Cornish historian and poet. Originally an undergraduate at Christ Church, and now a Fellow of All Souls, Rowse had not met Betjeman during the latter's time at Oxford, despite their network of mutual friends, which included the likes of Maurice Bowra, the 'brightest begonia in the parterre there in my time'[56] (as Rowse described the famous don, the one 'who got John Betjeman ... on the right road'[57] in life), and even G.D.H. Cole, founder of the University's Labour Club. Rowse's name was already linked inextricably to his native Cornwall – his *Tudor Cornwall* was published to general acclaim in 1941, and his more controversial autobiography *A Cornish Childhood* came out a year later, in 1942. Critical reaction to the latter was mixed, not least in Cornwall where many readers were offended by what they saw variously as a smug, ill-humoured and egotistical parade of diverse prejudices, aimed in particular at the family and at religion. Rowse had been hurt by such assessments. Coming on top of his 'rejection', as he saw it, by the Cornish electorate in the General Election of 1935, when he had failed to win the Falmouth and Penryn seat for Labour, he had decided to turn his back on Cornwall. He resigned his parliamentary candidacy in June 1943, and let it be known that henceforth he would not speak on any subject to any public audience in Cornwall, ever again. He even toyed with the idea of preventing his books from being sold in Cornish shops.[58]

In the end, of course, Rowse relented, and by the early 1950s was again giving talks to meetings in Cornwall, albeit sometimes with misgivings and a heavy heart. Eventually, too, his Cornish enthusiasms returned, largely as a result of his experiences in the United States in the 1950s and 1960s where he learned with admiration and pride of the Cornish role in developing the North American mining frontier.[59] He even wrote a book on the subject, *The Cornish in America*, which appeared in 1969. Thereafter, he became something of a Cornish nationalist, fiercely asserting his own Cornishness and generally promoting the cause of Cornwall. Yet when he first corresponded with Betjeman, Rowse was still deep in the darkness and depression of his twin 'rejections' – of his book, and of his ambitions as a politician.

Betjeman, it seems, had made the first move, writing to Rowse from Ireland in May 1943 to say how much *he* had enjoyed *A Cornish Childhood*. Rowse was overwhelmed. He replied to Betjeman from Polmear Mine, his seaside villa near St Austell. 'My dear Betjeman', he began, 'I don't suppose you realized how great a pleasure y[ou]r le[tter] was going to give me when you wrote it. For you are one of the few contemporary writers whom I can admire without reserve, without any criticism to offer even'.[60] This was praise indeed from the famously caustic pen of A.L. Rowse; Betjeman had said exactly the right thing at the right time. Paradoxically, in writing to Rowse on the eve of his return from Ireland, anticipating already his renewed engagement with Cornwall, Betjeman had caught Rowse in the midst of his painful estrangement. Long years would pass before Rowse would feel fully restored and reconciled to Cornwall. But he was intensely grateful to Betjeman for writing so supportively. 'So you see how praise of my book from you has warmed my heart as nothing else has', he added appreciatively, 'save Elizabeth Bowen's review of it, who was wonderfully interesting and revealing even to me of myself':[61] (she had written tactfully in the *Tatler* that Rowse's seemingly haughty intransigence was a result of his Celtic blood, something that she as an Anglo-Irishwoman could understand, where an English reviewer might not).[62]

Rowse went on; 'Of course I know, as any writer does, that the book is good; & anybody can see that it is authentic'. But, he added, pointing the finger at those who had publicly criticised *A Cornish Childhood*, 'it was interesting to see how it posed a stumbling block to all the second rate – the local Bishop [Hunkin], the Nonconformists, Wilson Harris, Stephen Spender, Raymond Mortimer'. They 'loathed the asperities', he said, 'what they really wanted was humbug. Which, after all, is hardly surprising. But they'll never get that from me'. Rowse concluded angrily: 'And they had bloody well better look out – for the book is to be continued [in subsequent autobiographical volumes] and in time I shall come to them (as I shall come to you, with what a difference!).[63]

Betjeman was 'a man of genius', Rowse told him in the same letter. Betjeman had mentioned that he had embarked on a long poem about Tintagel. Here were shades of Tennyson and Hawker, perhaps, of Arthur and the Holy Grail, an indication that Betjeman was already planning excitedly his renewed embrace of all things Cornish. What became of the poem is not clear – perhaps the idea metamorphosed over time into *Summoned by Bells*, Betjeman's own childhood autobiography – but Rowse was clearly delighted. He told Betjeman to 'make the most of your gifts' and explained that news of the putative Tintagel poem 'was the best news I have heard for a long time'. He added that he thought Betjeman's 'Trebetherick' the best of all his poems to date – 'how often I've read it to people' – and explained that when his own collection *Poems Chiefly Cornish* came out shortly he would be sure to send a copy. All in all, it had been a remarkable letter, an outpouring of appreciation and thankfulness. And there was yet more; fulsome praise that Rowse rarely showered upon anyone: 'It seems to me that you have been fortunate in your work in a way that one cannot but envy. You have affected the taste of a generation, perhaps not yet widely but at any rate significantly, in a way that is only comparable to Ruskin or Horace Walpole or the Pre-Raphaelites'. It was, Rowse said, 'An astonishing achievement – all off your own bat too'.[64]

Here was encouragement, if any were needed, for Betjeman to refocus his interests on Cornwall. He had managed to say the right things to Rowse, and Rowse had reciprocated generously, conveying precisely what Betjeman needed to hear at that point, on the eve of his return from Ireland. Rowse had also expressed opinions – about the low-church Bishop of Truro, Joseph Hunkin (whom Betjeman would later criticise, albeit obliquely), and about Elizabeth Bowen, another of their mutual friends, greatly admired by both men for her Anglo-Irishness – which chimed exactly with Betjeman's, further laying the foundations for a developing friendship.

Rowse's encouragement of Betjeman's work was sincere and genuine. Ten years later, when the Tintagel poem had still not appeared, Rowse wrote to ask whether a forthcoming sojourn at Trebetherick 'might mean your finishing your long Arthurian poem'. He added, with feeling, 'I do hope so'.[65] By now, however, the Tintagel project had been shelved long-since, or perhaps subsumed in plans for *Summoned by Bells*. As early as 1945, Betjeman had told Rowse that he was thinking about a verse autobiography, and Rowse responded with instant enthusiasm, writing on New Year's Day 1946: 'Very much love and a mid-wife's interest in the long autobiographical Cornish poem. Do push it forward to a triumphant conclusion'.[66] When *Summoned by Bells* appeared finally in 1960, Cornwall was a central theme, although the autobiographical content had expanded now to cover the wider scope of Betjeman's childhood and adolescence. Here, perhaps, was the influence of *A Cornish Childhood*; perhaps Rowse the mentoring 'mid-wife' had indeed helped Betjeman to give birth to his own childhood autobiography.

'The Place they call The House / That shelters A.L. Rowse'

Certainly, there is little doubt that Betjeman had looked to *A Cornish Childhood* for inspiration, and in *Summoned by Bells* there are fleeting hints of that influence. Rowse, for example, had reflected on early Sunday-school outings to the beach at Pentewan, where the boys and girls paddled in the sea and played among the towans (dunes), just as Betjeman and his young friends had at St Enodoc. Rowse wrote whimsically of those visits: 'Dear Sunday School teachers of my childhood, of those innocent years before the War, thirty years ago – before the world, a red and sinister moon, had looked over the horizon at us'.[67] In its composition, and in its nostalgic sense of loss, there was an almost Betjemanesque quality, a foretaste perhaps of Betjeman's 'Safe Cornish holidays before the storm' and 'before the dark of reason grows'. Rowse's Anglo-Catholic sympathies also appealed to Betjeman, as did Rowse's defence of Jack Bucknall, the 'Anglo-Catholic Socialist' (as Rowse called him) who had been curate at St Austell before his incumbency at Delabole, and Betjeman no doubt appreciated Rowse's brief portrait of 'Blisland, sweet grey granite village around its beech-strewn green, the church with its painted screens and images a sanctuary of Anglo-Catholicism'. There was even reference to 'sweet Uffington' in *A Cornish Childhood*, together with a neat description of Charlestown church, near St Austell: 'a pretty little Victorian Gothic building, all Early English lancet windows and pitch-pine pews, very G.S. Street, very Betjeman'.[68] Betjeman repaid the compliment in *Summoned by Bells*, with his own reference to Christ Church, Oxford: 'The place they call The House / That shelters A.L. Rowse'.[69]

Here was a spirit of mutual appreciation that both men cultivated. Rowse encouraged Betjeman to spend more time in south Cornwall, in the St Austell Bay area – both to expand Betjeman's knowledge of Cornish history and topography, and to relieve the oppression of Rowse's self-imposed isolation. But at first he did not invite him to stay at Polmear Mine, (where his widowed mother's presence created a hostile atmosphere that he did not like uninitiated visitors to experience). Instead, he made enquiries locally about suitable lodgings. But it was just after VE Day, and suddenly the celebratory mood that gripped Britain led to a mini-boom in the Cornish holiday trade, as war-weary folk allowed themselves a short respite from austerity. Rowse tried to get Betjeman into the Pier Guest House at Charlestown but in a postcard dated 30 July 1945 reported sadly that it was 'hopelessly booked up *till the second half of Sept.*'. Alas, he added, 'I am the sadder because I want intelligent conversation'.[70]

Over the years, such invitations continued. 'I'd love to see you', Rowse would write, on one occasion explaining that 'I went to Launcells [later to become one of Betjeman's favourite haunts in North Cornwall] one lovely spring Sunday in April: the stream tinkled away among the withies, & celandines and violets were out in the hedges – and we thought of you and Parson Hawker'.[71] Another time, in January 1946, when he had just sent Betjeman a copy of his *West Country Stories* – 'I long to know what you think of its Cornishry', he said – Rowse reported another North Cornwall foray. 'Do you know that dark tiled, shadowed red sandstone house at Harlyn', he inquired, 'with its heavy rustic pediment and everything going to decay – just where you turn round to go up that tamarisk lane straight as a die to Trevose Head?'.[72] He had gone there just before Christmas, he explained, and was now writing a story about it. Later, in November 1948, Rowse was 'Delighted to know you're in Cornwall: the place feels better for your being here'. He again urged a visit to south Cornwall. He regretted 'that you have never seen the Luxulyan Valley – quite the most lovely spot in this part of Cornwall – with a sweet moorland granite church, and a nice naughty old character for incumbent'. He even relaxed his Polmear Mine rule, 'in case you want to see a bit of Cwll you haven't seen'. As he explained: 'If you can get to Bodmin, as you can easily by train or bus, there are buses to St Austell many times a day. And you come through that upheaved China Clay country of my poem "Bus-Ride". If you have time to manage it, I could put you up for the night and return you safely the next day'.[73] Next year, in July 1949, Rowse let Betjeman know that he was down from Oxford for the vacation, in case he wished to call in: 'I shall be in my right-little, tight-little villa on the channel side of Cornwall ... sticking at my enormous book on the Elizabethan Age'.[74]

As well as reporting his own literary activities, Rowse encouraged Betjeman in his. Even if meeting up in Cornwall could be difficult to arrange, they got together sometimes at Oxford, especially when Betjeman was working for the British Council at Oriel in 1945. Here they would compare notes, swapping ideas about forthcoming projects. In early 1946 Rowse wrote to say that 'I'm *longing* to see your 'Old Bats on New Balconies'.[75] This was Betjeman's latest collection *New Bats in Old Belfries*, published in December 1945, and the fact that Rowse felt able to make fun of the title was a measure of the warmth of the relationship they had established. (By now letters were signed-off with 'Yours ever Leslie' [Rowse's preferred first name] or 'Love, A.L.').[76] Rowse was also urging another collection, a book that would bring together Betjeman's writings and broadcasts on topography and architecture. He floated the idea in May 1945 and again in August 1948, writing shortly after to remind Betjeman that he had agreed to the project: 'Don't forget it's a promise'.[77] By early 1949, Rowse had refined the suggestion further, so that the collection would now contain 'all the Cornish pieces and broadcasts that I love so much'.[78] This was the volume *First and Last Loves*, which appeared in 1952, containing among other things Betjeman's essays on Blisland, St Endellion, Looe, Port Isaac, and Padstow. This, more than anything, was literary evidence of Betjeman's renewed commitment to Cornwall. Meanwhile, Rowse had also secured a contribution from Betjeman on 'Victorian Provincial Life' for his edited volume *The West in English History*, published in 1949, for which he sent Betjeman a much appreciated royalty cheque for seven guineas in June of that year.[79] Later, in 1968, Rowse reproduced a short extract from Betjeman's *First and Last Loves* in his own *A Cornish Anthology*, part of the Padstow essay dealing with the 'Obby 'Oss.[80]

Betjeman responded to Rowse's encouragement. The conception and completion of *Summoned by Bells* may, as noted above, owe something to Rowse's influence. At any rate it was in Cornwall that Betjeman at last finished this *magnum opus*. As he wrote from Trebetherick to his wife Penelope on 10 February 1960, in the mock Cockney-cum-Irish-cum-Berkshire they reserved for their own correspondence, 'This morn OI FINISHED THE EPIC'.[81] But Betjeman also reciprocated, over the years encouraging Rowse in *his* efforts. Understanding that Rowse was saddened by the literary establishment's failure to recognize him as a serious poet, Betjeman went out of his way to praise his poetic efforts. When Rowse sent him a copy of his newly-published *Poems Partly American* in December 1958, Betjeman replied promptly on Christmas Day. 'I think the best poem of all is the one on the death of your mother', he said, adding appreciatively that 'What is so wonderful about your Cornish poems is that they are all *South* Cornwall'.[82] In particular, the 'final stanza of Cornish Spell made me almost cry with admiration and memory', he confessed, the tender sense of loss conveyed in the poem, with its mixture of nostalgia, regret and foreboding, reminding him of his own childhood days at Trebetherick. As Rowse had written: 'What is this sweet and summer smell / That hangs in hedge and field as well / And speaks of what I cannot tell / But what is dead – a honeyed spell'.[83]

Betjeman's admiration did not diminish with the years. 'God bless you dear a great Cornish writer' he wrote to Rowse in 1967.[84] Later, in 1975, he insisted that 'There are no things more enjoyable than a good poet in an old friend', adding subsequently that 'You must be the only historian who has written truly topographical poetry'.[85] Likewise, in 1980 he wrote that 'Your road to Oxford poems are a constant pleasure to me: so are your vigour and Cornishness'.[86] Moreover, as Poet Laureate, Betjeman more or less insisted that Rowse should produce a definitive collection of all his poetry. Thus commanded, Rowse had published in 1981 his *A Life: Collected Poems*: 'I am grateful to the Poet Laureate', he admitted, 'for repeatedly urging me to bring together my Collected Poems: without encouragement I might not have tackled the job'.[87]

Much earlier, in 1953, Rowse had moved into Trenarren, the country house on St Austell Bay that he had coveted since childhood. His mother now in a nursing home (and soon to pass away), Rowse had the great house to himself, and was exuberant. He could not wait to tell Betjeman about it. 'Well', he wrote, 'I have been and Equipped myself with rather more than I bargained for – a country house with 26 rooms – 14 bedrooms – inhabited chastely by me and my Cornish housekeeper, a vast echoing wing for each'. There was also a wonderful garden. 'I'm up to my eyes pruning & hooking & picking & spading & raking', he said, 'until the hands that never rocked the cradle can scarcely hold the pen'. But he was still working hard on literary tasks, he added: 'I've got *two* books coming out this autumn'. As before, he wanted to share all this with Betjeman, and invited him down to his new home: 'Do come to see it. It's a lovely spot, w.end of St Austell bay'. And, as before, he wanted to show Betjeman more of his south Cornwall: 'do come and see me and I'll take you to see the incumbent of that … church you liked so much – Rev Fox Harvey, vicar of Biscovey or St Blazey G[ate]'.[88]

'A.L. Rowse … first opened my eyes to south Cornwall'

Betjeman had managed occasional visits to Polmear Mine but Trenarren was altogether a more attractive prospect, and visits became more frequent. As Rowse remembered it, 'He would come over to lunch, sometimes with Penelope, both at Polmear Mine above Charlestown and later at Trenarren'.[89] Sometimes, indeed, Betjeman stayed over at Trenarren, for a long weekend or a few days mid-week, with or without Penelope, and here, at last, was the opportunity for Rowse to really introduce him to south Cornwall:

A North Coast man, he didn't know the Victorian churches around St Austell, so when he came over from Trebetherick I took him to the little barn-like church of Biscovey, with its Street tower, and the 'Good Shepherd' at Par; also the pretty church of my poem, 'Passion Sunday in Charlestown Church', which he specially liked, for in addition to Oxford, Cornwall, and architecture, we had poetry in common – though I was rather cagey about that, he a full-time professional, not averse to baring his soul in public.[90]

Writing in 1964, Betjeman acknowledged that it was 'my friend A.L. Rowse, who first opened my eyes to south Cornwall'.[91] Rowse had widened his vision, encouraging him from the limits of his North Cornwall, and with all the authority and inner knowledge of the 'insider' had pulled back the veil, revealing the secret mysteries – or at least hidden, sequestered spots – that might otherwise elude the visitor for ever. Betjeman, for instance, had discovered Herodsfoot and Hessenford, both in their deep, wooded south Cornish valleys, both with their mid-1850s churches by G.E. Street ('the Tractarian architect *par excellence*',[92] as Rowse termed him). Likewise, he had come to know Constantine parish, much loved by Rowse, with its 'Oyster beds ... woods and creeks of the many-vistaed Helford River in the south', and the 'earth works on the hilltops, marshes and moors and quarries for granite in the north'. There was nearby Gweek, he wrote, with its 'early Georgian looking manor house of Trewardreva', and Port Navas, 'a wooded tropical looking cove on a creek', the 'scene of Quiller-Couch's song "Helford River"' – as Rowse had no doubt told him.[93] Further east was Lansallos, another spot beloved by Q [Quiller-Couch], a 'scattered village in a valley', where on the coast the 'water is clear and deep'. And 'from Lansallos Head, above the little beach of Lansallos Cove, a huge view westward extends from the four-hundred-foot hilltop right across St Austell Bay to Black Head' – hard by Trenarren, where Rowse lived.[94] Thanks to Rowse, Betjeman had come to know many parts of Cornwall with all the intimacy of an 'insider'; it lent a renewed sense of 'belonging', for which Betjeman was grateful. He had even inherited Rowse's deep admiration for the writing of Sir Arthur Quiller-Couch, so much part of the literary landscape of south Cornwall, an influence that Jon Stallworthy would later detect in Betjeman's own work.[95] Cornwall was now, Betjeman confessed to Rowse, 'the only place I ever want to be in'.[96]

Betjeman was genuinely fond of Rowse, and vice versa. 'Upon occasion', Rowse wrote affectionately, 'John and I went church-crawling in Cornwall. I can see him now, the schoolboy excitement with which he fitted the key into the south door, bending down with "What *will* it be like inside". Or, again, his popping down quite unselfconsciously on his knees to say a prayer, leaving me standing'.[97] And they genuinely admired each other's work, especially their poetry. As Rowse emphasized, 'Cornwall and poetry were far more intimate bonds between us than architecture or people'.[98] Indeed, he wrote, in an essay devoted to 'The Poetry of John Betjeman', that 'Betjeman is a complete poet – *the whole of his life is in his poetry*'.[99] Betjeman was likewise effusive. '[What a] very good a topographical poet you are', he wrote to Rowse, especially on 'Cornwall – where you are unbeatable ... all the Cornish ones ... are the best you have done'.[100] Betjeman was also prepared to sing Rowse's praises to third parties, as in November 1950 when he wrote to Anne and Arthur Bryant that 'Most of the history I have read by modern writers (always excepting Leslie [Rowse]) is unreadable, because the authors have not bothered to put it into decent, rhythmic prose'.[101] For Rowse, as in his own work, Betjeman thought, poetry and prose were inextricably – and quite properly – entwined.

Nonetheless, despite the friendship, shared interests and mutual admiration, there were differences in temperament between the two men. Betjeman was, according to Rowse, 'in company cheerful and gay, full of jokes, but when alone given to melancholy, needing solace and support',[102] a contrast that Rowse might have seen in himself – although he would never have considered himself a 'joker', nor ever admitted requiring help. Similarly, with Betjeman its was 'Anything for a lark – larks all the time', and Rowse (being 'rather prim', as he confessed) was almost glad that he had not known him during Oxford undergraduate days: 'I would have disapproved of him wasting his time ... neglecting his tutorials and getting sent down for failing Divvers (Divinity, of all things)'.[103] Moreover, Betjeman was 'religious, but given to doubt and depression', said Rowse. Rowse's own doubts were more profound, he regretted, (political enemies in the 1930s had dubbed him an atheist), although he enjoyed the theatre and liturgy of High Church mass. He had described himself to Betjeman as 'an unbelieving "Anglo-Catholic"' (having admitted as much to Archbishop Lang in the 'thirties')[104], and Betjeman knew instinctively what he meant. 'I *hope*, that is all', wrote Betjeman in reply, 'Faith, Hope and Charity – and the greatest of these is Hope'. Rowse pondered these words, and then observed bleakly: 'There is the difference between two old friends: I am without hope, I despair'.[105]

To this despair was added, Rowse thought, the differences in their attitude to Cornwall. Betjeman, following his return from Ireland, was anxious to renew his embrace of all things Cornish. Rowse, meanwhile, had turned his public face against Cornwall. As he wrote enviously to Betjeman in late 1948: 'You don't have the love-hate complex that makes it so difficult for me'.[106] Envy, indeed, became an ever greater part of their relationship as the years passed. Rowse admitted his unfortunate tendency to fall out with old friends, and at times his friendship with Betjeman became strained. He envied Betjeman his knighthood, and as Betjeman grew in literary and popular stature, so Rowse was liable to become more irritated. Even the much requested visits to Trenarren could become moments of irritation, as in August 1956 when Betjeman and Penelope had come to stay. Rowse noted in his diary that early one Sunday morning he had had to drive Penelope, now a Roman Catholic convert, to 'the little RC church on the bypass at St Austell'. Rowse observed: 'Penelope has arrived early to make her confession before Mass, the silly. I hope she enjoys it as she enjoys food, everything: what a rigmarole'.[107] Inevitably, some of Rowse's irritation with Penelope rubbed off on his friendship with Betjeman, not least when she wrote to Rowse (no doubt without Betjeman's knowledge or sanction), asking for a loan of £400 to finance a visit by 'our Paul' (their son) to America.[108] Rowse refused – immediately and indignantly.

Later, as Betjeman's close association with Cornwall became ever more ingrained in the public imagination, so Rowse was likely to become annoyed by what he saw as this presumption of 'Cornishness'. Indeed, as Rowse pursued his own, belated rapprochement with Cornwall – asserting his identity as '100 per cent Cornish', the 'Voice of Cornwall', and 'the greatest living Cornishman' – so he was increasingly liable to be upset by what he saw as competing claims to his Cornish mantle.[109] Even the posthumous publication in 1984 of *Betjeman's Cornwall* (a modest collection of already well-known Cornish poems and essays) caused distress. 'We have had Daphne du Maurier's *Vanishing Cornwall*, Winston Graham's *Poldark's Cornwall*, and eventually *Betjeman's Cornwall*', fumed Rowse, 'none of them Cornish; all of them having adopted Cornwall'. In case people had forgotten, he reminded them that 'I am the real thing, 100 per cent Cornish: when is someone going to see that a "Rowse's Cornwall" would be a different matter – history, antiquities, villages, crevices, holes and corner, relics, what is beneath: the *real* Cornwall'.[110] Suitably enraged, he did indeed set about *A.L. Rowse's Cornwall*, to be published in 1988.

'I wish they hadn't said I was a Cornishman'

Earlier, in 1974, there had been friction of a sort when Betjeman and Rowse collaborated over the book *Victorian and Edwardian Cornwall from Old Photographs*. When the book appeared the introductory blurb explained that 'Sir John Betjeman and Dr A.L. Rowse are the two most eminent living Cornishmen – the one by adoption, the other by birth'.[111] Here the foreigner took precedence over the native, the knighthood over the honorary doctorate. Rowse was furious, and Betjeman was appalled. 'I wish they hadn't said I was a Cornishman', he wailed, explaining hastily to Rowse that 'I have always been a furriner. But I am v. proud to be linked to you'.[112] As a peace offering, he left Rowse in his Will a large model of St Mary's church at Penzance, made out of shells, and in years to come Rowse gave the model pride of place in the hallway at Trenarren, just inside the entrance door. Here, perhaps, was Rowse's way of saying 'no harm done', and, after this hiccup, friendly relations were restored. In 1976, for example, Rowse had written to Betjeman to say how much he had enjoyed his television programme on the Victorian diarist, Francis Kilvert. Betjeman had replied graciously by suggesting that the producer, Patrick Garland, 'who did the Kilvert programme would make a lovely Hawker programme with you. In fact he ought to make several programmes with you'. In an amusing aside, further evidence that the friendship had been patched up, Betjeman revealed that very many years before Patrick Garland's 'father was sent by my father to Paris with me to teach me about sex with ladies but it failed because I fell ill'.[113] It was a tale calculated to delight Rowse. After Betjeman had died, Rowse wrote in his personal copy of Betjeman's *Uncollected Poems*: 'Oh, how I miss him! Life is poorer without him'.[114]

Nonetheless, Betjeman had learned to be wary of Rowse and his ways. He 'is a very strange character',[115] he had confided to a friend in 1966, and in his early visits to Polmear Mine had been introduced to some of Rowse's eccentricities. In September 1949 he had written to Anne Barnes, reporting that 'we had a happy time at Trebetherick',[116] and describing a visit to Polmear Mine where Gerald Berners was a houseguest. Berners, who lived at Farringdon, not far from Uffington, was another of their mutual friends, a composer and writer of note (Betjeman wrote his entry in the *Dictionary of National Biography*) to whom Rowse had been introduced by Lord David Cecil. A confirmed bachelor, Berners had written 'a naughty skit' (as Rowse described it) entitled *The Girls of Radcliffe Hall*. 'Miss Radcliffe Hall', Rowse explained, 'was a Lesbian of an old-fashioned sort, who was much in the news at the time for the childish prosecution of her novel, *The Well of Loneliness*.[117] It was a story calculated to amuse Betjeman, with his own professed sympathy for homosexuality, and he readily accepted the invitation to visit the two men at Polmear Mine, that 'small house outside St Austell and near St Just-in-Roseland' as he inaccurately described it to Anne Barnes. He took his friend Anthony West (son of Rebecca West and H.G. Wells) with him. It was a mistake – or at least there were awkward moments. 'Anthony West, who came with us, called the house St Queer-in-Rowseland', reported Betjeman bemusedly.[118] Rowse later described the visit rather sourly, recalling the time 'when Gerald Berners was staying with me in Cornwall, and John Betjeman brought Anthony to lunch. All I remember of the occasion', he noted, 'was John's exclamation, seeing Johannesberger on the bottle of wine, "And South African, by Jove!", to Gerald's reproach: "he should have known better"'. Rebecca West, who 'had a complex about Anthony', according to Rowse, got to hear of the visit and wrote to Rowse to complain that he had taken Anthony's side in the family quarrel; unwittingly drawing Betjeman into the dispute.[119] Betjeman learned to be careful.

Betjeman's long and occasionally bumpy relationship with A.L. Rowse had been a significant element of his post-war re-engagement with Cornwall, and the means by which he had gained an intimate 'insider' knowledge of Cornish byways far from the tourist trail. There were, however, limits to the degree of 'Cornishry' that Rowse was prepared to afford Betjeman – part of a wider uncertainty, perhaps, as to the extent to which Betjeman might be considered an 'insider' in Cornwall (see chapter six) – but, by the time of the *Old Photographs* volume incident in 1974, it no longer mattered. Betjeman, happy still to acknowledge himself as 'furriner', had long since effected his rapprochement with Cornwall. Cornwall was again, as it had been in his childhood, a place of refuge, of healing and liberation.

'I ... regard Cornwall as home'

The pattern of frequent holidays, established soon after the war, continued. Candida Lycett Green recalls that 'We went for two weeks every summer to Trebetherick' – normal family holidays on the beach (Betjeman even tried his hand at body surfing), and reunions with the old circle of friends. These holidays were 'the highlight of our year', she recalled, and it seemed that Betjeman's prayer to St Enodoc was being answered, that his children, Paul and Candida, were enjoying the same happy days that he had known in his own childhood. 'We learnt to swim in the same rock-pools and shrimp in the same sandy ones', she remembered, 'We watched big seas by the same blow-hole and dammed the same freshwater stream under Bray Hill; we took the ferry to Padstow'. They would visit Lord and Lady St Germans at Port Eliot, and made friends with the 'reclusive and eccentric' vicar of Warleggan, the Revd Densham. They were part of the Cornish scene.[120]

There were occasional gaps in the cycle. In August 1951, for example, Betjeman wrote to Anne Barnes from Alderney to admit sadly: 'Can't afford Cornwall this year. It is heartbreaking. This place for its duty-free spirits, high cliffs, cobbled streets and remote unspoiledness is no substitute at all'.[121] But next year he was back into the rhythm, writing to Cecil Beaton, the photographer, from Trebetherick, to report that 'I am having the last week of my holidays here amid "bad luck", "good shot", "played" ringing over tamarisks from the tennis courts'. Here were 'fresh young schoolboys and schoolgirls dodging about and ageing schoolmasters plunging into the "foam bearded Atlantic" and cocktail parties in the villas and a good round of golf in the morning'.[122] It was all very jolly, like a return to those days of long ago before the Great War, a world away from the metropolitan world of journalistic copy deadlines. ('I am in Cornwall till next Sunday, then horrible old London',[123] he wrote to Elizabeth Bowen on one occasion). He was back again in the summer of 1953, and again in the November, with a succession of visits throughout the 1950s and into the 1960s.[124] In June 1956 he told Anne Barnes that 'I ... still regard Cornwall as home and have to see it every year'. Similarly, in August that year he explained to Laurence Whistler that 'I always find I like poetry most when I am in Cornwall and can feel and think and see again'.[125] And in similar vein, he reminded his friend Peggy Thomas of the aptness of her remark; 'that Trebetherick is like an unsuccessful love affair, always having to be broken up because of outside hostile circumstances'. He added, 'I always enjoy Cornwall more than anything that happens to me in the year and this year I can say that I enjoyed myself more than ever. My! How we laughed!'. And, he said, he longed 'to live there for ever'.[126]

In fact, he had almost been offered a job in the autumn of 1944, working for the BBC in its Devon and Cornwall area.[127] In the event, he plumped for the more attractive prospect of employment with the British Council, forgoing the opportunity to live and work in the environs of Exeter or Plymouth, if not Cornwall itself. It may be simply that the British Council position was more exciting. Or perhaps the BBC post seemed too provincial, or perhaps, so soon after his return from Ireland, he was not yet ready – or sufficiently enthused – to relocate to the far west. Again, it is not clear whether he came to regret this decision. But we do know that, by the 1950s, he was increasingly determined that, if he could not live full-time in Cornwall, then he would spend as much time as possible there, preferably in a house of his own. As early as March 1948 he had written to Alan Pryce Jones from Trebetherick, glorying in his distance from the metropolis. There 'seems to be all Bodmin Moor between me and barbarity', he wrote: 'I am shocked to find how easily I can be consoled by place'.[128] Three years later, in June 1951, he wrote to Anne Channel, insisting that 'I do want to buy a house in Trebetherick. Nowhere else. Not even Rock or Polzeath'.[129] Soon word was out that Betjeman was house-hunting in Cornwall, and even Rowse got to hear of it eventually: 'Somebody told me that you are really coming to live in Cornwall, or were equipping yourself with a house at Trebetherick. Is this so much to be welcomed news true? I do hope so'.[130]

In the end, it was not until December 1959 that Betjeman acquired 'Treen', a typical Trebetherick type property in Daymer Lane, with a view out across Daymer Bay. It was exactly what he wanted; Anne Channel had searched dutifully on his behalf, and had found the perfect house. It was another life-altering moment for Betjeman; the fruition at last of his long-held ambition, acquisition of a property of his own in Cornwall. Significantly, despite the importance (and cost) of the purchase, he did not tell his wife Penelope until after the transaction was completed. Predictably, she was furious – not only because such an important decision had been made behind her back but also because it marked another milestone in their growing estrangement. She wrote, with prescient knowledge: 'I do most *deeply* resent the fact that you bought the cottage in Cornwall without letting me know anything about it ... Your heart is in Cornwall and you had much better go there'.[131]

'bracing and witty and kind and keen on drink'

From the earliest days, the marriage of John and Penelope Betjeman had been turbulent. In many ways, they had quite separate interests (she, having lived in India, was a passionate student of the Subcontinent; she also adored horses, animals that Betjeman disliked), and their union may simply have been a case of 'opposites attract'. Certainly, not long into his marriage he had begun to express misgivings. In December 1936, for instance, he wrote to his old flame Wilhelmine Creswell (Billa Harrod, as she became). 'I wish quite often that we had got married', he confided, 'You are just my cup of tea and we would have laughed such a lot. But Pethrillappy [Penelope] is very nice.

I can't have my cake and burn the candle at both ends'.[132] But sometimes
he tried to. There were rumours of flings and affairs – some platonic, some
not – even as late as the 1960s and 1970s when he was alleged to have
had a liaison with his old friend Margie Geddes, whom he had first met in
1929. According to Margie: 'He was a highly sexed man, practically till his
death'.[133] Intriguingly, Betjeman had once written to Michael Redington,
producer for Associated TV's religious programmes, to suggest – only
slightly tongue-in-cheek – some moral topics worthy of debate:

> Why can't we have two wives? When a man has ceased to love his wife
> and falls in love with another woman, why can't he have her as well?

> What's wrong with picking up Tarts? Is it worse if a woman entices away
> a man than a man enticing away a woman?

> Some of my best friends are 'queer' – are they likely to go to Hell?

> I am told that my body is a Temple of God and I must love my fellow
> creatures. I go mad about my female neighbours in their pretty Summer
> dresses and wish to possess them. Why is this wrong?

> What is the difference between lust and love? [134]

Embedded is this series of amusing questions were issues that deeply
troubled Betjeman, the cause of continuing angst and guilt. In 1951, long
after the flaws in his marriage had become apparent (their incompatibility
was made deeper by Penelope's decision during 1947 to convert to Roman
Catholicism), he met Lady Elizabeth Cavendish at a dinner party. The
mutual attraction was immediate, despite their disparities in ages (she was
born in 1926), and Betjeman wrote shortly to George Barnes to explain that
Elizabeth was exactly his kind of girl: 'bracing and witty and kind and keen
on drink'.[135] Initially, Penelope did not make much of this new friendship
– she was used to Betjeman's crushes and dalliances – but in meeting
Elizabeth, Betjeman had found his life-long companion. In 1951 the Betjeman
family had moved to Wantage, in Berkshire, and in 1954 Betjeman rented
a flat in London – ostensibly to meet the increasing demands of his work
in the capital but, of course, also to be near Elizabeth and to ensure time
together on their own. Likewise, sojourns in Cornwall were increasingly
opportunities to escape with Elizabeth, rather than the family holidays of

earlier years. As Candida Lycett Green explained, by the 1960s 'When my father was in Cornwall or in London ... he was with Elizabeth; and when he was at our home in Wantage ... he was with my mother'.[136]

The relationship between John Betjeman and Lady Elizabeth Cavendish (who was also Princess Margaret's Lady-in-Waiting, and daughter of the Duke of Devonshire), was one of the establishment's best kept secrets, especially in the early days. It was an open secret in Betjeman's circle but was kept out of the press, by and large, and hidden from public view, avoiding any whiff of scandal. It was also assumed to be a platonic, even if extremely close, friendship. 'Freckly Jill' Menzies, Betjeman's former secretary, considered that it 'was a very respectable affair and there was no adultery',[137] and Penelope herself thought the same. She met Margie Geddes in the 1970s, and told her that 'It's the eternal triangle Margie, but I don't think there is any sex in it. He is past that now'.[138] Earlier, Betjeman had himself told A.L. Rowse that 'We have ruled out sex', and Rowse was happy to believe him. Rowse did not much approve of heterosexual relationships anyway, and thought that 'sex makes fools of us all'.[139] He saw Betjeman's friendship with Elizabeth in essentially practical terms. 'Elizabeth Cavendish kindly took him in hand', he wrote, 'and tidied him up. I dare say Penelope got tired of keeping him in order – a full-time job – and rather fancied a career for herself'.[140] Nonetheless, others thought otherwise, and when Betjeman and Elizabeth visited George and Anne Barnes for overnight stays, they were always presented with a double bed. 'I *do* hope he's fucking her!', Anne Barnes was reputed to have exclaimed on one occasion.[141]

Whatever the precise details of their intimacy, there was no doubt of the significance of Trebetherick as bolt hole for Betjeman and Elizabeth. The purchase of 'Treen' was a strategic move which, as well as fulfilling Betjeman's ambition to own a house in Cornwall, provided the perfect hideaway. In October 1963, for example, he wrote excitedly to T.S. Eliot to say that Elizabeth was coming down to stay with him at 'Treen'.[142] Visits became ever more frequent. In 1967 Betjeman was in Cornwall during January, February and May. In the following year, 1968, he was down in January, February, March, May, October, and November, writing to his friend Elsie Avril on 15 January to explain that 'I go to Cornwall tomorrow (Treen, Trebetherick, Wadebridge – Kathleen Rosevear's cottage as was) till Sunday week to recover from having done too much badly in too little time'.[143] The next year, 1969, Betjeman was at 'Treen' during January, March, May, June, July, August and November. He wrote to Mary Wilson, wife of the Prime Minister, on 14 January, delighting in the solitude and freedom: 'It rains here without stopping. Trevose Head fog-horn moans, the sea mist is down, the silence is profound. I feel fairly secure'. In early April he wrote to her again, this time from Wantage: 'Oh were I by the waves and rocks and sapphire sea ... I will have to go to Cornwall and write for most of May'. Likewise, in June 1970, writing to Mary from London, he added: 'I hope to go to Cornwall ... for ten days. Isn't it a relief that waves still break, estuaries fill up and flowers bloom and the steady friends who are inanimate remain'.[144]

Betjeman was now genuinely dividing his time between Cornwall and London (and Wantage), and Elizabeth had become his constant companion. Together, they explored Cornwall, visiting Betjeman's childhood haunts but also seeking out and getting to know new places in south Cornwall and beyond. Elizabeth proved a gifted amateur photographer, and a number of her Cornish photographs appeared as illustrations in Betjeman's newly re-written Shell Guide to Cornwall published in 1964. There was the village green at Blisland, Beeny Cliff at Boscastle, countryside near St Endellion, Port Quin (near Port Isaac), Daymer House (near Trebetherick), the Methodist chapel at Trelill in St Kew parish – all Betjeman's old favourites – together with more distant places, such as Warleggan, Dozmary Pool and the mysterious Devil's Jump at Advent (all on Bodmin Moor), St Day church in the mining country near Redruth, the Tamar at Landulph, and the south-east Cornish villages of Tideford and Landrake.[145] Together, these illustrations provided a window into the meanderings of the two lovers as they made their way through Cornwall, intimations of their happy excursions from 'Treen' to places near and far.

At Trebetherick, in his own home, alone with Elizabeth Cavendish, Betjeman had experienced a new kind of 'liberation' and healing. But, as in those early childhood days, the exhilarating sense of freedom could sometimes be fleeting, and insecurities would return. Penelope was never far from his thoughts, and he was often racked with feelings of guilt and indecision. He was still writing to her as 'My darling Plymmi'[146] (one of his nicknames for her) until the early 1980s, almost to the eve of his death. There was no question of a divorce. But there was also no question of their living together, or of him giving up Elizabeth. Indeed, Betjeman's medical records, increasingly voluminous towards the end of his life, routinely cited Elizabeth as 'Next of Kin', with the explanatory designation 'friend', a measure of the primacy and permanence of their relationship.[147] As Betjeman tried to explain to Billa Harrod, 'I have lived so long apart from Penelope that Elizabeth now loves me more than anyone else in the world ... In all this awful storm of misery, the one thing I cling to is my love for Penelope *and* Elizabeth who has given up marriage and a family life with her own children, out of love for me'.[148]

At first, Penelope was often driven to anger by Betjeman's double life. When he announced in December 1956 that he might not be down at Wantage with her and the children for Christmas, she was enraged. She wrote to him on the 20th: 'If you won't come down for Christmas ... then DON'T. I am FED UP WITH YOUR BULLYING FOR NEARLY THIRTY YEARS AND AM AT LAST GOING TO TAKE A STRONG LINE'. She added: 'I'M DAMNED if I am going on with you in this perpetual dichotomy with insomnia, hysterical nerves, fear of losing your reputation etc etc ... Take it or leave it. ELISABETH [sic] or ME'.[149] Likewise, in June 1961 Penelope was again infuriated by what she saw as Betjeman's hypocrisy, duplicity and indecision. 'I know this is going to make you VERY angry', she wrote, stating her position very clearly – 'you are trying to get the best of both worlds: 1) leading a full sacramental life and trying to combine it with 2) what can honestly only be described as an adulterous relationship'. She accepted his word that his relationship with Elizabeth was entirely chaste but 'It seems to me cowardly of you not to have sex as well'.[150] Yet, in the midst of this tirade, Penelope was beginning to recognize and accept the reality of the situation. She would remain Betjeman's wife but, she had to acknowledge now, his first love was Elizabeth, and would remain so. In which case, she decided, she would rebuild her own life anew, devoting her energies and enthusiasm to the pursuit of *her* first love: India and the study of all things Indian. She wrote touchingly:

> When I am away from you I LOVE you and I ALWAYS SHALL and I shall write to you every week of my life. The great thing for you and E[lizabeth] is that I shall NOT feel left out of the eternal triangle because I have INJER [India] and I know I can make a fascinating life for myself out there ... I know you would never marry her unless I died.[151]

Time With Betjeman

Thereafter, Penelope did indeed focus her attention on her Indian studies, and she left Wantage in 1972 (when the family home was given up; another milestone), purchasing a cottage at Hay-on-Wye as part of her strategy for reshaping her life. She put a brave face on things publicly. In August 1972 she was interviewed by the *Listener*. 'Happy life? Yes, I think extremely happy',

17. John Betjeman and Elizabeth Cavendish relax at 'Treen', Betjeman's house at Trebetherick, during the making of the television version of *Summoned by Bells* in 1976, produced to mark the Poet Laureate's seventieth birthday.

she said: 'you might call it a stormy marriage, but fundamentally John and I are extremely fond of each other and I shall be terribly sad if he dies first and he'll be very sad if I die first'.[152] Betjeman, meanwhile, had become ever more ensconced in Cornwall. In 1973 he was at 'Treen' in January, February, March, April, May, June, September, October and December, interspersed with short spells in London, and 1974 he was there during February, March, April, June and October. In 1972 he had been appointed Poet Laureate, and, fittingly, news of the honour came through when he was at Trebetherick. He walked alone, as he had so many times since those childhood days, along the beach at Daymer Bay, contemplating the enormity of the situation. He was worried, he admitted, that 'better poets' would be annoyed. 'My feelings were of humility', he said, 'I was surprised and then pleased, and when I was pleased I said yes'.[153] The *New York Times* telephoned, finding him 'in the sunshine of Cornwall', as he had put it, 'thinking some stuff up'. *The Times* of London tracked him down at Trebetherick, where it discovered him 'Dressed in his characteristic rough coat and baggy trousers, with his bare feet in red slippers up before the fire'. He remarked, said the newspaper, 'on the silence of the night' and urged: 'Listen to the waves ... You can hear the high tide on the beach a few hundred yards away. This is where I spent the happiest days of my childhood'.[154] Quietly, privately, serenely, he was enjoying the personal triumph of his elevation as Poet Laureate – and savouring the appropriateness of his being in Cornwall.

Increasingly, in the years ahead, in the words of Candida Lycett Green, Betjeman 'took refuge at Treen in Cornwall with Elizabeth, surrounded by his Trebetherick friends'. He 'needed Elizabeth more and more', she added, particularly in the late 1970 and early 1980s as his disabilities – especially Parkinson's disease – began to take hold.[155] He became yet more nostalgic and melancholy: 'I wish we were all in Cornwall and walking along at low tide from Daymer to Rock, whatever the weather', he would write to old friends.[156] A heart attack in 1978 and a stroke in 1981 showered further disabilities upon him but he rallied (his Australian pal, Barry Humphries, wrote in admiration that he had the strength of 'a Mallee Bull'[157]), and he made with producer Jonathan Stedall a remarkable series of television programmes, *Time With Betjeman*, which was broadcast during 1983. The last of these showed Betjeman in his contented retirement at Trebetherick. 'Lovely, here', he whispered, as he gazed across his Cornish garden at 'Treen'. Cornwall was at its sultry, summery best as Betjeman, wheelchair-bound, contemplated the riot of exotic plants before him. 'Finished?', asked Stedall; 'Yes', said Betjeman, as if summing up his life.[158]

Betjeman died the next year, in May 1984. He had come down to Cornwall for a break, seriously ill as he was, and had overheard arrangements – so the story goes – for him to be returned to London by ambulance. There and then he made the decision to die in Cornwall. 'I know that at that point that he decided he wanted to die at Treen', wrote Candida Lycett Green. Moreover, added Elizabeth Cavendish, 'his fear of death' – a major preoccupation for so many years – 'seemed to go'. He passed away peacefully on the morning of 19 May 1984, comforted by his childhood toys, Archie the teddy-bear and Jumbo the elephant. It was a glorious Cornish spring day, as Elizabeth observed: 'He died on the most beautiful sunny morning with sun streaming into the room ... none of us moved for nearly an hour afterwards and the sense of total peace was something I shall never forget'.[159]

CHAPTER SEVEN

'Jan Trebetjeman, The Cornish Clot'

John Betjeman Goes Native

'Cornwall is a Duchy', insisted John Betjeman, writing in 1958: 'It is separated from England by the picturesque Tamar Valley, and has more sea coast than anywhere else in Britain'.[1] Like 'Q' – Sir Arthur Quiller-Couch – and other writers of the period, Betjeman used the term 'Duchy' to emphasize this distinctiveness and to suggest Cornwall's cultural and constitutional distance from England. Ignoring the tedious legal pedantry that worried over whether 'Duchy' was territorially coterminous with 'County', and why the Duchy as an institution owned more land outside Cornwall than within, Betjeman understood that the term was fundamentally a badge of 'difference'. True, there were times when, for Betjeman, Cornwall would become a 'County', or might be considered 'West Country', or could even be 'in' England but not 'of' England'. But at root Betjeman never wavered in his view that 'Cornwall is a foreign country'.[2]

Like Wales, Cornwall was 'abroad', with a far-away exoticism that made it seem like Spitsbergen or Honolulu. Here was 'the Celtic kingdom of Cornwall', said Betjeman, 'Not another county: another country'.[3] There were links with Brittany, exemplified in the 'holy island' (as he called it) of St Michael's Mount: 'What Mont St Michel is to Brittany, this is to Cornwall'.[4] Indeed, he added, the 'Cornish are the same sort of Celts as the Welsh and Bretons'.[5] And it was vital, Betjeman thought, that other people should appreciate, acknowledge and celebrate this Cornish difference: 'You must know', he told his listeners in a radio broadcast in February 1939, 'if you don't know Cornwall, that it is not like England – not even now, with all its bungalows and tea places'.[6] In his first Shell Guide to Cornwall, published in 1934, Betjeman had tried to convey this separateness to the general English-speaking reading public. The 'mystery, popularly known as "Celtic Twilight", which hangs over the Highlands of Scotland and over Wales and Ireland, also hangs over Cornwall', he told his readers, 'it makes the county still strange and different from anywhere else in England'.[7]

It was a message repeated time and again, and it was persuasive. Listeners, viewers, readers, colleagues and companions, all deferred to Betjeman's insistence that Cornwall was a land apart. Betjeman's close friend, the railway writer C. Hamilton Ellis, was entirely convinced by the oft-repeated message, taking trouble in his various histories to acknowledge the distinction between Cornwall and England. In his *Four Main Lines*, for example, published in 1950, he explained to *his* readers how the old London and South Western Railway had in its early expansionist days almost secured 'a monopoly of all south-western England *and* the Duchy of Cornwall'.[8] Five years later, it was a distinction Hamilton Ellis was still careful to observe, describing in another of his railway books the Great Western's 'route to the West of England and Cornwall'.[9] Such was the reach of Betjeman's influence.

'Cornish is a Celtic language'

An essential component of this difference, Betjeman considered, was the Cornish language. Cornwall's loss of political independence, he lamented in his Shell Guide, had spurred the decline of Cornish, although 'many words and phrases survived in the West of Cornwall'. Moreover, he added, despite the fate of the language, in Cornwall 'the *Saws* (the same as the Scottish *Sassenach*) or Englishman is even to this day looked upon as a "foreigner"'. Betjeman had studied Welsh, the language of his Meyrick forefathers, at Oxford (and was later to learn Irish when in Ireland during the war), and his scholarly knowledge of the Celtic tongues was made plain in the Cornwall guide. 'Cornish is a Celtic language', he explained authoritatively, 'like [Scots] Gaelic, Welsh and Irish'. He continued: 'The Celtic languages are divided into two groups. The first and older group is called Gaelic, and consists of Irish Gaelic, Scottish Gaelic and Manx. The second is called Brythonic, and consists of Welsh, Cornish and Breton'. Moreover, he added, 'The so-called "Ancient Britons" spoke the language of this second group, and, even today, it is said that a Breton onion-seller can understand Welsh as it is spoken in South Wales'.[10]

Echoing Henry Jenner, whose *Handbook of the Cornish Language* had appeared in 1904, Betjeman considered that 'there is no great literature surviving, of any great interest, in the language'. He knew of the existence, however, of 'three religious plays ... a life of St Meriasek, written in 1504, the Lord's Prayer, the Ten Commandments and some Scripture quotations

... a secular story and a seventeenth-century account of the Creation of the World'. Moreover, he insisted, 'nine-tenths of Cornish place names are in Cornish, and it is useful to know a few words in Cornish and the primary rules of its grammar so as to be able to translate the name of the place where you happen to be, or, if you are going to live in Cornwall, to give your house a Cornish name'.[11] Betjeman listed a few common place-name elements and then, remarkably, provided what must have been surely the first explanation of 'mutation' in the Cornish language to be provided for a mass, popular readership:

> You must remember that mutation happens very often. That is to say B becomes V as in Goon-vean (bean), or P; C(K) becomes G as in Cargelli (celli), and, more rarely H: D becomes Th as in Car-thew (du), and J; F becomes V; G is sometimes left out altogether or becomes W or C or K or Q; M becomes V; P becomes B, and T becomes D. This is not unreasonable or capricious, but merely a grammatical rule.[12]

From Cornish language, it was a short step to discussion of Cornish saints, already one of Betjeman's favourite subjects, not least from his reading of Sabine Baring-Gould. 'St Erth was a pagan chief whom St Patrick converted among hoots of ribald laughter', he reported in the Guide, while 'St Erney cures your headaches if you pray to him; when he died the birds heaped up leaves and twigs over his grave to form a little beehive hut'. Then there was 'St Uny [who] lost his belt and a fox got tangled up in it', and 'St Ewe, who was a martyr, [and] sailed away from Britain alone in a boat made of quartz which is still preserved in Brittany'. These were pleasant, attractive tales, Betjeman observed, but, light-hearted as they seemed, they held a deeper meaning. Although 'we may doubt the truth of the stories', he argued, 'we cannot doubt the courage and zeal of the saints'. As he was to emphasize time and again in the years ahead as he elaborated his pan-Celtic sympathies: 'It was through them that Ireland and Wales remained the last havens of learning during the dark ages, and through them that Cornwall, Wales and Ireland were civilized hundreds of years before ... England'.[13]

In conception, format and appearance, Betjeman's 1934 Shell Guide was, for its time, revolutionary. As William S. Peterson, Betjeman's bibliographer, has remarked, it was 'a new kind of guidebook ... deliberately quirky in both content and topographical style'.[14] It also reflected Betjeman's personal enthusiasms, such as his penchant for nineteenth-century engravings (admitted in *Summoned by Bells*, where he described his fondness for books of 'steel engravings' and 'folios of architectural plates'). There was, for example, on page 19 an engraving of St Mawgan church and Lanherne nunnery, reproduced from J. Britton's and E.W. Brayley's 1831 volume, *Cornwall Illustrated in a Series of Views*. Indeed, Betjeman even borrowed this title for his Guide, for good measure also employing in his book a facsimile reproduction of part of the title page from the 1831 volume. The Guide sold well, with a second edition in 1939, but had gone out of print by the end of 1941.

More than twenty years later, in 1964, Betjeman produced an entirely re-written edition of his Shell Guide to Cornwall. It was longer, better crafted and better illustrated but it retained something of the flavour of the original, still entertaining and often amusing in a sometimes slightly off-beat way, rather than the entirely dry-as-dust approach that Betjeman despised in other guides. Despite all the changes that had overtaken Cornwall since his first Guide, Betjeman was keen once more to elaborate his particular theme – Cornwall as a land apart. In this new version he was concerned to avoid the medievalist focus of so many other contemporary guides (not least Pevsner's), together with what he imagined to be their humourless pedantry. Overwhelmed with work, and with a series of new Shell Guides to oversee, he had at first devolved the task of drafting a new text to H.J. Wilmott, an antiquarian enthusiast and news editor on the staff of the *Cornish Guardian* newspaper who had published with J.C. Trewin a delightful volume of their correspondence, entitled *London-Bodmin*.[15] Betjeman gave Wilmott a free hand but when the manuscript arrived, he was appalled. It was exactly what he did not want. He had to write diplomatically to Wilmott, explaining that 'I do not think ... it necessary to say quite so much about the mediaval [sic] associations', and pointing out that the 'ownership of manors and the like have been done so many times before'.[16] Wilmott tried again, but the revised draft was even worse. Tactfully, Betjeman released Wilmott from his task, and finished the job himself – at Trebetherick during September 1962, with the help of John Piper, the series' co-editor.

'north Cornwall, where I was brought up as a child'

In a masterly introduction to the new-look Shell Guide, Betjeman charted and critiqued the changes (for the worst) that had happened since the first version was published: the impact of the motor car, road widening, electricity poles and wires, more tourists, and so on. But he also penned a new sketch of Cornwall's history and people, from the early Celts, 'who were Christians before the Saxons', to today when: 'The old and beautiful Cornwall is now mostly to be found on foot or in a small car by those skilled in using the 1-inch ordnance survey map'. The historical experience of the Cornish had been 'a hard struggle for existence', he said: 'The Saxons and the Normans tried to hold them down with forts and castles. They did not take kindly to the Reformation, nor to Cromwell, and most of them stood out for King Charles'. Their livelihood 'since Roman times' had depended chiefly on mining, but they 'were also farmers and fishermen'. In the eighteenth century, their 'religious faith was awakened by John Wesley and to this day the majority of Cornish are Methodists'. They even 'had their own brand of it', added Betjeman, 'the Bible Christians, a sect whose chief light was Billy Bray, the converted tin miner'. Nonetheless, the Anglican 'revival of the see of Cornwall and the building of the cathedral in Truro in the '80s turned the gaze of Christians to Brittany, where the feasts of so many Cornish saints were still kept'. And, Betjeman explained, from 'the 1880s artists were coming from England into Cornwall and settling in St Ives and Newlyn and painting not only the scenery but the people. Some, like Stanhope Forbes, made the journey via Brittany'.[17]

Betjeman's observation that the Newlyn School painters were interested in people as well as scenery was astute. Often, for literary and artistic visitors to Cornwall, the Cornish were all but invisible, at best part of the backdrop. In common with such 'outsiders', Betjeman was drawn to land- and seascapes: the 'picturesque Tamar Valley', the 'sea coast', and the fact that 'the Celtic field system makes the Duchy look different from England'.[18] But, more unusually, he was interested in the people too, and here, like the painters of the Newlyn School, he was in something of a minority among those early visitors. Patrick Taylor-Martin, in his 1983 study of Betjeman and his work, imagined that in the Cornwall of Betjeman's boyhood, 'the natives were primitive children of nature'.[19] Yet this was never Betjeman's perception. Despite his 'Celtic Twilight' enthusiasm, he stopped short of depicting the Cornish as an exotic 'other', and instead his instinct was to claim common cause with the locals. In his early childhood days at Trebetherick, he reflected years later, 'there were many Cornish still resident' in the area: 'Charlie Mably who collected golf balls on the course and lived at the oldest house; Tom Buse, who, with his wife and daughters ran the Haven Boarding House at which first we stayed, and drove the jingle to take us to the station'. There was the 'old farm at the top of the hill owned by Francis Mably and another one, lower down, farmed by Tom Blake'. They co-existed with the holidaymakers who visited year-on-year,

18. John Betjeman wanders across the *towans* (sand dunes) at 'his' St Enodoc.

and with those who had moved down to settle permanently in Cornwall. 'We were a family', Betjeman insisted, 'though not related. We were all equal, and the Cornish inhabitants – the Buses, the Mablys, the Coxes, the Males, the Champions, the Camps and many others in the shops and farms were all part of us'.[20] Likewise, when he produced his first Shell Guide to Cornwall in 1934, he was careful to include Cornish recipes given to him by his Cornish neighbours – Mrs Mably at Trebetherick, and Mrs Tremaine at Trevanger farm – a touch of authenticity but also a device to demonstrate intimate connection with the indigenous community.[21] These good ladies were his friends.

Sometimes Betjeman admitted to himself that Trebetherick was really just 'a suburb by the sea and for all our crabbing, fishing and bathing, nothing to do with the real Cornish who regarded us as the foreigners we still are'.[22] He was also, as we have seen, prepared to admit publicly his non-Cornish credentials, to confess time and again that he was a 'foreigner'. In 1969, for example, he told Cornish journalist Michael Williams that: 'I am not a native of Cornwall, but a suburban Cockney'.[23] He was also, he confessed to A.L. Rowse, 'an emmet',[24] a pejorative Cornish dialect word meaning 'ant' that was applied by the locals to tourists and (sometimes) in-migrants. Yet, as we have also seen, Betjeman was desperate to 'belong', and even as he denied being Cornish, so he sought to acquire Cornishness, partly by adopting his Cornish persona – 'Jan Killigrew Trebetjeman'; even 'Jan Trebetjeman, the Cornish Clot'[25] – and partly through the discovery of his Welsh descent and the later cultivation of multiple Celtic allegiances. It was a complex paradox that Betjeman himself struggled to understand. 'There's something in most of us that wants to be what we aren't', he said, 'a Cornish fisherman, a Cornish boatbuilder or sailmaker. We wear navy-blue jerseys and sou'westers if we can. We want to be taken as natives. That's because we feel need of solitude and roots'. Did the Cornish welcome him into their company, he wondered, or were they merely playing along with him, for their own profit and amusement? 'We listen guilelessly to sailors' yarns', he said: 'The shrewd Cornish – independent, proud – cash in on the foreigners: and small blame to them'.[26] He wanted to be like them; and if he could not, he understood their motives and forgave them.

In his desire to 'belong', and to acquire that patina of Cornishness, Betjeman would sometimes stretch the truth a little, the periodic Cornish holidays of his boyhood transformed into something like permanent residency. In April 1937, in a radio broadcast, he talked vaguely of 'the part of Cornwall where I used to live'.[27] Likewise, 'I had the inestimable privilege of spending most of my childhood in Cornwall', he wrote in 1944 in a review of A.L. Rowse's *West Country Stories*.[28] Later still, in a BBC television programme in 1959, he described the journey by car 'to north Cornwall, where I was brought up as a child',[29] neatly insinuating a Cornish childhood without having to offer explanations or caveats. So successful were such assertions, that even today one website devoted to Cornwall's history can announce confidently that: 'Sir John Betjeman, poet and television personality, was born in Cornwall'.[30]

'Know what a beam engine is?'

Betjeman could also deploy a proprietorial tone, asserting a specialist knowledge of Cornwall, as he had in 1957 when he replied authoritatively to the publisher John Foster White about where to stay and what to see when visiting Cornwall (see pp. 27–8). Similarly, despite his self-confessed ineptitude with anything practical or mechanical, he struck the pose of a Cornish engineering instructor – someone out of the Camborne School of Mines, almost – as he explained in a film in 1955 the workings of the beam-engine at Crofton Pumping Station on the Kennet and Avon Canal in Wiltshire. He told viewers that water had been pumped into the canal for

150 years 'by one of the oldest steam engines still working in the world: a Cornish beam engine'. He continued, magisterially: 'Know what a beam engine is? While you're looking at its beautiful rhythmic motion, I'll try to tell you'. The beam itself was 'like the top of a pair of scales', he said, 'and the beam's worked up and down by a steam piston on one side, which operates a suction pump on the other'. And so, he added: 'Down goes the rod on the pump side, carried down by its own weight: the steam piston draws it up again and the pump sucks out water, which is eventually spurted into the canal'.[31] Perhaps the viewers understood.

Although, as we know, Betjeman was drawn overwhelmingly to Celtic revivalist imaginings of Cornwall, he was also prepared (as the Crofton commentary indicated) to acknowledge the place of engineering and mining in Cornish history and heritage. The engine-houses and chimney stacks that dominated Cornwall's former tin and copper-mining districts were, he said, 'memorials to the Cornish engineers. Men like Trevithick and Hornblower, who in the eighteenth century improved on stationary steam engines for pumping up water out of wet mines ... And hauling up minerals from a thousand feet below'.[32] These were the times when St Day, between Redruth and Truro, was 'one of the chief mining towns of Cornwall'. Its streets, he said, were 'once like Oxford Street, a century and more ago, to ill-paid tin miners. After long hours in the hot wet granite passages below the earth they'd look into these shop windows, they and their poor families, gazing and gazing and longing to buy'. But these times were long gone, he explained, and now, with the mines abandoned, a 'silence always hangs about St Day'. Yet it too, like the engine-houses and chimney stacks, was a memorial to past glories: 'For all its melancholy, St Day is now the least spoiled town in Cornwall'.[33]

Betjeman also found in the old mining landscapes that *frisson* of 'happy terror' that he had already detected in rural North Cornwall (see p. 71); a sinister hint of the dangers that lurked among the mine dumps and open shafts, and might trap the unwary. 'For all its empty open look this desolate country is dangerous to walk on', he said: 'Underneath it is a honeycomb of miles of passages in the hot granite. Some shafts go down 2,000 feet. One false step and you might find yourself plunged into black, hot silence'.[34] But in his uneasiness Betjeman betrayed his ambivalent attitude to industrial Cornwall. He was prepared, as we have seen, to celebrate the mining and engineering past, and to recognize the iconic status in the history of Cornwall of engine-houses, chimney stacks and towns like St Day. But for him it was not the 'real' Cornwall that he had encountered elsewhere

– deeply rural, and deeply 'Celtic' – and when he visited the urban mining heartland of Camborne and Redruth there was much to disconcert him. 'The sort of wasteland of garages, small factories, hoardings and shacks and cafes which intersperse the main road between Redruth and Camborne and turn this area into Cornwall's Slough', he explained, 'have as their centre Illogan Highway and Pool'.[35] He hoped, perhaps, as in his famous poem about the real Slough, that 'friendly bombs' might fall to obliterate this industrial eyesore. But if they had, they would have destroyed the surviving buildings along that main road of East Pool and Wheal Agar mine – including two Cornish beam-engines, still *in situ* in their engine-houses – which in the early 1960s, when Betjeman was writing, were already in the care of the Cornish Engines Preservation Society, and later passed to the National Trust on account of their national and international significance. Betjeman had failed to spot their existence, let alone their importance.

'splendid white cones of the china clay pits'

Betjeman was similarly ambivalent about the china clay country of mid-Cornwall. He again understood the iconic value of this singular landscape to its natives, not least his friend A.L. Rowse and the poet Jack Clemo, but struggled to appreciate it himself. He managed to extol the 'splendid white cones of the china clay pits, with the milky green lakes below them'[36] that, he said, dominated the landscape in St Stephen-in-Brannel parish. But he was less enthusiastic about 'the sunless northern slopes of the china clay district' around Bugle and Carthew, with its rows of 'grey late Victorian cottages, brick and slate chimney stacks, grocers shops, chapels, heathery waste land and main roads with heavily loaded lorries'.[37] In St Austell itself, capital of the clay country, he disapproved mildly of the 'many executives' with their 'parked cars outside the various office buildings of the big china clay combine in the town'. St Austell was prosperous, he acknowledged, listing the many uses for china clay ('pottery, face powder, size, calico and shiny art paper to name a few') but he regretted that 'Mostly St Austell has had to cave in to the chainstores and the china clay combine's demands'. Some important historic buildings had survived in the town, he said, but it was in the parish's coastal strip outside the clay country that 'at Porthpean … and Trenarren beyond it, where A.L. Rowse lives, unexpectedly the old Cornwall survives'.[38]

Most of all, Betjeman was critical of the environmental damage that he imagined the clay industry was inflicting on Cornwall. He explained that the 'white silica waste, when the clay has been extracted, is lifted up on to tips and makes this lunar landscape of mountains around St Austell'. He added (inaccurately) that 'Nothing will grow on these white tips', and that the escaping 'white waste will continue to pollute brown streams, and plunge on to streak the southern estuaries with creamy mud'.[39] He was thinking especially of the aptly named White River that flowed from St Austell down to the sea at Pentewan, where the water was stained milky white, the china-clay particles providing a strange buoyancy for swimmers who were not afraid to venture into the murky waves. As much as the mass tourism and 'development' that Betjeman so abhorred in his own North Cornwall, here in the St Austell area was environmental destruction that had to be stood up to – someone had to take on the 'big china clay combine' that ran the district as if it were a personal fiefdom. He said so to A.L. Rowse, and Rowse – in an uncharacteristically tactful moment – was able to act as something of a go-between, mediating between Betjeman and Sir Alan Dalton, chief executive of the clay combine, who also happened to be a friend of Rowse.

Betjeman wrote to *The Times* in July 1970 to protest about china clay waste dumped in the sea.[40] He had found an important ally in Air Marshall Sir John Tremayne, another Rowse acquaintance, and together Betjeman and Tremayne investigated the environmental impact of china clay waste along the south coast, around St Austell Bay. 'What about the pollution of the river and sea by the China Clay Co.?', Betjeman demanded angrily of Rowse. As Betjeman reported, he and Tremayne had been 'down your way … looking at the filthy scum of china clay on Pentewan beach, and how many more streams than the St Austell White River are white'.[41] As Rowse acknowledged, 'White River' was a modern appellation, derived from the clay pollutants; 'its old name was Cober, which simply means stream, represented still by the place-name Gover at the head of it'. Like Clemo, Rowse appreciated the iconic value of the clay country, but he could also be extremely critical of it and its unrelieved modernity. He was well placed, therefore, given this ambivalence, to act as mediator. 'I did my best to be an honest broker between Air-Marshal Tremayne and Sir Alan Dalton', he wrote, 'both friends. In the end the militant Air-Marshall won'.[42]

As Rowse observed, the clay company had by then already become much more 'public-spirited and conservation-minded', and as a result of Betjeman's actions 'the streams are now flowing clearer'. Rowse had always thought 'clay detritus … completely harmless'. But he too was glad to see clean water, and was rather pleased that Sir Alan Dalton (a keen gardener, Rowse explained) and his clay company had also 'planted trees galore and covered sand-burrows with rhododendrons and lupins, purple and gold, bless them'.[43] Rowse, it seems, was proud to have done his bit. Yet, perversely, in this moment of victory, Betjeman could also observe gloomily that tackling the clay combine was really just one small advance in the face of the overwhelming threats that now faced Cornwall. 'All the same', he said, in the final analysis 'I prefer polluted streams to streams of visitors',[44] answering the question he had posed back in 1964 in his television broadcast 'One Man's County' when he had wondered out-loud whether it was the clay industry or the tourist trade that posed the greater long-term environmental danger.

'I do not wish to offend Mr Betjeman'

In his role as environmental campaigner, Betjeman had taken a keen interest in planning issues in Cornwall. As early as 1938, he had complained that the 'Cornish coast is becoming a huge suburb', insisting that 'This must be checked'. Building should be confined to certain designated areas, he said, with the rest of Cornwall 'left undeveloped'.[45] Significantly, his address book in the 1950s, otherwise devoted mainly to friends, acquaintances and work colleagues, also included H.W.J. Heck, the chief planning officer at Cornwall County Council.[46] Heck's successor at County Hall in Truro, C.J. Barrington, even found his way onto Betjeman's Christmas card list in 1964.[47] In 1963 Betjeman had been one of thirty-nine signatories to a letter to The Times complaining about plans by the Admiralty 'to use approximately 355 acres of moorland, at Zennor in Cornwall, for troop training in connexion with helicopters'. Other signatories included A.L. Rowse, Benjamin Britten, Arthur Bryant, the writer F.E. Halliday, the artist Patrick Heron (who lived at Zennor), the sculptors Barbara Hepworth and Ben Nicholson, the potter Bernard Leach, and many other luminaries from the world of art, music and literature, most with Cornish connections of one sort or another. Together, they objected that the 'land concerned includes three rocky hills of exquisite grandeur'. As they pointed out, 'nearly all this land was recently placed under restrictive covenants to the National Trust by its various private owners'. Moreover, 'since it lies at the heart of a uniquely beautiful region which has been protected by a National Parks Commission order, we sincerely hope that the Admiralty will withdraw their application and look elsewhere'.[48]

A rather stunned Admiralty did indeed back off. As in other campaigns he had supported, Betjeman had demonstrated the power of concerted action by informed and well-connected activists designed to embarrass 'the establishment'. He had also displayed his faith in the National Trust as an institutional safeguard of natural and historic heritage, not least in Cornwall. At Trebetherick, he had arranged for parcels of land owned by the Betjeman family to pass to the National Trust, protecting the locality from further development, and ensuring that his part of North Cornwall 'has been kept in its natural state not by the government or any private landlord but by the National Trust'.[49] In a BBC television broadcast in 1959, he recalled the role played by the Trust in preserving the peace and integrity of nearby Pentire. 'I remember the consternation there was when this piece of headland – Pentire – came up for sale', he said, 'but local people subscribed to buy it and gave it to the National Trust, so that it is now an open space for ever for all to enjoy'. But, he was quick to add, 'it's not a useless open space'. Far from it: 'The National trust owns Pentire farm', he told his viewers, 'the old farmhouse on the left – and the newer house, in simple storm-resisting style'. Here, he added, farmers 'with the good Cornish name of "Old" have looked after this land for generations and made a living from it ... snug in a hollow in this windswept peninsula'. Here they were, 'Cornish father and Cornish son', farming 'wild and wonderful' country on the Atlantic Ocean's edge, high above the tumbling sea where 'only seals can bask safely in these merciless waters'.[50]

Elsewhere in Cornwall, Betjeman continued, the community had felt the benign hand of the National Trust. What 'do you do with a great country house like Cotehele if you inherit it and like it and can't afford to keep it?', he asked: 'Rather than let it become a ruin, anything. A fifteenth-century Cornish manor, it was accepted by the Treasury in lieu of death duties from Lord Mount Edgcumbe and the Treasury handed it on to the Trust'. In similar manner, he explained, 'St Michael's Mount in Cornwall was a gift from its owner, Lord St Levan. Lanhydrock, with its woods, seventeenth-century gatehouse and formal gardens, was given by Lord Clifden'.[51] Here was a tradition that Betjeman approved (and indeed had played some small part in), and when in 1967 he was approached by the regional committee of the National Trust in Cornwall to pen a verse in support of the campaign – Enterprise Neptune – to preserve the British coastline, he was delighted. He set to with a will, his poem 'One and All' (later republished as 'Delectable Duchy') contrasting the pristine North Cornish coast of his early childhood with the 'tired', 'over-hired' and 'pathetic sight' that was 1960s tourist Cornwall (see pp. 24–6). It was an eleventh-hour call to arms that Betjeman imagined would galvanize the informed public, encouraging all those who valued Cornwall to rally round at last in a concerted effort to prevent the final despoliation of the land they loved. It was a critical moment, a not-to-be-missed opportunity.

But the regional committee of the National Trust did not see it that way. One Trust member, quoted in *The Times*, thought Betjeman's effort 'poetic licence run amok'. For surprised readers, taken aback perhaps by the strength of such criticism, the newspaper explained that 'Mr Betjeman's poem describes ... a grim picture of a county overrun by the litter of tourists, and where beauty spots have been spoiled by caravan sites and holiday development'. This was not a description that had appealed to N.J. Savage, one of the regional committee members, who announced that Betjeman's especially commissioned poem had now been rejected by the Trust! This was because, said Savage, the verse 'was felt to be against the best interests of the Neptune campaign, which is aimed at saving 900 miles of British coastline'. As Savage complained, it was considered that the poem 'gives the impression that Cornwall is already spoilt beyond redemption. If people are to led to believe this', he insisted, 'then they will see no point in helping the campaign'. Although 'I do not wish to offend Mr Betjeman,' Savage continued, 'I think his poem is a poetic licence highly exaggerated'. Nonetheless, *The Times* reported, Savage had 'said he would like Mr Betjeman to write another poem painting Cornwall as a county of beautiful, unspoilt coves which could be in danger of being ruined'. Not surprisingly, Betjeman declined, his faith in the National Trust dented. Lord Antrim, the chairman of the Trust, intervened to 'investigate the rejection by the regional committee of the Trust in Cornwall of a poem ... specially written by John Betjeman', but it was too late.[52]

'a firm supporter of the anti-nuclear movement in Cornwall'

Campaigning for the National Trust would always be a genteel occupation, and Betjeman in his vociferousness had overstepped the mark. It was an episode that had revealed his subversive side, his willingness to strike poses that would discomfort cautious or conventional opinion. Moreover, as he had demonstrated in the china clay campaign, his environmentalism was more than skin deep, and went beyond the preservation offered by the National Trust to embrace more radical critiques of governmental policy and planning. In that sense, although he often denied it, Betjeman was a political activist. He was, for example, a committed anti-nuclear campaigner (he had been

frightened by the sinister nuclear plant at Harwell in Berkshire), and in
Cornwall he lent his support to the Cornish anti-nuclear movement. There
were concerns about the possible presence of nuclear weapons at military
establishments in Cornwall (something the government would neither
confirm nor deny), and there were long-standing fears about other potential
nuclear activities. There were suggestions, for example, that Cornwall
might be a suitable location for the storage underground of nuclear waste,
and there were periodic proposals for the establishment of a nuclear power
station in Cornwall.

In the autumn of 1979, the UK Atomic Energy Authority announced
its intention to investigate three possible Cornish sites – at Gwithian, the
notorious Nancekuke (which already had a bad press as home of the Ministry
of Defence's chemical and biological warfare establishment), and Luxulyan in
mid-Cornwall. Mebyon Kernow (MK), the Cornish nationalist movement,
led the foundation of what was hailed at the time as a 'rainbow alliance' of
green activists, the Cornish Anti-Nuclear Alliance (CANA), which set about
organizing an effective campaign to frustrate the investigations. Lessons were
learned from Breton nationalists attempting to block similar plans at Plogoff
and Le Pellerin in Brittany, and there was a bold programme of direct
action to prevent the exploratory work – on one occasion Bill Heck, son of
the former chief planning officer, climbed to the top of a drilling rig near
Luxulyan to plant a Cornish flag in protest at the proposals. Shortly after,
plans for a nuclear power station in Cornwall were dropped.[53] Although
illness had prevented Betjeman from playing an active role in these later years
of his life, when the nuclear threat in Cornwall was acute, local campaigners
valued his moral support and appreciated the weight of his opinion. Indeed, at
his funeral at St Enodoc in May 1984, one of the wreaths placed at Betjeman's
grave was from the local branch of the environmentalist group, Greenpeace.
As the *Western Daily Press* newspaper reminded its readers: 'Sir John was a
firm supporter of the anti-nuclear movement in Cornwall'.[54]

Likewise, Betjeman was a strong critic of modern 'agribusiness',
especially its use of pesticides and other chemicals, and the spread of
battery farming. In Cornwall, he deplored the destruction of ancient
Cornish hedges, so much a part of the distinctive landscape and important
wildlife habitats. He knew that Robert Stephen Hawker had introduced
the modern harvest festival at Morwenstow in North Cornwall (see p. 45),
and in his spoof 'Harvest Hymn' Betjeman produced a critique of modern
farming methods as powerful as his angry lament for the demise of the
'Delectable Duchy':

We spray the fields and scatter
          The poison on the ground
So that no wicked wildflowers
          Upon our farm be found.
We like whatever helps us
          To line our purse with pence;
The twenty-four-hour broiler-house
          And neat electric fence.

All concrete sheds around us
          And Jaguars in the yard,
The telly lounge and deep-freeze
          Are ours from working hard.[55]

Betjeman was also prepared to put his money where his mouth was, carefully husbanding the little piece of land around his house 'Treen', at Trebetherick. In the gales of February 1978 a large elm had come down, and Betjeman was keen to see it replaced. He wrote to Archie Polkinghorne, the local builder, explaining that 'I think trees are more important in Trebetherick than houses. In fact they are essential, Cornish elms (*ulmus cornubiensis*) in particular'. He went on, explaining to Polkinghorne that 'I would like to see a little spinney of Cornish elms and ash and sycamores across the back garden of Treen and the bottom garden of St Enodoc cottage'. Asking him to do the job, Betjeman urged Polkinghorne to find tall saplings, so that they would soon grow to maturity. 'I would like to see them before I die', he wrote, 'and to know that this little bit of the lane will still be Cornish'.[56]

Earlier, in the 1960s, Betjeman had been especially worried about the impact of the Beeching Axe in Cornwall. He was by then Vice-President of the Railway Development Association. A seasoned campaigner, he knew that opposition to Dr Beeching's plans – in the rest of Britain as well as in Cornwall – would have to be tough and rigorous. It would not be enough to oppose the wholesale closure of railway routes on purely sentimental grounds, and sound economic and social cases would have to be made to persuade a sceptical government heavily influenced by the 'road lobby' that Britain's secondary routes had a viable future. As Betjeman put it: 'I love branch lines because they are little quiet worlds of peace and seclusion. But in order to try and preserve them, we have got to be what is called *practical!*'.[57] In fact, it was not merely the quiet rural backwaters that were threatened.

The Somerset & Dorset, which linked Bath to Bournemouth and provided an important corridor for through connections to the Midlands and North of England, was a major secondary route earmarked for closure. The line was one of Betjeman's favourites and in 1963 he made a television programme about it, broadcast on the BBC, concluding with the cautionary note: 'In ten years' time, when the roads are so full of traffic we'll be going by train again, you'll be grateful you still have a railway to your town. Don't let Dr Beeching take it away from you'.[58] But Betjeman's support, other than winning the appreciation of railway enthusiasts and an enduring place in the iconography of the 'sad forgotten S&D' (as he called it), did nothing to save the railway.[59] It closed in March 1966. The political case for its survival (complicated by inter-regional rivalries within British Railways) had not been made sufficiently strongly. It was also a long, sprawling, infrastructurally complex but undercapitalized route that was in any case unlikely to survive in the then current climate.

'the brute Beeching'

Precisely the same could be said of the North Cornwall railway. Even more than the Somerset & Dorset, the North Cornwall was close to the heart of John Betjeman (see pp. 28–36). Earliest childhood memories included train journeys to Wadebridge and Padstow, and the route between those two towns, along the Camel estuary, was, he said, the most beautiful he knew. The remote wayside stations of Egloskerry and Tresmeer were, as T.W. Roche said, immortalized in Betjeman's *Summoned by Bells*, and the line itself – with its distinctive green Southern Railway coaches in the heart of otherwise Great Western dominated territory – lent a particular identity to the North Cornwall district it served. Indeed, in its territorial extent, as we have seen, it almost defined Betjeman's North Cornwall. The Beeching assault then, when it came, was a hard blow for Betjeman. At first, as in his estimation of the Somerset & Dorset, he imagined that the North Cornwall was so vital a lifeline in that area that commonsense would surely prevail and the route be saved. The Beeching plan had called for the closure of the entire route west of Okehampton, including the two branch railways westwards from Halwill Junction – the 'main' line to Wadebridge and Padstow, and the shorter stretch to Bude. In Cornwall and West Devon, local opinion mirrored Betjeman's disbelief.

However, there were those who took the threat seriously. In February 1964 Gilbert Nelson wrote to Betjeman from Bude to congratulate him on his Somerset & Dorset television programme. But he also expressed his forebodings about the Beeching Axe in Cornwall. Monstrous the plans might be but they had a certain momentum, now that the closures had begun, that would make them difficult to stop. 'How sad to think that the Beeching axe is felling these West Country lines', said Nelson as he surveyed the devastation beyond Cornwall, 'I wonder what will happen at the end of the present year if the Bude and Padstow lines are cut down too'. Now in his seventy-sixth year, Nelson admitted that he was 'still … a boy regards trains', and that thirty years ago he and his son had built a model railway, based on the old Great Western, which he still operated and which 'Dr Beeching cannot touch'.[60] Betjeman was delighted. 'I must thank you for your charming letter about the old S. and D.', he replied, 'I envy you living at Bude'. He added that he had recently been twice to Bude by train, and that the branch seemed perfectly viable: 'so far as I can see, the brute Beeching has not yet deprived us of our lines down there and if he does I don't see how the narrow roads are going to cope with the summer traffic'. Yet he sensed the awful logic of Nelson's letter, and with an almost audible sigh of resignation asked Nelson, when he was out walking his dog on the cliffs, to 'remember me to the Atlantic rollers … and every station between you and Halwill Junction'.[61]

The Labour victory in the 1964 general election raised the hope that the Beeching cull might be reversed, or at least halted. Barbara Castle, the new Minister of Transport, promised as much but in reality the process had already gone too far. Castle had devised a new set of 'social criteria' for considering closures but, focussing as these did on specific localities, they rarely addressed wider strategic issues. The Southern line from Waterloo to Padstow had been deemed to duplicate the (Great) Western route from Paddington to Penzance, despite the fact that these served widely different areas, and in officialdom this view prevailed. Betjeman's beloved 'Atlantic Coast Express' was withdrawn in September 1964, little more than six months after Gilbert Nelson has written his prescient letter, and thereafter it was downhill all the way for the route of the 'ACE'. Local efficiencies, such as the introduction of single-car railbuses on the shuttle service between Bodmin North and Boscarne Junction on the line between Bodmin and Wadebridge, made little difference, and the whole North Cornwall system was finally closed to passengers on 30 January 1967. The only stump to survive, a forlorn result of Castle's 'social criteria', was the short remnant of the Callington branch between Gunnislake and Bere Alston.

Here, like the Somerset & Dorset, had been a long, sprawling, infrastructurally complex but undercapitalized route, hampered by long-standing rivalries between the Southern and the (Great) Western, which even Betjeman's patronage could not save. One observer, David Henshaw, would write later that 'areas of north Cornwall were now as far from a railhead as the remotest corners of Wales'.[62] Another, S.H. Austin, offered his thoughts ('after Betjeman', as he put it) in the style of *Summoned by Bells*:

> Come Petrol, spirit of the traveller's joy:
> Whereas my forbears packed their trunks
> And settled to a porter's salute to journey,
> I load my own magic carpet, self-piloted,
> And once more it's the open road for me.
> And those deadly twins, Free Choice and
>   Market Forces.[63]

Now, as Austin observed, the 'empty trackway, wind in the willow-herb, / Winds up from Egloskerry to Tresmeer/ Through indifferent and encroaching fields, / Past farms whose sons await with eagerness / The motorway link'. Yet Betjeman's inability to affect the fate of the North Cornwall did not mean that he was entirely impotent as anti-Beeching campaigner west of the Tamar. The Railway Development Association had been determined to save the branch line from Liskeard (on the Penzance mainline) to Looe, on the south coast. A short, self-contained line (with the additional economic consideration of a large china clay processing plant at Moorswater), the branch was an altogether more viable proposition than the sprawling North Cornwall (or Somerset & Dorset). In March 1966, as the hard-pressed Labour government fought another general election to improve its slim majority, Betjeman saw his chance. He put his full weight behind the Association's campaign, and this time the railway was saved. Years before, he had written that 'Wherever there was a space in Looe for a car park there *was* a car park. And it was full'.[64] Now the powers-that-be were persuaded by such rhetoric, that Looe simply could not survive without its rail link, such were its topographical constraints between steep hills on either side of the harbour and estuary.

Significantly, perhaps, in preparing the case for the Liskeard to Looe branch, the Railway Development Association had put Betjeman in touch with John Finlayson.[65] Finlayson was spokesman in Cornwall for Transport 2000, the local branch of the UK pressure group dedicated to achieving a balanced, coordinated public transport policy, in particular by supporting the railways and resisting the road lobby. But Finlayson was also a senior member of Mebyon Kernow, the Cornish nationalists, and was active in its Pendennis (Falmouth) branch. Not yet exactly a political party, MK was beginning to outgrow the pressure group role it had sketched for itself at its foundation in 1951, and was already fighting local elections in Cornwall. Taking its cue from Plaid Cymru (Welsh nationalist) and Scottish National Party by-election victories in 1966 and 1967, which saw Gwynfor Evans and Winnie Ewing returned to Westminster, MK began to evolve into a more overtly party-political organization, with self-government for Cornwall 'in domestic affairs' its principal aim. In 1968 it published its economic development policy document, *What Cornishmen Can Do*. Strategic objectives included a University of Cornwall (which would be achieved initially, it was argued, by co-locating the Falmouth School of Arts and Camborne School of Mines together 'somewhere in the Falmouth-Camborne-Truro area'), and a comprehensive transport policy for Cornwall. In the aftermath of Beeching's cuts, 'Bus services on narrow winding roads have proved no substitute (e.g., Bodmin-Padstow, Fowey-Lostwithiel)' for the lines that had closed. These closures would 'destroy social life' in remote areas, MK claimed, and had already served 'to encourage more (and older) cars on to roads ill-suited to heavy traffic'. The railways in Cornwall could be made to pay their way, insisted MK, and if British Rail was not up to it, then 'Cornwall itself should be given the opportunity to run its own services'.[66]

Betjeman's contacts with John Finlayson, however fleeting, illustrated their common ground on transport policy (not least their collective effort to save the Liskeard-Looe line). Moreover, as in Betjeman's later support for the anti-nuclear movement in Cornwall, such contacts suggested a degree of sympathy with the aims of Mebyon Kernow, at least in these areas. Indeed, the battle to save the railways in Cornwall had become increasingly 'political', and as Betjeman and MK worked to oppose the closure of the North Cornwall system, so the Conservative MP for Truro was actively supporting the abandonment of local lines on the (road lobby) grounds that it was better to spend government money on improving roads rather than subsidizing unremunerative branch lines.[67] He said so authoritatively to a stunned and demoralized audience at a public meeting at Wadebridge in September 1964, helping to seal the fate of the 'route of the *ACE*'.

'I know some people call me reactionary'

Such thinking appalled Betjeman. But did this mean that he supported Mebyon Kernow? A public figure whose radio broadcasts and television appearances had made him 'teddy bear to the nation',[68] as *The Times* was to put it, Betjeman knew that he appealed to a wide range of opinion and could not afford to display overt party-political allegiances. He was prepared to nail his colours to the mast in preservation or environmental matters, taking on the 'establishment' if necessary, but he always claimed no interest in party politics. If there were evidences, then they could be contradictory. In his undergraduate days at Oxford he had been a member of G.D.H. Cole's Labour circle, and his mix of Quakerism, Anglo-Catholicism and William Morris enthusiasms established a lifelong admiration for eccentric Christian socialists such as Conrad Noel, the 'Red' vicar of Thaxted, and Jack Bucknall at Delabole. He was a close friend of Mary Wilson, wife of Harold Wilson, Labour Prime Minister in the 1960s and 1970s, referring to her husband affectionately as 'the Leader'. He opposed the Beeching Axe and sought to expose the influence of the 'road lobby' in the Conservative government of the early 1960s, a clash exemplified in his (unsuccessful) tussle with Harold Macmillan to save the Euston Arch. (This became, as Alan Clarke put it, 'a particular *cause célèbre* amongst conservationists who wondered if the minister even understood the meaning of the term "Conservative"'[69]).

Yet Betjeman's defence of the rural railway system was part of a wider nostalgia that could sometimes appear sentimentally reactionary. Here, perhaps, was an old-fashioned Toryism, rooted in the countryside and opposed to 'progressive' ideas, and to change generally. As Betjeman admitted to the (Labour-supporting) *Daily Herald* newspaper in March 1961, 'I know some people call me reactionary because I don't believe in progress'. But that did not mean that he did not approve of changes for the better that had been achieved in people's lives since the war. 'Some things of course are much better', he readily conceded: 'People are better housed, on the whole. They're brighter in the head ... That appalling sense of insecurity has been almost eliminated. And the National Health Service is a really wonderful achievement'. And yet, he continued, 'if the Left is to be identified with dreaming of the future, or with the myth of human equality, then I am on the Right. Although we are all equal in the eyes of God, we are patently not equal to each other'.[70] Here was a confession that might gladden the heart of the Conservative Party, seeking perhaps to co-opt the public's favourite poet to its cause. But Toryism as it was to develop in the years ahead, especially in the 1970s under Margaret Thatcher's leadership in Opposition and then as Prime Minister (she was in office when Betjeman died in 1984), was to develop a hue that was in many respects anathema to Betjeman.

Thatcherism was supposed by its critics to appeal to the mythical 'Essex man' – self-motivated, hard-nosed, driven by 'targets', and sceptical of 'society' (as Thatcher herself was) and of any responsibility the individual might be expected to have towards it.[71] This was exactly the imagined type lampooned by Betjeman in his poem 'The City', which had appeared in his collection *Mount Zion* as early as 1932. Here he had scorned 'Business men with awkward hips / And dirty jokes upon their lips', and 'Young men who wear on office stools / The ties of minor public schools'. Likewise, in his infamous 'Slough', there were 'the bald young clerks who add / The profits of the stinking cad'. Much later, in 'Executive', he had satirized the 'young executive. / No cuffs than mine are cleaner', who owned 'a Slimline brief-case' and used 'the firm's Cortina'. This was 'a liaison man and partly P.R.O. / Essentially I integrate the current export drive / And basically I'm viable from ten o'clock till five'. Not above 'some mild developing', the young executive would, with 'luncheon and a drink or two', 'fix the Planning Officer, the Town Clerk and the Mayor'.[72] And so it went on, Betjeman comprehensively disparaging the very type with whom, in popular estimations of political allegiance in 1970s and 1980s, Thatcherism would so often be associated. Again, Betjeman was too ill to express any opinions on this, even if he had wanted to, but the 'Essex man' caricature of Thatcherite Toryism seems uncomfortably close to those stereotypes he had already deployed so effectively.

Party-political allegiance, then, perhaps genuinely did not sit well on Betjeman's complex, sometimes paradoxical, set of beliefs and prejudices. 'Politics don't interest me much', he repeated to the *Daily Herald*, 'except' (he added a little disingenuously) 'that I have discovered the one way to muck up a plot to ruin a building or a bit of countryside is to get a question asked in Parliament'.[73] Betjeman may have eschewed party politics, but, even by his own admission, he was certainly a shrewd political operator. He had demonstrated this ability repeatedly in campaigning, in Cornwall and beyond. Moreover, despite protestations that he took no notice whatsoever of 'the news', he was also a sharp observer of political events. In Ireland during the war this attribute had been a key to his success as Press Attaché to the UK Representative (see pp. 110–15), allowing him to develop a keen appreciation of the subtlety and nuances of Irish politics. Later, after the War, and when he had returned to Britain, he was likewise alerted to the rise of Scottish, Manx and Welsh nationalism. Hardly discernible at first to the average observer, especially in England, the emergence of Celtic nationalism was quick to attract Betjeman's interest, even sympathy.

'a Cornish Nationalist and Manx Republican'

It was not surprising, then, that Betjeman took notice of the foundation of Mebyon Kernow in 1951. Just as his interest in the post-war stirrings of Scottish and Manx nationalism had prompted his *alter egos*, 'Iain MacBetjeman' and 'Ewan Quetjeman', so now he also became 'Jan Trebetjeman The Celebrated Cornish Nationalist' or plain 'Jan Trebetjeman The Cornish Nationalist', or even 'Jan Trebejteman Stage Cornishman and Art Worker'.[74] Likewise, in the *Spectator* in June 1954, when he temporarily took over a regular column by 'Strix' (Peter Fleming), Betjeman explained to readers that: 'If the flavour of these paragraphs is a little different this week, that is because Strix has been laid low with an attack of malaria. His place has been taken by a Cornish Nationalist and Manx Republican who signs himself Jan Trestrix'.[75] All this was tongue-in-cheek, of course, and not to be taken too seriously. Or was it? As Rowse had observed, it was never quite clear with Betjeman whether he was being serious or not, and that behind the light-hearted jokings and absurdities were often subjects about which he cared passionately, that 'guying things that he really held seriously', a device (Rowse said) that so often 'took simpletons in'.[76]

Betjeman never joined MK, and probably had never considered doing so. His attitude was no doubt akin to that of Alderman K.G. Foster (another acquaintance on the Betjeman Christmas card list), the one-time chairman of Cornwall County Council who had robustly repulsed attempts by Plymouth City Council to annexe parts of south-east Cornwall. As Foster had explained: 'Although I am not a member of Mebyon Kernow, I am sure we are all attempting to achieve the same purpose ... Any effort or movement to keep our entity and maintain our viability would always have my support'.[77] It was a position that Betjeman understood, and with which he probably concurred. It was in marked contrast to that of Daphne du Maurier, one of Betjeman's contemporaries and another 'outsider' who had taken Cornwall to heart, also looking for mechanisms to 'belong'.

Going further than Betjeman, du Maurier had joined Mebyon Kernow as an associate member,[78] and in 1969 wrote an article for the movement's journal *Cornish Nation*, insisting that a form of self-government for Cornwall was achievable within the next decade.[79] Yet, despite this public affirmation of Cornish nationalism, in private her membership remained a bit of a giggle. As she wrote to her friend, Oriel Malet, in November 1967: 'Oh, I forgot to tell you, I have been made a Member of the Nationalist Party of Cornwall, called *Mebyon Kernow* (Sons of Cornwall) and given a badge to wear, and a thing to stick on my car, and I can hardly wait to blow up the [Tamar] bridge, like your Welsh Nationalists!'.[80] Later, in February 1969, she reported to Malet that 'I'm having fun with the Cornish Nationalists, *Mebyon Kernow*'. Referring to her piece in *Cornish Nation*, she added that 'I wrote the article for their paper, and am all in with the editor, and now it seems that MK are vaguely in league with the Welsh Nationalists, and the Breton ones too, and the Bretons have a black and white flag, like ours'. It was all a bit of fun, although one spoilsport – 'some anti-MK man' – had written to warn her off. 'Do you realize', he said, 'that you are playing with fire by joining MK?'.[81]

Perhaps she did. At any rate, du Maurier's fiction, at least until the appearance of her last work *Rule Britannia* in 1972, was entirely devoid of nationalist constructions of Cornwall, political or cultural, while comments in her non-fictional *Vanishing Cornwall*, published in 1967, seemed critical rather than supportive of Cornish nationalism. 'That stalwart band of Cornish nationalists, Mebyon Kernow', she wrote, 'would ... put the people into black kilts, speaking the old Cornish language, with a Parliament west of the Tamar. The vision is idyllic but hardly practical'.[82] Moreover, the Cornish nationalists themselves never quite accepted that she was really one of their number. In 1964 the journalist Geoffrey Moorhouse had noted that nationalists 'take a dim view of the romantic image of Cornwall put about by the likes of Daphne du Maurier',[83] and her associate membership of MK did not seem to make much difference to this opinion. Even A.L. Rowse, who in his later (Cornish nationalist) years courted friendship with du Maurier and affected an appreciation of her books, never really deviated from his view that her novels were 'Perfect shopgirls'' fiction, with *Vanishing Cornwall* the work of 'an inveterate romancer'.[84] There was in Rowse's disdain, however, a touch of misogyny (he was similarly dismissive of the Cornish writer, Anne Treneer). Indeed, until the comprehensive rehabilitation of du Maurier's work in recent years by a new generation of feminist scholars, the prevailing assessment was that her stories were merely 'Gothic romance'. As Sally Beauman put it, reflecting on the treatment accorded du Maurier's *Rebecca*, 'enduring popularity has not been matched by critical acclaim'.[85]

It is not clear whether Betjeman and du Maurier compared notes about her membership of Mebyon Kernow, or indeed about anything else much at all. Despite much apparently in common – she was to the south Cornish coast around Fowey what he was to North Cornwall; 'Daphne du Maurier Country' as opposed to 'Betjemanland' – there is little to suggest social or professional contact between the two. As Rowse had noted, Betjeman's many published book reviews were almost always favourable or supportive, as though he was perpetually afraid to upset friends and colleagues, or even aspiring authors whom he did not yet know. He did not want to make enemies unnecessarily.[86] But he had made an exception to the rule when du Maurier's novel *The Parasites* came out in 1949, writing a scathing review in the *Daily Herald*, the tone of which so incensed Victor Gollancz (du Maurier's publisher) that he penned (but never sent) an angry retort in which Betjeman was accused of '*bloody* rubbish'.[87] That *The Parasites* had a strong autobiographical strand may have contributed to du Maurier's hurt; perhaps inhibiting, even preventing, further contact between the two writers. After Betjeman's death, when such things no longer mattered, du Maurier was asked to contribute to *My Favourite Betjeman*, published in 1985 in aid of the Parkinson's Disease Society.[88] Encouraged to select her favourite Betjeman poem, she chose 'Cornish Cliffs' which, with its contrast between metropolitan England and their adopted Cornwall, stood at last for what they had in common: 'More than in gardened Surrey, nature spills / A wealth of heather, kidney-vetch and squills / Over these long-defended Cornish hills'.[89]

Ironically, Betjeman's work had also suffered at the hands of critics who saw it as lightweight and inconsequential. Even *Summoned by Bells* attracted mixed reviews, with lukewarm receptions from the likes of the poet John Wain and an anonymous reviewer in *The Times* (possibly Geoffrey Grigson). 'Fuck Wain and that prig in *The Times* who was probably Griggers', exclaimed Betjeman in anger and distress.[90] Yet Betjeman was a male, and his work was not so easily sneered at, sidelined or categorized as that of Daphne du Maurier. Likewise, in Cornwall Betjeman was not subject to the blanket suspicion that was sometimes cast on du Maurier. Although he had never sought to flirt openly with Mebyon Kernow, his sympathy with nationalist perspectives in local campaigns against the Beeching Axe and nuclear power were well known. He also shared MK's anti-metropolitan hostility to Whitehall and officialdom, and long before Cornish nationalists had coined the pejorative term 'Devonwall', Betjeman had warned of the bureaucratic tendency to eradicate individual identities and merge services, whereby Devon would become merely 'South-West Area One', and Cornwall 'South-West Area Two'.[91] Moreover, in contrast to du Maurier, Betjeman had unreservedly and consistently embraced the Cornish Celtic revival that underpinned modern Cornish nationalism, and had given it widespread literary expression. To that extent, Betjeman was a significant literary voice for nationalist imaginings of Cornwall, in a way that du Maurier never could be.

Additionally, as we have seen (pp. 21–3), Betjeman was quick to acknowledge his complicity in the forces that threatened to overwhelm Cornwall, and readily confessed to being 'part of the problem'. His poem 'Delectable Duchy', the one that had so thoroughly alarmed the National Trust, was also evidence of his willingness to speak out against the despoliation of Cornwall, of his courage to suggest that – unless something radical was done to achieve a more fundamentally sustainable economy – rampant, unrestrained tourism would ultimately destroy the Cornish environment. Significantly, at the same time that Betjeman was making this outspoken proposition, so MK too was calling for a more sustainable Cornwall. Part of this sustainability would be a limit on population growth – not only the vast annual summer influx that frightened Betjeman but also the growing in-migration that by the late 1960s was beginning to turn around Cornwall's century-long experience of population loss. In a process described by Ronald Perry and other observers of Cornish socio-economic change as 'counter-urbanization', thousands of people from 'up-country', especially from the Midlands and the south-east of England, relocated to Cornwall in the closing decades of the twentieth century.[92] Many came on individual initiative, not a few as a result of happy holiday experiences, but others in the mid and late 1960s were re-settled in Cornwall in towns like Bodmin as part of an 'Overspill' project managed by Greater London Council, a plan that provoked much hostility in Cornwall. MK spearheaded Cornwall-wide opposition to 'Overspill', leading to its rejection by Camborne-Redruth council and to the election in April 1967 at St Day and Lanner of Colin Murley as MK's first official County Councillor, standing on an anti-'Overspill' ticket.[93]

'Hengist and Horsa rape while Betjeman holds her down'

Together, 'counter-urbanization' and 'Overspill' galvanized Cornish nationalist opinion, and by December 1971 the MK magazine *Cornish Nation* was observing indignantly that in-migrants were taking the best jobs and the best houses, with the indigenous Cornish relegated to menial tasks (or unemployment) and poorer housing in in-land districts.[94] The coastal areas in particular, it was alleged, were being given over to second-homes or luxury houses that locals could not afford. Betjeman was sympathetic to such opinion, attempting as always to make amends for being part of the problem. But for one observer at least, the poet Victor Elphick, the crisis that was now upon Cornwall had its roots in those early Edwardian days, when families such as the Betjemanns had first identified Cornwall as a place suitable for holidaying and retreat, second-homes and boarding houses. It was they who had opened the Pandora's box of Cornish tourism.

In a television programme *Muses with Milligan*, Betjeman had complained once more that Cornwall was being ruined by tourism, and he had announced that he no longer visited in summer because he could not bear the tourist hordes.[95] Here Betjeman was speaking about himself but he was also, as he had done before, expressing his sympathy for the locals who had to endure the summer invasion too. Betjeman was glad that in the winter months the majority of visitors went home, leaving Cornwall in peace. Now the Cornish could regain what was properly theirs, while the more sensitive, better informed type of visitor might creep in unannounced and 'out of season' to see what Cornwall and the Cornish were really like: 'The Duchy becomes its native self in winter, and that is the time to see it'. Similarly, Betjeman was pleased that the majority of summer visitors was attracted to the coastline, leaving the interior relatively untouched. 'Inland, Cornwall is mercifully considered dull', he wrote, so that the tourist masses did not yet know that 'The wooded inland valleys like those of the Allen, Camel, Inny, Fowey and Lynher ... are remotest and loveliest Cornwall'.[96]

For Elphick, who had watched the programme, this was close to hypocrisy, and in his lingering annoyance he penned a parodied version of Betjeman's 'Trebetherick', which duly appeared in *Cornish Nation* in March 1973:

> How sad, John Betjeman says, that Cornwall's not the same.
> He'll go in winter, yes, but not in summer-time,
> Because it is no longer the place he loved when young.
> But is it any wonder that his Cornish dream has gone?
> Was it not smothered by his overwarm embrace,
> Her Celtic culture covered by his bosom on her face?
>
> Blesséd be St Enodoc, blessed be the wave,
> Blesséd be the springy turf, we pray, pray to thee.
> Ask for our children all the happy days you gave
> To Ralph, Vasey, Alastair, Biddy, John and Me.
>
> Betjeman's kin and class and other middle-rankers,
> Civil servants from Madras, pensioned urban bankers,
> Panama-hatted, perspired in tea-shopped Cornish town.
> Tramway engineers, retired, smug, well-off, nut-brown,

Their villas yucca lined, tamarisk and fuchsia hedge.
Betjeman and his kind were the Anglo-Saxon wedge.

Blesséd be St Enodoc ... etc

They it was who had laid the golf courses, invented
Surfing at Newquay, made gift-shops popular, rented
Cottages, cashed in on brass piskies and Joans-the-Wad
Made in darkest Birmingham. Then Saxon feet, rough-shod,
Trampled Kernow's landscape, where Piran's flag had flown.
Hengist and Horsa rape while Betjeman holds her down.

Sunset over Praa Sands and Pentewan's milky sea,
Glimps'd through caravans, but never more for me.
Soulless, the widen'd road cutting through Tresillian,
And car-park broad where Devons grazed in Goran.
Architect-planned boxes up ev'ry silent creek,
By God and St Enodoc! Overspill at Gweek?

Forgotten is St Enodoc, the wave is any wave,
Concrete covers springy turf. What did we pray to thee?
That our children should lose all the happy days you gave,
To Tom, Dick and Harry and London-by-the-sea?[97]

It seems unlikely that Betjeman ever read Elphick's poem. If he had done so, he would have been saddened by the attack but would have agreed, quite possibly, that Elphick had a point.

Elphick may indeed have had a point. But the bitter irony conveyed in his poem was itself ironic. Not only might Betjeman actually have agreed with him, but Elphick had made precisely the same observations (in almost identical language) about the crisis facing Cornwall as Betjeman had done in his own work. Betjeman and Elphick were, to that extent, on the same side, as perhaps Elphick realized. But, for all his admissions of guilt, Betjeman had not been forgiven by Elphick. Moreover, despite all his efforts to claim common cause with Cornwall and the Cornish, and to acquire that patina of Cornishness and those multiple Celtic allegiances, Betjeman had failed to convince Elphick of his credentials. 'Betjeman and his kind were the Anglo-Saxon wedge', said Elphick uncompromisingly, 'Hengist and Horsa rape while Betjeman holds her down'.

'the writer of the Guide is not a Cornishman'

Here, then, were signs that, despite everything, John Betjeman could be as unpopular with Cornish nationalists as Daphne du Maurier – despite even his campaigning on Cornish issues and his advocacy of Cornish Celtic revivalism. As early as July 1934, one irritated reader had written to the Architectural Press to complain about Betjeman's Shell Guide to Cornwall. 'As I am a Cornishman', wrote the critic, 'and was born there 59 years ago and I am down there once or twice a year and have visited practically every town and village in Cornwall I think I can claim to have a little knowledge of it'. Armed with this superior understanding, he went on to complain that it is 'quite evident the writer of the Guide [Betjeman] is not a Cornishman and really knows little about it'. For example, he said, Betjeman had failed to find anything of architectural interest in Lostwithiel, while anyone with even a nodding acquaintance with the town would know its church, 'with the finest spire in Cornwall', and the 'very ancient building called Stannary Hall, where all the tin in Cornwall used to be brought to be weighed and taxed in the middle ages'. Even the Cornish recipes provided by Mesdames Mably and Tremaine failed to impress: Betjeman had forgotten to mention 'gurtymeat', a favourite dish that 'every Cornish woman knows all about'.[98]

Here Betjeman was castigated for both his presumed non-Cornishness and the alleged sketchiness of his knowledge of Cornwall. These were twin criticisms that were aimed at him periodically over the years. In March 1974, for example, the Revd William G. West wrote to Betjeman, asking whether 'you know anything about the Hocking family', the Cornish novelists. He thought Betjeman a Cornish expert, he said, hence the inquiry, but nonetheless 'was a little surprised' to find Batsford (the publishers) describing him in their current catalogue 'as one of "the most eminent living Cornishman"'.[99] This was, in West's opinion (shades of A.L. Rowse), taking literary licence a little too far. Sometimes, too, Betjeman could be a little cavalier with the facts, more interested in telling a good story well rather than getting bogged down in tedious detail. In August 1965, for example, he had described the parish church at Shaldon in Devon in a BBC television programme. He singled out for particular praise the beautiful interior screen, made, he said, of slate. Alas, he was mistaken, as one viewer told him in no uncertain terms. The material was not slate but Polyphant stone, from the famed Polyphant quarry at Lewannick, near Launceston in Cornwall. This was a serious error, and the onus was on Betjeman to put the record straight: 'I would be most grateful to have the false impression re-stone corrected, which I repeat is definitely *not slate* but true Cornish Polyphant stone'.[100]

However, this periodic scolding did not amount to sustained criticism of Betjeman's Cornish credentials. Pedantic correction by readers, listeners and viewers was one of the occupational hazards faced by all writers and broadcasters, and Betjeman's share of such criticism was probably no worse than that aimed at other prominent public figures. Indeed, hostile correspondence was more than matched by a stream of appreciative letters, many originating from Cornish addresses. Betjeman's television series, *Time With Betjeman*, made and broadcast in the late evening of his life, provoked an outpouring of affectionate messages. 'I never fail to consult your *Cornwall* whenever a sound opinion is needed on any place', wrote Paul Richards of St Austell in March 1983, adding that 'I hope the planners and council officials have been watching the films – as a lover of Cornwall you too know how much has been lost in recent years in the name of progress. My own town of St Austell is a superb example'.[101] W.C. Worden also wrote from St Austell, remembering former days when he had worked at Lower Trebetherick farm, and had gone out ferreting for rabbits with Betjeman's father, Ernie: ('Unfortunately, his hearing was a great handicap'). Now, alas, Worden added, echoing Betjeman's fears, 'most of the meadows with their tamarisk hedges as far away as Greenaway have ... become building sites for mostly holiday homes'.[102] Another correspondent, this time from Boscastle, wrote to say that he had 'especially liked the parts filmed at Trebetherick as, being Cornish, we knew it well',[103] and from Luckett, near Callington, 'a small red-head and her family of fans' expressed their appreciation: '*Thank you* and thank you', they wrote.[104] Muriel Williams, from Penryn, felt likewise: 'There is something about this county that brings out the best in people'.[105]

In such snapshots was glimpsed the genuine regard with which Betjeman was held in Cornwall. 'Well, Good Poet, know of my esteem', wrote Frank Sutton from St Austell: 'Accept my whey as plaudit for your cream'.[106] Even in nationalist circles, the vehemence of Elphick's condemnation was rarely repeated. There were those, such as Chris Nancollas, writing in the nationalist magazine *An Baner Kernewek/The Cornish Banner*, who by the early twenty-first century could complain that the transformation of Padstow into 'Padstein' – the up-market world of Rick Stein restaurants – was merely the latest manifestation of a trend started by Betjeman and his ilk. 'I blame John Betjeman myself', said Nancollas.[107] But the magazine's editor, James Whetter, struck a different note in the November 2006 edition of *An*

The Lord Lieutenant, President
and
Council of the Cornwall Historic Churches Trust

request the pleasure of your company

at

PORT ELIOT, ST. GERMANS
(by kind invitation of Lord Eliot)

FRIDAY, 22nd OCTOBER
at 7 p.m.

———————

Poetry to be read by

SIR JOHN BETJEMAN
Poet Laureate

who will be introduced by
Dr. A. L. ROWSE

Pasty supper, wine, beer   Black tie

19. Sir John Betjeman, part of the Cornish scene – a poetry reading by the Poet Laureate at Port Eliot, hosted by Lord Eliot and the Lord Lieutenant of Cornwall, and introduced by Dr A.L. Rowse.

Baner Kernewek. Celebrating the hundredth anniversary of Betjeman's birth, Whetter penned an affectionate article that ranged across Betjeman's life and work, carefully pointing out the myriad Cornish connections, concluding that 'his life can be seen as a triumph' and noting with satisfaction that 'it was in the land that he loved that he died and was buried'.[108]

Earlier, in the summer of 1988, when the passing of John Betjeman in May 1984 was still fresh in memory, Donald R. Rawe – author, poet, playwright, publisher, Cornish bard and Mebyon Kernow activist – was moved to contribute a lengthy poem to the magazine *Cornish Scene*, couched in Betjemanesque language and implicitly affirming Betjeman's vision of Cornwall. In this context, imitation was emphatically the sincerest form of flattery: doubly so, since Rawe himself was a native of Padstow and had written the definitive history of the 'Obby 'Oss.[109] As *Cornish Scene* explained, the poem was 'somewhat reminiscent of *Summoned by Bells*', and likewise celebrated the North Cornwall of Betjeman's (and Rawe's) childhood and youth: 'Down swerving high-hedged lanes we reach St Kew / Where beeches lord barely over a mildewed manor house / And a cheerful pub keeps the old church company'.[110]

'Mercifully Preserved!'

Nearly twenty years later, Bert Biscoe, another Cornish activist (Independent member of Cornwall Council, chair of the Cornish Constitutional Convention, and much else) was also moved to put pen to paper. He had alighted upon the telling phrase 'mercifully preserved',[111] employed by Betjeman in his 1964 Shell Guide to Cornwall to describe his relief that the delightful late Georgian crescent, Walsingham Terrace, in the centre of Truro, had been spared redevelopment. An accomplished poet, Biscoe redeployed the phrase as title for a poem he had written, soon to be performed at Carruan farm, near Polzeath in North Cornwall, at an event held to commemorate the hundredth year since Betjeman's birth. Conceived by Betjeman's daughter, Candida Lycett Green, the 'birthday party' at Carruan attracted a wide range of Cornish performers – Cornish dancing, wrestling, brass bands – as well as a large audience from near and far. Biscoe shared the stage with 'Bishop Bill' Ind, the popular Bishop of Truro, reading his poem to the scores of assembled Betjeman enthusiasts. He had also read the poem on BBC Radio 3, who had commissioned it as part of the BBC's commemorative Betjeman season, achieving UK-wide exposure for his particular evocation of John Betjeman in Cornwall.

Significantly, Biscoe's 'Mercifully Preserved!' was not an uncritical portrayal of John Betjeman. Indeed, like Betjeman himself, the poem conveyed a certain ambiguity, an enigmatic quality that was at once both critical and affectionately supportive. Here was no laudatory celebration, but neither was the poem hostile or accusing. Imagined as a 'fictional account of the visit to Truro by Sir John Betjeman during which he saved Walsingham Place from demolition', Biscoe's poem exposed the paradoxes inherent in Betjeman's conservation work in Cornwall. On the one hand, Betjeman's intervention – in Walsingham Place, as in countless other campaigns – won the gratitude of those with fewer strings to pull, those whose voices counted for less in the corridors of power, and who otherwise might not have prevailed against officialdom. And yet, on the other hand, as Biscoe understood, such conservation could also fly in the face of the aspirations of ordinary people, who saw in 'redevelopment' not a threat to historic architecture but instead an opportunity to acquire modern amenities – running water, flush lavatories, and so on. As Biscoe explained in his poem, after the Second World War people in Truro, as elsewhere in Cornwall and Britain, demanded an improved quality of life, including those basic modern amenities that – in Cornwall especially – were often sadly lacking. In Truro, said Biscoe, the cry was 'Comprehensive redevelopment', and the city council – receiving the message loud and clear from the local electorate – set about planning far-reaching demolition and renewal. But the scale of the proposals caused alarm, even among advocates of new amenities: 'And we started to think we might've made a mistake./ They was talkin' 'bout scattin' the whole bleddy town t'bits! / Thay 'ad pictures of how things could look – / More like Thunderbirds than Trurra! There was "hell up"!'.

Then, at the eleventh hour, John Betjeman appeared:

> I remember some old bloke off the telly –
> Big black hat – maybee 'ee wore a cape like Dracula –
> I can't recall – stood up in Walsingham Place
> Mrs Wass'name – she heard all the commotion
> And was too embarrassed to come out of her privy –
> she moved up Trelander – Council gave 'er a house –
> Died of walkin' up that hill day after day – wore 'er out!
>
> Old Boy! He had a walking stick. Marched around town
> Like he owned the place – 'Comprehensive Development' –
> He said it like 'ee was swearing, you! He stood up
> By Mallett's store, poking his finger in the Mayor's chest –
> 'You simply cannot knock down this Crescent –
> its too beautiful – you people think that progress
> means cancelling the past and making multi-story car parks!'

His point well made, Betjeman was soon off to the station to catch his train. But 'Missus Wass'name' emerged from her privy to demand her council house. 'I want runnin' water', she exclaimed, 'I want a toilet, not a privy! And a television! / This place d'drive me round the bend – bleddy furriners /Comin' down 'ere, chuckin' themselves about'. In the end, of course, a compromise was struck. Walsingham Crescent was 'mercifully

20.   John Betjeman and Jonathan Stedall during the making of the television series *Time With Betjeman* in 1983. Despite his increasing disabilities, Betjeman is relaxed and contented in his adopted Cornwall.

preserved', and plans to rip the heart out of Truro were moderated. 'Missus Wass'name' got her new council house up the hill, out of town, with its running water and television. But, alas, it killed her.[112]

More than Victor Elphick, Bert Biscoe had caught the complexity of John Betjeman and Cornwall, and indeed of modern Cornwall itself. The conflict between development and conservation, in its many guises, had been at the heart of debate in post-war Cornwall. That Betjeman was sometimes embroiled at the centre of the controversy was a measure of his engagement with Cornwall and Cornish issues. Disingenuously, he had posed as 'Jan Trebetjeman, the Cornish Clot',[113] suggesting an air of simple rustic passivity. But, as ever, this was a guy, for the reality was that he cared passionately for Cornwall and was prepared to make a stand for his adopted land. Even A.L. Rowse, his temperamental friend, recognized this. Despite his insistence that Betjeman could never be really Cornish, Rowse admitted that he was 'utterly devoted to Cornwall'.[114] Others acknowledged that this was so, and there were those, perhaps more generous than Rowse, who insisted now that '"foreigner" the poet [Betjeman] never was'.[115] His daughter, Candida Lycett Green, sensed this too. In selecting Carruan, perched high above Polzeath with views across to Pentire, as the venue for the Betjeman commemorations in 2006, she explained that 'I could think of no better place to celebrate what would have been his 100th birthday'. Her father had had 'an enduring love of Cornwall', she said, and 'I wanted the whole event to be incredibly Cornish ... about Cornwall, young people and poetry'. And, she added, happily: 'I think the Cornish are proud of my father. They claim him as one of their own'.[116]

'When People talk to me about "The British" ... I Give Up'

In June 1984, shortly after John Betjeman's death, Stanley Eveling – the Edinburgh playwright, critic and academic – wrote an appreciation of the late Poet Laureate in the *Scotsman* newspaper. Reviewing Betjeman's life and work, Eveling sought to capture the essence of the man, to tease out what he was really like. He thought he had him pretty well summed up. 'John Betjeman had no interest in either politics or the news', concluded Eveling confidently. 'Nor was he a man of deep religious conviction', he added, 'though he had a lightly whimsical hope that it wasn't all nonsense'.[1] Betjeman, it seems, had protested too much, and Eveling had been taken-in, just as A.L. Rowse knew people would be, by Betjeman's deliberate ambiguity, his making light of things he held seriously. As Rowse had insisted: 'The point is our Poet Laureate is not as simple as some people think'.[2] As we have seen, Betjeman was in many ways deeply 'political', from navigating his way skilfully through the complexities of Irish affairs during the Second World War to campaigning passionately on environmental issues in Cornwall. He understood the origins and nature of Celtic nationalism – in Wales, Scotland, the Isle of Man and, of course, Cornwall – as well as in Ireland, and was sympathetic to these several causes, having cultivated his own Celtic identities, partly in compensation for the shaky foundations of his own Englishness, as he saw it. He was also, as we have again seen, in many ways deeply 'religious', espousing a 'Celtic Christianity' and Anglo-Catholicism that, he imagined, rooted him in Cornwall and offered the prospect of redemption from the many sins he felt so acutely.

Occasionally, Betjeman let his guard down, a moment of plain speaking providing sharp insight into his inner thoughts. In February 1943, for example, during a BBC Home Service broadcast, he had told his listeners that: 'When people talk to me about "the British", as though they were all the same, I give up'.[3] His wartime experiences in Eire had reminded him of the marked, sometimes stark, differences between Ireland and England. But more than that, he recognized that there were significant differences between England on the one hand, and Wales, Scotland, the Isle of Man, and Cornwall on the other. Stripped of its Imperial context, 'British' had little meaning, thought Betjeman, and if the constituent parts of these islands were to be celebrated, then they would have to be treated as separate entities, and not as some generalized whole. 'Betjeman's Britain', with its snappy alliteration, was a title that would have appealed to publishers. But Betjeman studiously avoided it, and it was not until after his death that a collection of his writings (and later a video) with that so obvious label at last appeared.[4]

Today, in the era of devolution, with a Parliament in Scotland, Assemblies in Wales and Northern Ireland, and even a newly-won unitary Cornwall Council (in which Mebyon Kernow, the Cornish nationalists, are represented), the deconstruction of 'Britishness' is commonplace, even *de rigueur*. But in 1943, at the height of the war and when the conflict had not yet turned decisively in the Allies' favour, Betjeman's suggestion that 'the British' did not exist as a homogeneous people was deeply subversive. Even J.B. Priestley, as passionate an advocate of 'Englishness' as any other, was persuaded to promote 'Britishness' instead as his patriotic duty, as part of the war effort. As his biographer, John Baxendale, has observed, by 'England' Priestley 'really did mean England, showing little interest in Scotland and Wales, although for the duration of the war he temporarily adjusted his focus to "Britain"'.[5] Betjeman, however, despite his appreciation of the importance of wartime propaganda (or perhaps because of it), was not to be moved.

'Séan O'Betjemán', 'Iain MacBetjeman', 'Ewen Quetjeman', 'Jan Killigrew Trebetjeman', and even (on one occasion) 'Deirdre O'Betjeman', were faintly silly *alter egos*, self-styled nomenclatures that smacked of dilettantism and the theatre of the absurd. But here, again, Betjeman was making light of serious commitments. These comic nicknames disguised the personal significance of his Celtic allegiances, making fun of himself and concealing the depth of his support for Celtic causes. But once more, there were flashes of occasional plain speaking. In 1946, for example, just after the war and with his Irish sojourn still fresh in memory, Betjeman could write with an angry passion that could not fail to impress: 'When the Act of Union was passed in 1800, when Ireland ceased to have her own Parliament in Dublin, when Grattan's hopes were frustrated and the dupes and lackeys of Castlereagh sold Ireland to England, a civilisation passed'. Then, he said, 'Dublin ceased to be a capital and became a provincial city', and not 'until the Easter Rising of 1916 was she a capital again'.[6] Betjeman had regretted the Act of Union; more controversially, he welcomed the Easter Rising, with the violent rupture of the United Kingdom that it precipitated.

In viewing the United Kingdom in this way, of eschewing any idea of 'the British people', Betjeman was ahead of his time. In April 1968, one H.W.J. Edwards wrote to the *Tablet*, explaining that now, thankfully, the recent by-election victories of the Welsh and Scottish nationalists might allow England to be itself at last, that the 'habit of flying the English flag rather than the Union Jack might catch on', and that 'the English have the chance of seeing just where their bounds shall be set: the Marches, the Cheviots and the Tamar'.[7] It was a view that Betjeman might have shared; indeed, he had already played his part in anticipating the identity politics of 'post-Britishness'. To that extent, Betjeman was an early advocate of the way these islands are so often viewed today, as 'a multi-national state'[8] (as Richard Rose once dubbed it) comprising some half-a dozen or so 'nations' – depending how these were defined, and who was doing the defining – a perspective elaborated at length in Norman Davies' monumental volume *The Isles*, published in 1999.[9]

For Betjeman, as we have seen, Cornwall was an integral part of this territorial complexity. Indeed, Cornwall epitomized this complexity, its 'in England' but not 'of England' status a paradoxical hybridity that appealed to Betjeman, reflecting the uncertainties and ambiguities of his own personal identity. Moreover, just as Betjeman was prepared to speak plainly on the subject of Irish independence, so he would insist over and over again that Cornwall was not England, that Cornwall was a Duchy, that Cornwall was a Celtic kingdom, and so on. In so doing, he espoused a vision that mirrored that of Cornish nationalism, a perspective that could not fail to impact on the way the 'multi-national state' was viewed over time. As Arthur Aughey has observed in his *The Politics of Englishness*: 'Of course, Cornish nationalism remained a minority taste ... but, if one took the argument according to regional identity seriously, the case it made was critical'.[10] Or, as Tom Nairn has put it: 'Beyond the familiar Scotland-Ireland-Wales triad there now lies the question of Cornwall'.[11]

Betjeman had played his part in placing Cornwall alongside this 'triad'; in his writings, his broadcasts, and in his campaigning over many years. For some, like Michael Williams, the Cornish author, Betjeman had thus earned the right to be considered: 'Cornish to the bone – in heart and spirit anyway'.[12] June Lander, another Cornish writer, thought so too. In her account in the *Western Morning News* of Betjeman's funeral, she wrote approvingly that the late Laureate had always insisted that Cornwall was 'not part of England, but a separate country'.[13] It was an opinion that had earned John Betjeman his Cornish credentials. But uncertainties and ambivalence remained, not least for Betjeman himself, who, so desperate to 'belong', to be 'John Trebetjeman, The Celebrated Cornish Nationalist', confessed still to being merely a 'foreigner', an 'emmet'.

A.L. Rowse had not attended Betjeman's funeral; deterred, he explained, by the 'raging Atlantic rain and wind'. But, one 'Sunday afternoon not long after I went to visit his grave', he said, 'a day that somehow seemed more in keeping', with people picnicking in the glorious sunshine or strolling across the sands at Daymer Bay, boats bobbing out on the blue sea. He found Betjeman's grave just inside the lych-gate, 'surrounded by tamarisks ... flowers wilting in the hot sun, a plain wooden cross: JOHN BETJEMAN'. Close by was his mother's headstone, and inside the little church itself, 'there on the right is the Cornish slate tablet to his father, beneath which John sat or knelt'. Rowse pondered the tablet for a moment: 'Ernest Edward Betjemann of Undertown in this parish'. As he moved away, he mused on its significance. 'There is the ambivalence', said Rowse, going to its core, 'the two German nns'.[14]

Notes

Preamble: 'The Sky Widens to a Sense of Cornwall'

1. A.N. Wilson, *Betjeman* (London, 2006); Bevis Hillier, *John Betjeman – The Biography* (London, 2006).
2. *The Times*, 25 August 2006.
3. John Betjeman, *Collected Poems* (London, 1984), pp. 303–4 ('Old Friends').
4. Frank Delaney, *Betjeman Country* (London, 1985), pp. 35–8.

Chapter One: John Betjeman as 'foreigner'

1. John Betjeman, *Summoned by Bells* (London, 1962), p. 87.
2. Betjeman (1962), p. 87.
3. John Betjeman, *Collected Poems: Enlarged Edition* (London, 1984a), p. 67 (from 'Trebetherick').
4. Betjeman (1984a), p. 99 (from 'Saint Cadoc').
5. Simon Jenkins, *England's Thousand Best Churches* (London, 1999), p. 82.
6. John Betjeman, *Cornwall: A Shell Guide* (London, 1964), p. 86.
7. Betjeman (1984a), p. 232 (from 'Greenaway').
8. Betjeman (1984a), p. 334 (from 'The Hon. Sec.).
9. *Western Morning News*, 23 May 1984.
10. *Daily Express*, 23 May 1984.
11. Jonathan Stedall, *Where On Earth is Heaven?* (n.p., 2009), p. 372.
12. Michael Williams, *People and Places in Cornwall* (Bodmin, 1985), p. 10.
13. Stedall (2009), p. 372.
14. *Guardian*, 23 May 1984.
15. Bevis Hillier, *Betjeman: The Bonus of Laughter* (London, 2004), pp. 580–2.
16. *Sunday Telegraph*, 3 June 1984.
17. A.L. Rowse, *Memories and Glimpses* (London, 1986), p. 476.
18. Rowse (1986), p. 476.
19. Rowse (1986), p. 476.

20. Rowse (1986), p. 476.

21. Rowse (1986), p. 510.

22. Rowse (1986), p. 476.

23. Betjeman (1962), p. 88.

24. Williams (1986), pp. 10–12.

25. Williams (1986), p. 9.

26. Williams (1986), p. 17.

27. Anon, *William Morris: An Illustrated Life* (Andover, n.d.), p1.

28. see Roy Hattersley, *The Edwardians* (London, 2004).

29. cited in Brenda Maddox, *The Married Man: A Life of D.H. Lawrence* (London, 1994), p. 189.

30. see Philip Payton, *D.H. Lawrence and Cornwall* (St Agnes, 2009).

31. Alan M. Kent, *The Literature of Cornwall: Continuity, Identity, Difference 1000–2000* (Bristol, 2000), pp. 174–6.

32. See Michael Bartholomew, *In Search of H.V. Morton* (London, 2004).

33. J.B. Priestley, *English Journey* (London, 1934).

34. John Baxendale, *Priestley's England: J.B. Priestley and English Culture* (Manchester, 2007), p. 80.

35. *Saturday Review*, 27 March 1926.

36. *Saturday Review*, 27 March 1926.

37. Simon Jenkins, 'Introduction', in H.V. Morton, *In Search of England* (London, 1927; repub. 2002), p. viii.

38. Morton (1927; 2002), p. xx.

39. Morton (1927; 2002), p. xix.

40. Morton (1927; 2002), p. xvii.

41. Morton (1927; 2002), p. xviii.

42. Morton (1927; 2002), p. xvii.

43. Morton (1927; 2002), p. xvii.

44. Morton (1927; 2007), p. xx.

45. Morton (1927; 2007), p. 13.

46. Morton (1927; 2007), p. xx.

47. Morton (1927; 2007), pp. 20–1.

48. Morton (1927; 2007), p. 21.

49. Morton (1927; 2007), p. 135.

50. Morton (1927; 2007), pp. 26–30.

51. Rowse (1986), p. 476.

52. Betjeman (1962), p. 28.

53. John Betjeman, 'Coming Home, or England Revisited', BBC Home Service, 25 February 1943; see also Stephen Games (ed), *Trains and Buttered Toast* (London, 2006), pp. 138–9.

54. Games (ed.) (2006), p. 14.

55. Games (ed.) (2006), p. 14.

56. David Milsted (ed.), *Brewer's Anthology of England and the English* (London, 2001), p. 26.

57. Milsted (ed.) (2001), p. 27.

58. Patrick Taylor-Martin, *John Betjeman: His Life and Work* (London, 1983), p. 9.

59. Taylor-Martin (1983), p. 10.

60. Norman Vance, 'Foreword' in Greg Morse, *John Betjeman: Reading the Victorians* (Brighton, 2008), p. vii.

61. 'Kelsmscott', BBC Home Service, 4 May 1952; see also Candida Lycett Green (ed.), *Coming Home: An Anthology of Prose* (London, 1997), pp. 302–6.

62. *Daily Telegraph*, 22 August 1960.

63. *Daily Telegraph*, 22 August 1960.

64. *Daily Telegraph*, 22 August 1960.

65. Betjeman (1962), p. 96.

66. 'St Protus and St Hyacinth, Blisland, Cornwall', BBC West of England Home Service, 21 July 1948; see also Games (ed.) (2006), p. 238.

67. Jenkins (1999), p. 25.

68. cited in Timothy Mowle, *Stylistic Cold Wars: Betjeman versus Pevsner* (London, 2000), p. 127.

69. Mowle (2000), p. 126.

70. Mowle (2000), pp. 76–92.

71. Mowle (2000), p. 92.

72. Mowle (2000), pp. 35–54.

73. Mowle (2000), p. 21.

74. Taylor-Martin (1983), p. 50.

75. Dennis Brown, *John Betjeman* (Plymouth, 1999), p. 36.

76. Morse (2008), p. 158.

77. A.N. Wilson, *Betjeman* (London, 2006), p. 11.

78. Wilson (2006), p. 7.

79. Wilson (2006), p. 11.

80. Betjeman (1962), p. 4.

81. Candida Lycett Green, *John Betjeman: Letters, Volume One: 1926–1951* (London, 1994), p. 95.

82. Bevis Hillier, *Young Betjeman* (London, 1988), p. 122.

83. Taylor Martin (1983), p. 25.

84. *The Times*, 24 August 2006.

85. James Vernon, 'Border Crossings: Cornwall and the English (Imagi)nation', in Geoffrey Cubitt (ed.), *Imagining Nations* (Manchester, 1998), p. 153.

86. Bernard Deacon, *A Concise History of Cornwall* (Cardiff, 2007), p. 2 and backcover notes.

87. Morton (1927; 2007), p. 83.

88. Morton (1927; 2007), p. 83.

89. Morton (1927; 2007), p. 83.

90. Morton (1927; 2007), p. 113.

91. Morton (1927; 2007), p. 113.

92. Wilkie Collins, *Rambles Beyond Railways, or Notes in Cornwall taken a-foot* (London, 1851), p. 124.

93. W.H. Hudson, *The Land's End: A Naturalist's Impressions of West Cornwall* (London, 1908; repub. 1981), p. 34 and p. 142.

94. Rowse (1986), p. 477.

95. Rowse (1986), p. 477.

96. Rowse (1986), p. 477.

97. Rowse (1986), p. 477.

98. Betjeman (1962), p. 79.

99. Marion Bowman, 'Cardiac Celts: Images of the Celts in Contemporary British Paganism', in G. Harvey and C. Hardman (eds.), *Paganism Today* (London, 1996).

100. Hillier (1988), p. 7.

101. see Patrick Hutton, *I Would Not Be Forgotten: The Life and Work of Robert Stephen Hawker 1803–1875* (Padstow, 2004), pp. 11–13.

102. 'Hawker of Morwenstowe', BBC Home Service, 7 October 1945; see also the *Listener*, 18 October 1945, and Lycett Green (ed.) (1999), p. 186.

103. Stedall (2009), p. 392.

104. John Hurst, 'Literature in Cornwall', in Philip Payton (ed.), *Cornwall Since the War: The Contemporary History of a European Region* (Redruth, 1993), p. 297.

105. Hurst (1993), p. 297.

106. Kent (2000), p. 219.

107. Kent (2000), p. 220, p. 221.

108. 'One Man's County: John Betjeman Looks at Cornwall', ITV, 22 January 1964; see also John Betjeman, *Betjeman's Cornwall* (London, 1984b), p. 20; and Candida Lycett Green (ed.), *Betjeman's Britain* (London, 1999), p. 37.

109. 'Padstow', BBC Third Programme, 6 February 1949; see also John Betjeman, *First and Last Loves* (London, 1952), pp. 217–225; Betjeman (1984b), pp. 68–78; and Games (ed.) (2006), p. 301.

110. 'Seaview', BBC West of England Programme, 11 May 1938; see also Games (ed.) (2006), p. 107.

111. 'Residents', BBC West of England Programme, 27 April 1938; see also Games (ed.) (2006), p. 105.

112. Lycett Green (ed.) (1999), p. 11.

113. *Architectural Review*, 73, April 1933, pp. 153–8; see also Lycett Green (ed.) (1999), p. 43.

114. 'Visitors', BBC West of England Programme, 22 April 1938; see also Games (ed.) (2006), p. 95.

115. 'One Man's County', ITV, 22 January 1964; see also Betjeman (1984b), p. 26; and Lycett Green (ed.) (1999), p. 42.

116. 'One Man's County'; Betjeman (1984b), p. 26; Lycett Green (ed.) (1999), p. 42.

117. *Cornish Review*, 1 January 1967; John Betjeman, *A Nip in the Air* (London, 1974), pp. 21–2.

118. Betjeman (1984a), pp. 379–8.

119. 'Victorian Provincial Life', BBC Home Service, 24 May 1949; see also Games (ed.) (2000), p. 38.

120. 'Victorian Provincial Life'; Games (ed.) (2000), p. 38.

121. Uffington Museum Betjeman Collection[UMBC]/Correspondence/Betjeman to William Collins, 11 April 1953; see also Candida Lycett Green (ed.), *John Betjeman: Letters, Volume One: 1926 to 1951* (London, 1994), p. 37.

Chapter Two: Imagining North Cornwall

1. Uffington Museum Betjeman Collection [UMBC]/Correspondence/Betjeman to John Foster White, 7 August 1957; see also Candida Lycett Green (ed.), *John Betjeman: Letters, Volume One: 1926 to 1951* (London, 1994), p. 128.

2. UMBC/Correspondence/Betjeman to John Foster White, 7 August 1957; Lycett Green (ed.) (1994), p. 128.

3. As in the early 1960's ITV programme 'Swindon and North Lew', one of the 'lost' Betjeman films subsequently shown on Channel 4 in 1994 and in 1995 distributed as a video *Betjeman Revisited*.

4. 'Padstow', BBC Third Programme, 6 February 1949; see also John Betjeman, *Betjeman's Cornwall* (London, 1984a), p. 68; and Stephen Games (ed.), *Trains and Buttered Toast* (London, 2006), p. 294.

5. 'Padstow', 6 February 1949; Betjeman (1984a), p. 68; Games (ed.) (2006), p. 293.

6. 'Padstow', 6 February 1949; Betjeman (1984a), p. 68; Games (ed.) (2006), pp. 293–4.

7. 'Padstow', 6 February 1949; Betjeman (1984a), p. 68; Games (ed.) (2006), p. 294.

8. T.W.E. Roche, *The Withered Arm: Reminiscences of the Southern Lines West of Exeter* (Bracknell, 1967), p. 5.

9. Roche (1967), p. 48.

10. John Betjeman, *Cornwall: A Shell Guide* (London, 1964), p. 65.

11. Roche (1967), p. 48.

12. Roche (1967), p. 5.

13. John Betjeman, *First and Last Loves* (London, 1952), p. 75.

14. For example, see John Betjeman, 'The Railheads of London', in Bryan Morgan (ed.), *The Railway Lover's Companion* (London, 1963), pp. 242–54; 'By Steam Train to Kensington, *Punch*, 25 August 1954; 'Royal Railway Carriages', *Listener*, 9 March 1961; 'Great Central Railway, Sheffield Victoria to Banbury', *New Yorker*, 31 March 1962; 'End of the Line' (a review of H.A. Vallance, *British Branch Lines* and Roger Calvert, *The Future of Britain's Railways*), *Spectator*, 9 July 1965.

15. UMBC/Correspondence/L.TC. Rolt to Betjeman, 15 July 1950; UMBC/ Misc/Talyllyn Railway Preservation Society Membership Card, 1965; see also John Betjeman 'Foreword' in L.T.C. Rolt, *Railway Adventure* (London, 1953; 2nd edn 1961), pp. xix–xx.

16. Exeter University Library Special Collections [EUL] Betjeman Library/C. Hamilton Ellis, *The Midland Railway* (London, 1953); see also Hamish Riley-Smith (ed.), *The Betjeman Library: A Catalogue of the Library of Sir John Betjeman* (Swanton Abbot, 1996), item 3904.

17. EUL Betjeman Library/T.W.E. Roche, *The Withered Arm* (Bracknell, 1967); Riley-Smith (1996), item 3932.

18. 'Padstow', 6 February 1949; Games (ed.) (2006), p. 293.

19. John Betjeman, *Summoned by Bells* (London, 1960), p. 33.

20. John Betjeman, *London's Historic Railway Stations* (London, 1972), pp. 74–85.

21. Betjeman (1960), p. 33.

22. Betjeman (1960), p. 33.

23. Stephen Austin, *Atlantic Coast Express* (London, 1989), p. 8.

24. *Listener*, 28 March 1940.

25. John Betjeman, 'Introduction', in George C. Perry (ed.), assisted by Graham Norton and Christopher Bushnell, *The Book of the Great Western* (London, 1970); see also Stephen Games (ed.), *Tennis Whites and Teacakes* (London, 2007), p. 217 & p. 220.

26. Games (ed.) (2007), p. 217.

27. UMBC/Correspondence/Betjeman to Peggy Thomas, 26 September 1958; see also Lycett Green (ed.) (1994), pp. 146–7.

28. London and South Western Railway, *By the Cornish Seas and Moors: Holidays in King Arthur's Land* (London, 1915).

29. Gilbert Thomas and David St John Thomas, *Double Headed: Two Generations of Railway Enthusiasm* (Newton Abbot, 1963, 2nd edn 1981), p. 134.

30. Roche (1967), pp. 31–5; D.W. Winkworth, *Southern Titled Trains* (Newton Abbot, 1989), pp. 21–49; Stephen Austin, *Portrait of the Atlantic Coast Express* (London, 1997), pp. 9–23.

31. Cited in Alan Bennett, *Southern Holiday lines in North Cornwall and West Devon* (Cheltenham, 1995), p. 81.

32. Hugh Miners and Treve Crago, *Tolzethan: The Life and Times of Joseph Hambley Rowe* (Bude, 2002), p. 16.

33. *Ceremonies of the Gorsedd of the Bards of Cornwall*, (n.p., n.d), pp. 7–11.

34. See Philip Payton, *Cornwall: A History* (Fowey, 2004), chapters 10 and 11.

35. See Philip Payton, *The Cornish Overseas: A History of Cornwall's Great Emigration* (Fowey, 2005), chapter 2.

36. John Murray and the Survey Committee, *Devon and Cornwall: A Preliminary Survey* (Exeter, 1947), p. 63.

37. Betjeman (1964), p. 7.

38. 'Rhyme and Rhythm', BBC Home Service, 26 January 1947; see also Games (ed.) (2007), p. 399.

39. 'Jacob Epstein', in Hector Bolitho (ed.), *Twelve Jews* (London, 1934); see also Candida Lycett Green (ed.), *Coming Home: An Anthology of Prose* (London, 1997), p. 61.

40. 'Yesterday's Fiction', BBC Home Service, 21 August 1944; see also Games (2006), pp. 140–1.

41. Claire Tomalin, *Thomas Hardy: The Time-Torn Man* (London, 2006), pp. 99–111.

42. See Kenneth Phelps, *The Wormwood Cup: Thomas Hardy in Cornwall* (Padstow, 1975), p. 1; p. 70; p. 84; p. 89.

43. Phelps (1975), p. 101.

44. Cited in Melissa Hardie (ed.), *A Mere Interlude: Some Literary Visitors in Lyonnesse* (Penzance, 1992), p. 153.

45. Cited in Hardie (ed.) (1992), p. 151.

46. Betjeman (1964), p. 55.

47. Betjeman (1964), p. 55.

48. Charles Henderson, *The Cornish Church Guide* (Truro, 1928), p. 114.

49. Betjeman (1964), p. 55.

50. John Betjeman, 'Hardy and Architecture', in Margaret Drabble, *The Genius of Thomas Hardy* (London, 1976); see also Lycett Green (ed.) (1997), p. 472.

51. Betjeman (1976); Lycett Green (ed.) (1997), p. 473.

52. 'Victorian Provincial Life', BBC West of England Home Service, 24 May 1949; published in modified form in A.L. Rowse (ed.), *The West in English History* (London, 1949), p. 172; see also Candida Lycett Green, *Betjeman's Britain* (London, 1999), p. 66 (also modified); Games (ed.) (2006), p. 37.

53. Brenda Duxbury and Michael Williams, *King Arthur Country in Cornwall* (Bodmin, 1979), p. 22.

54. Douglas Williams (ed.), *Thread of Gold: A History of Freemasonry in the Province of Cornwall 1752–2002* (Truro, 2002), p. 29, pp. 102–4, pp. 288–9, p. 327.

55. Betjeman (1964), p. 112.

56. Betjeman (1964), p. 111.

57. Betjeman (1964), pp. 111–2.

58. Betjeman (1964), p. 112.

59. Betjeman (1964), p. 112.

60. 'Beside the Sea', BBC2 television, 25 December 1969; see also Stephen Games (ed.), *Betjeman's England* (London, 2009), p. 67.

61. Betjeman (1964), p. 112.

62. Betjeman (1964), p. 112.

63. Betjeman (1964), p. 114.

64. Betjeman (1964), p. 22.

Chapter Three: Hawker, Baring-Gould and 'Betjeman Country'

1. J.C. Trewin, 'Preface', in Muriel Hawkey (ed.), *A Cornish Chorus* (London, 1948), p. xiv.

2. John Betjeman, *Cornwall: A Shell Guide* (London, 1964), p. 86.

3. Betjeman (1964), pp. 86–8.

4. Nicholas Orme, *English Church Dedications: With a Survey of Cornwall and Devon* (Exeter, 1996), p. 106.

5. Patrick Hutton, *I Would Not Be Forgotten: The Life and Work of Robert Stephen Hawker1803–1875* (Padstow, 2004), p. 37.

6. Hutton (2004), pp. 68–9.

7. Michael Williams, *Following the Famous in Cornwall* (Bodmin, n.d. c.1974), dustcover notes by John Theobold.

8. Hutton (2004), p. 170.

9. Cited in A.L. Rowse, *The Little Land of Cornwall* (Gloucester, 1986), p. 264.

10. H. Miles Brown, *The Catholic Revival in Cornish Anglicanism: A Study of the Tractarians of Cornwall 1833–1906* (St Winnow, 1980), p. 21.

11. Miles Brown (1980), p. 58.

12. 'The Parson Hawker of Morwenstow', BBC West of England, 7 February 1939; see also Stephen Games (ed.), *Trains and Buttered Toast* (London, 2006), p. 162.

13. 'Hawker of Morwenstowe', BBC West of England, 7 October 1945; see also Candida Lycett Green (ed.), *Coming Home: An Anthology of Prose* (London, 1997), p. 188; Candida Lycett Green (ed.), *Betjeman's Britain* (London, 1999), p. 77.

14. 'Hawker', 7 October 1945; Lycett Green (ed.) (1997), p. 188; Lycett Green (ed.) (1999), p. 77.

15. 'Hawker', 7 October 1945; Lycett Green (ed.) (1997), p. 186.; Lycett Green (ed.) (1999), p. 74.

16. Philip Payton, *The Cornish Overseas: A History of Cornwall's Great Emigration* (London, 2005), pp. 58–9.

17. C.E. Byles, *The Life and Letters of R.S. Hawker* (London, 1905), p542; see also Mark Stoyle, *West Britons: Cornish Identities and the Early Modern British State* (Exeter, 2002), pp. 175–80.

18. 'Hawker', 7 October 1945; Lycett Green (ed.) (1997), p. 187; Lycett Green (ed.) (1999), p. 75.

19. 'Hawker', 7 October 1945; Lycett Green (ed.) (1997), p. 187; Lycett Green (ed.) (1999), pp. 75–6.

20. 'Hawker', 7 October 1945; Lycett Green (ed.) (1997), p. 187; Lycett Green (ed.) (1999), p. 76.

21. 'Hawker', 7 October 1945; Lycett Green (ed.) (1997), p. 188; Lycett Green (ed.) (1999), p. 76.

22. 'Hawker', 7 October 1945; Lycett Green (ed.) (1997), p. 188; Lycett Green (ed.) (1999), p. 77.

23. Hutton (2004), p. 36.

24. 'Hawker', 7 October 1945; Lycett Green (ed.) (1997), p. 189; Lycett Green (ed.) (1999), p. 79.

25. Hutton (2004), p. 35.

26. Piers Brendon, *Hawker of Morwenstow* (London, 1975), p. 70.

27. Brendon (1975), p. 168.

28. Hutton (2004), pp. 52–4.

29. Brendon (1975), p. 173.

30. 'The Parson Hawker', 7 February 1939; Games (2006), pp. 161–2.

31. 'Hawker', 7 October 1945; Lycett Green (ed.) (1997), p. 189; Lycett Green (ed.) (1999), p. 78.

32. Hutton (2004), p. 142.

33. Hutton (2004), p. 168.

34. Hutton (2004), p. 167.

35. Hutton (2004), p. 175.

36. 'Hawker', 7 October 1945; Lycett Green (ed.) (1997), pp. 188–9; Lycett Green (ed.) (1999), p. 77.

37. 'Hawker', 7 October 1945; Lycett Green (ed.) (1997), p. 189; Lycett Green (ed.) (1999), p. 77.

38. Hutton (2004), p. 196.

39. 'Sabine Baring-Gould', BBC West of England Home Service, 21 September 1945; see also Games (2006), p. 194.

40. Sabine Baring-Gould, 'Colour in Composition', *Atlanta*, Vol. 6, 1892, p. 240.

41. John Betjeman (edited by Nigel Kerr), *Guide to English Parish Churches* (London, 1958; new edn. 1993), p. 125.

42. John Betjeman, 'The Face of Devon', in Lycett Green (ed.) (1999), pp. 31–2; originally published in *Devon: Shell Guide* (London, 1936).

43. Betjeman, 'The Face of Devon' (1999), p. 31.

44. 'Baring-Gould', 21 September 1945; Lycett Green (ed.) (1997), p. 166; Games (ed.) (2006), p. 192.

45. 'Baring-Gould', 21 September 1945; Lycett Green (ed.) (1997), p. 167; Games (ed.) (2006), p. 192.

46. Betjeman (Kerr) (1958, 1993), p. 125.

47. Orme (1996), p. 177.

48. Bickford H.C. Dickinson, *The Parish Church, St Peter, Lew Trenchard & The Rev Sabine Baring-Gould* (Lew Trenchard, n.d.), pp. 11–2.

49. 'Baring-Gould', 21 September 1945; Lycett Green (ed.) (1997), p. 165; Games (ed.) (2006), p. 190.

50. 'Baring Gould', 21 September 1945; Lycett Green (ed.) (1997), p. 165; Games (ed.) (2006), pp. 190–1.

51. 'St Petroc', BBC West of England Home Service, 11 July 1949; see also Games (ed.) (2006), p. 204.

52. 'St Petroc', 11 July 1949; see also Games (ed.) (2006), p. 204.

53. John Betjeman, 'Introduction', in W.E. Purcell, *Onward Christian Soldier: A Life of Sabine Baring-Gould* (London, 1957), p. v.

54. Betjeman (1957), p. v.

55. Betjeman (1957), p. vi.

56. Betjeman (1957), p. v.

57. Betjeman (1964), p. 30.

58. Sabine Baring-Gould, *A Book of the West: Cornwall* (London, 1899, repub. 1981), p. 74.

59. Betjeman (Kerr) (1958, 1993), p. 125.

60. Baring-Gould (1899, 1981), p. 5.

61. John Betjeman, *Summoned by Bells* (London, 1960), p. 87.

62. Baring-Gould (1899, 1981), p. 165.

63. 'St Petroc', 11 July 1949; Games (2006), p. 208.

64. Betjeman (1957), p. vi.

65. Betjeman (1957), p. vi.

66. Betjeman (1957), p. vi.

67. 'Baring-Gould', 21 December 1965; Lycett Green (ed.) (1992), p. 165; Games (2006), p. 190.

68. Purcell (1957), p. 179.

69. Simon Trezise, *The West Country as a Literary Invention: Putting Fiction in its Place* (Exeter, 2000), p. 39.

70. Betjeman (1957), p. vi.

71. Baring-Gould (1899, 1981), pp. 272–3.

72. Sabine Baring-Gould, *The Vicar of Morwenstow: Being a Life of Robert Stephen Hawker* (London, 1899; 12th edn 1949), p. 93.

73. Baring-Gould (1899,1981), p. 273.

74. Baring-Gould (1899, 1981), p. 273.

75. Baring-Gould (1899, 1981), p. 266.

76. Baring-Gould (1899, 1981), pp. 89–95, pp. 141–3.

77. Baring-Gould (1899, 1981), pp. 85–6.

78. Baring-Gould (1899, 1949), p. 38.

79. 'The Parson Hawker', 7 February 1939; Games (2006), p. 163.

80. Betjeman (1960), p. 33.

81. John Betjeman, *Collected Poems: Enlarged Edition* (London, 1984b), p. 235 (from 'The Dear Old Village').

82. 'Coast and Country', BBC West of England Home Service, 1 July 1949; published as 'St Endellion' in Betjeman (1952), p. 208; see also John Betjeman, *Betjeman's Cornwall* (London, 1984), p. 49; Lycett Green (ed.) (1997), p. 242.

83. 'Coast and Country', 1 July 1949; John Betjeman, *First and Last Loves* (London, 1952), p. 208; Betjeman (1984), p. 49; Lycett Green (ed.) (1997), p. 242.

84. 'Coast and Country', 1 July 1949; Betjeman (1952), p. 208; Betjeman (1984), p. 49; Lycett Green (ed.) (1997), p. 242.

85. 'Coast and Country', 1 July 1949; republished as 'Port Isaac' in Betjeman (1952), p. 213; see also Betjeman (1984), p. 38; Lycett Green (ed.) (1999), p. 51; Games (2006), p. 259. There are variations from the original script in the published editions, except for Games (2006) which reproduces the text as broadcast.

86. 'Coast and Country', 1 July 1949; Betjeman (1952), p. 213; Betjeman (1984a), p. 38; Lycett Green (ed.) (1999), p. 51; Games (ed.) (2006), p. 259.

87. 'Coast and Country', 1 July 1949; Betjeman (1952), pp. 213–5; Betjeman (1984a), pp. 38–43; Lycett Green (ed.) (1999), pp. 52–3.

88. Betjeman (1952), p. 214; Betjeman (1984a), p. 39; Lycett Green (ed.) (1999), p. 52.

89. 'Coast and Country', 1 July 1949; Games (ed.) (2006), p. 261. Other published versions [Betjeman (1952), p. 217; Betjeman (1984a), p. 44; Lycett Green (ed.) (1999), p. 54] end with the alternative phrase: 'across the green and gently rolling harbour flood'.

90. 'St Protus and St Hyacinth, Blisland, Cornwall', BBC West of England Home Service, 21 July 1948; see also Games (ed.) (2006), p. 237. Other published versions of this broadcast [Betjeman (1952), pp. 179–182; Betjeman (1984a), pp. 59–62] are significantly abridged.

91. 'St Protus and St Hyacinth', 21 July 1948; Games (ed.) (2006), pp. 237–9.

92. 'Padstow', BBC Third Programme, 6 February 1949; Games (ed.) (2006), p. 293. Other published versions of this broadcast [Betjeman (1952), pp. 217–225; Betjeman (1984a), pp. 68–78) are also abridged.

93. 'Padstow', 6 February 1949; Games (ed.) (2006), p. 295–301.

94. 'Faith in the West', BBC West of England Home Service, 1 February 1957; poem republished as 'St Petroc' in Kevin Gardner (ed.), *Poems in the Porch: The Radio Poems of John Betjeman* (London, 2008), pp. 123–9.

95. Gardner (ed.) (2008), p. 30.

96. 'Faith in the West', 1 February 1957; Gardner (ed.) (2008), p. 129.

97. 'Faith in the West', 1 February 1957; Gardner (ed.) (2008), p. 123.

98. 'Faith in the West', 1 February 1957; Gardner (ed.) (2008), p. 124.

99. See Bevis Hillier, *Young Betjeman* (London, 1988), p. 89.

100. *Evening Standard*, 8 May 1936; see also Stephen Games (ed.), *Tennis Whites and Tea Cakes* (London, 2007), p. 185.

101. *Evening Standard*, 8 May 1936; see also Games (ed.) (2007), pp. 185–6.

102. 'Padstow', 6 February 1949; Games (ed.) (2006), p. 300.

103. A.N. Wilson, *Betjeman* (London, 2006), p. 121.

104. Betjeman (1960), p. 33, p. 40.

105. 'Victorian Provincial Life', 24 May 1949; Games (2006), p. 35.

106. Betjeman (1984b), pp. 66–7 (from 'Trebetherick').

107. 'The Parson Hawker', 7 February 1939; Games (ed.) (2006), p. 163.

108. 'Baring-Gould', 21 September 1945; Lycett Green (ed.) (1997), p. 164; Games (ed.) (2006), p. 189.

109. 'Baring-Gould', 21 September 1945; Lycett Green (ed.) (1997), p. 165; Games (ed.) (2006), p. 190.

110. 'Seaview', BBC West of England Programme, 11 May 1938: see also Games (ed.) (2006), p. 107.

111. See Donald R. Rawe, *Traditional Cornish Stories and Rhymes* (Padstow, 1971), pp. 24–25.

112. 'Seaview', 11 May 1938; Games (ed.) (2006), p. 107.

113. 'This I Believe', CBS, recorded 21 September 1953; see Games (ed.) (2007), p. 440.

114. Lycett Green (ed.) (1992), p. 17.

115. 'Padstow', 6 February 1949; Games (ed.) (2006), p. 293.

116. 'Padstow', 6 February 1949; Games (ed.) (2006), p. 263.

117. *Evening Standard*, 8 May 1936; Games (ed.) (2007), p. 186.

Chapter Four: Betjeman and *The Secret Glory*

1. John Betjeman, *Summoned by Bells* (London, 1960), p. 85.

2. Betjeman (1960), p. 66–7.

3. Betjeman (1960), p. 68.

4. Betjeman (1960), p. 67.

5. Exeter University Library Special Collections [EUL] Betjeman Library/Arthur L. Salmond, *Cornwall* (London, 2nd edn 1913). This was Betjeman's original

Methuen Little Guide, and is inscribed: 'John Betjemann March 1918'.
Intriguingly, he had not entirely abandoned the double *n* by that date. See also
Hamish Riley-Smith, *The Betjeman Library: A Catalogue of the Library of Sir John
Betjeman* (Swanton Abbott, 1996), item 2216.

6. Betjeman (1960), p. 85.
7. Betjeman (1960), pp. 85–6.
8. Betjeman (1960), pp. 86–7.
9. Betjeman (1960), p. 87.
10. Betjeman (1960), pp. 87–8.
11. Bevis Hillier, *Young Betjeman* (London, 1988), p. 122.
12. Derek Stanford, *John Betjeman: A Study* (London, 1961), p. 25.
13. Stanford (London, 1961), pp. 25–6.
14. Moira Tangye, *The Book of St Ervan* (Tiverton, 2006).
15. Tangye (2006), p. 112.
16. Tangye (2006), p. 113.
17. Tangye (2006), p. 113.
18. Tangye (2006), p. 112.
19. See Mark Stoyle, *West Britons: Cornish Identities and the Modern British State*
    (Exeter, 2002), chapter 8: '"A Monument to Honour" – The Cornish Royalist
    Tradition after 1660'.
20. A.C. Benson, *The Life of Edward White Benson*, (London, 1899), Vol. 1, p. 428.
21. David Everett, 'Celtic Revival and the Anglican Church in Cornwall, 1870–
    1930', in Philip Payton (ed.), *Cornish Studies: Eleven* (Exeter, 2003), p. 217.
22. H. Miles Brown, *The Church in Cornwall* (Truro, 1964, repub. Truro, 2005),
    p. 150.
23. Miles Brown (Truro, 1964, Truro, 2005), p. 150.
24. C.S. Phillips and Others, *Walter Howard Frere: Bishop of Truro – A Memoir*
    (London, 1947), p. 110.
25. Phillips & Others (1947), p. 117.
26. *Cornish Church Kalendar* (Truro, 1933), Preface, n.p.
27. A.L. Rowse, *Quiller Couch: A Portrait of 'Q'* (London, 1988), p. 199.
28. Miles Brown (Truro, 1964, Truro, 2005), p. 150.
29. A.L. Rowse, *A Cornish Childhood: Autobiography of a Cornishman* (London, 1942),
    p. 160.
30. Reg Groves, *Conrad Noel and the Thaxted Movement: An Adventure in Christian
    Socialism* (London, 1967), p. 304.
31. Catherine Lorigan, *Delabole: The History of the Slate Quarry and the Making of its
    Village Community* (Reading, 2007), pp. 138–46.
32. Bernard Walke, *Twenty Years at St Hilary* (London, 1935), p. 32.
33. Walke (1935), p. 33.
34. Walke (1935), p. 180.

35. Guy W. Hockley and W.R. Johnson, 'Truro', in Phillips & Others (1947), p. 88 & p. 87. Hockley died before the chapter could be published; it is not clear how much he was able to contribute to its compilation but it seems likely that the lion's share of the work fell to Johnson.

36. Hockley & Johnson (1947), p. 77–8.

37. Hockley & Johnson (1947), pp. 78–9.

38. Hockley & Johnson (1947), p. 80.

39. Hockley & Johnson (1947), p. 101.

40. Hockley & Johnson (1947), pp. 90–1.

41. Hockley & Johnson (1947), p. 96.

42. Hockley & Johnson (1947), p. 97.

43. Hockley & Johnson (1947), pp. 93–4.

44. Hockley & Johnson (1947), pp. 94–5.

45. Rowse (1988), p. 199.

46. Alan Dunstan and John Peart-Binns, *Cornish Bishop* (London, 1977), pp. 98–9.

47. Edwin Stark, *Saint Endellion: Essays on the Church, its Patron Saint and her Collegiate Foundation* (Redruth, 1983), p. 69.

48. Correspondence/Betjeman to Wilfred Johnson, 24 April 1949 (Private Collection of Mrs Elizabeth Bartlett).

49. 'Coast and Country', BBC West of England Home Service, 1 July 1949; John Betjeman, *First and Last Loves* (London, 1952), pp. 209–12; see also John Betjeman, *Betjeman's Cornwall* (London, 1984a), pp. 50–52; Candida Lycett Green (ed.), *Coming Home: An Anthology of Prose* (London, 1997), pp. 243–245; Candida Lycett Green (ed.), *Betjeman's Britain* (London, 1999), pp. 57–8.

50. Betjeman, *Cornwall: A Shell Guide* (London, 1964), p. 43.

51. Patrick Taylor-Martin, *John Betjeman: His Life and Work* (London, 1983), p. 35.

52. John Betjeman, *Ghastly Good Taste: or, a depressing story of the Rise and Fall of English Architecture* (London, 1933, repub. with additions 1970), pp. 32–3.

53. Betjeman (1964), p. 52.

54. Betjeman (1964), p. 52.

55. Kevin J. Gardner (ed.), *Faith and Doubt of John Betjeman: An Anthology of Betjeman's Religious Verse* (London, 2005), pp. xxi–xxii.

56. Gardner (ed.) (2005), p. 58.

57. Gardner (ed.) (2005), p. 58.

58. Gardner (ed.) (2005), p. 59.

59. S.P.B. Mais, *We Wander in The West* (London, 1950), p. 13. Mais was a topographical writer much admired by Betjeman, and appeared on his Christmas card list – see Uffington Museum Betjeman Collection [UMBC]/ Miscellaneous/ Christmas Card List c1964.

60. The timeless presence (and influence) of the White Horse in the life of Uffington is the central, linking theme in Jane Cooper and Sharon Smith, *The White Horse and the Village of Uffington* (Uffington, 2004).

61. Stephen King, *Just After Sunset* (London, 2008), p. 278.

62. See Sharon Lowena, "'*Noscitur A Sociis*': Jenner, Duncombe-Jewell and their Milieu", in Philip Payton (ed.), *Cornish Studies: Twelve* (Exeter, 2004), pp. 61–87.

63. Philip Payton, *D.H. Lawrence and Cornwall* (St Agnes, 2009).

64. Arthur Machen, *The Autobiography of Arthur Machen* (London, 1951), p. 120–1. This is the combined volume of Machen's two earlier autobiographical works: *Far off Things* (London, 1922); *Things Near and Far* (London, 1923).

65. Hillier (1988), p. 122.

66. Hillier (1988), p. 122.

67. Betjeman (1960), p. 87.

68. Elizabeth Rees, *Celtic Saints in Their Landscape* (Gloucester, 2001), pp. 69–76.

69. A. Lane-Davies, *Holy Wells of Cornwall* (Penzance, 1970), p. 79; P.O. Leggat and D.V. Leggat, *The Healing Wells: Cornish Cults and Customs* (Redruth, 1987), p. 22.

70. John Betjeman, *Collected Poems: Enlarged Edition* (London, 1984b), pp. 98–9 (from 'Saint Cadoc').

71. Hillier (1988), p. 192.

72. UMBC/Correspondence, Betjeman to John Piper, n.d. April 1966; see also Candida Lycett Green (ed.), *John Betjeman: Letters, Volume Two:1951–1984* (London, 1995), p. 303.

73. UMBC/Correspondence, L.T.C. Rolt to Betjeman, 15 July 1950.

74. John Betjeman, 'Foreword', in L.T.C. Rolt, *Railway Adventure* (London, 1953; new ed. 1961), pp. xix–xx.

75. Rolt (1953 & 1961), p. 86.

76. Byron Rogers, *The Man Who Went into The West: The Life of R.S. Thomas* (London, 2006), p. 60.

77. John Betjeman, 'Introduction', in R.S. Thomas, *Song at the Year's Turning* (London, 1955); see also Lycett Green (ed.) (1997), p. 323.

78. Rogers (2006), p. 210.

79. Greg Morse, *John Betjeman: Reading the Victorians* (Eastbourne, 2008), p. 14.

80. John Betjeman, *English Parish Churches* (London, 1958), p. 188; see also Lycett Green (ed.) (1997), p. 89.

81. Betjeman (1958), p. 189; Lycett Green (ed.) (1999), p. 90.

82. John Betjeman and John Piper, *Shropshire: A Shell Guide* (London, 1951), 'Introduction'; see also Lycett Green (ed.) (1999), p92.

83. *Spectator*, 21 October 1955.

84. 'Landscapes with Houses: Cardiff Castle', BBC Home Service, 18 May 1952; see also Lycett Green (ed.) (1999), p98.

85. *Spectator*, 3 August 1956.

86. Betjeman (1960), p. 87.

87. UMBC/Correspondence, Arthur Machen to Betjeman, 16 September 1943.

88. Machen (1951), p. 260.

89. Arthur Machen, *The Secret Glory* (London, 1922, new edn n.d. c.2005), pp. 43, 49.

90. Machen (1922 & n.d. c.2005), pp. 70, 100–1.

91. Betjeman (1960), pp. 19, 88.

92. Betjeman (1984b), pp. 181–2 (from 'Harrow-on-the-Hill').

93. Machen (1922 & n.d. c.2005), pp. 88–9.

94. Machen (1922 & n.d. c.2005), p. 118.

95. Machen (1922 & n.d. c.2005), p. 140.

96. Machen (1922 & n.d. c2005), pp. 142–3.

97. Betjeman (1984b), pp. 86–9 (from 'Myfanwy' and 'Myfanwy at Oxford').

98. Betjeman (1984b), p. 98 (from 'Saint Cadoc').

Chapter Five: Séan O'Betjemán and the 'Anglo-Celtic Muse'

1. Uffington Museum Betjeman Collection [UMBC]/Misc., unidentified cutting from the *Irish Times* (c.1972), interview by Tom McGurk.

2. Michael Harrison (ed.), *Under Thirty: Anthology* (London, 1939), p. 49.

3. Candida Lycett Green, *John Betjeman: Letters, Volume One: 1926–1951* (London, 1994), pp. 267–8.

4. Robert Welch (ed.), *The Oxford Companion to Irish Literature* (Oxford, 1996), pp. 609–11.

5. UMBC/Correspondence, Betjeman to Pierce Synott, 21 June 1926; Betjeman to Camilla Russell, 14 August 1931; see also Lycett Green (ed.) (1994), pp. 25, 73.

6. Welch (ed.) (1996), pp. 11–2.

7. Derek Stanford, *John Betjeman: A Study* (London, 1961), p. 141.

8. Helen Gardner (ed.), *The New Oxford Book of English Verse* (Oxford, 1972), pp. 463–5.

9. Welch (ed.) (1996), p. 143.

10. Gardner (ed.) (1972), pp. 464–5.

11. Welch (ed.) (1996), p. 144.

12. Cited in Michael O. Henry, 'Institutions for the Promotion of Indigenous Music: The Case for Ireland's *Comhaltas Ceoltoiri Eireann*', *Ethno-musicology*, Vol. 33, No. 1, p. 69.

13. UMBC/Correspondence, Betjeman to Penelope Betjeman, 25 September

1978; see also Candida Lycett Green (ed.), *John Betjeman: Letters, Volume Two: 1951–84* (London, 1995), p. 541.

14. Lycett Green (ed.) (1994), p. 19.

15. Lycett Green (ed.) (1994), p. 45.

16. Bevis Hillier, *Young Betjeman* (London, 1988), pp. 309–10.

17. Lycett Green (ed.) (1994), p. 45.

18. UMBC/Correspondence, Betjeman to Edward and Christine Longford (Pakenham), 31 July 1939; see also Lycett Green (ed.) (1994), p. 232.

19. UMBC/Correspondence, Betjeman to Elizabeth Bowen, 29 October 1938; see also Lycett Green (ed.) (1994), p. 216.

20. Lycett Green (ed.) (1995), p. 515.

21. UMBC/Correspondence, Betjeman to Patsy Zeppel, n.d. December 1967; see also Lycett Green (ed.) (1995), p. 242.

22. UMBC/Misc., Membership Card, Irish Peers Association, 1963.

23. UMBC/Correspondence, Betjeman to Camilla Russell, 14 August 1931; see also Lycett Green (ed.) (1994), p. 73.

24. UMBC/Correspondence/Betjeman to Camilla Russell, 26 August 1931; see also Lycett Green (ed.) (1994), pp. 75–6.

25. UMBC/Correspondence, Betjeman to Camilla Russell, 26 August 1931; see also Lycett Green (ed.) (1994), p. 75.

26. UMBC/Correspondence, Betjeman to Camilla Russell, 29 August 1931; see also Lycett Green (ed.) (1994), p. 79.

27. UMBC/Correspondence, Betjeman to T.S. Eliot, 21 July 1938; see also Lycett Green (ed.) (1994), p. 213.

28. UMBC/Correspondence, Betjeman to Bess Betjeman, 3 October 1938; see also Lycett Green (ed.) (1994), p. 215.

29. UMBC/Correspondence, Betjeman to Bess Betjeman, 3 October 1928; see also Lycett Green (ed.) (1994), p. 215.

30. S.J. Connolly (ed.), *The Oxford Companion to Irish History* (Oxford, 1998), p. 49; The Earl of Longford and Thomas P. O'Neill, *Eamon de Valera* (London, 1970), pp. 301–2.

31. UMBC/Correspondence, Betjeman to Michael Rosse (Earl of Rosse), 19 April 1933; see also Lycett Green (ed.) (1994), pp. 118–9.

32. UMBC/Correspondence, Michael Rosse to Betjeman, 20 April [1933].

33. UMBC/Correspondence, Michael Rosse to Betjeman, n.d. [April 1933?].

34. Peter Hart, 'The Protestant Experience of Revolution in Southern Ireland', in Richard English and Graham Walker (eds.), *Unionism in Modern Ireland: New Perspectives on Politics and Culture* (London, 1996), p. 81.

35. Longford & O'Neill (1970), p. 350.

36. Longford & O'Neill (1970), p. 351.

37. Bevis Hillier, *John Betjeman: New Fame, New Love* (London, 2002), p. 197.

38. *Irish Times*, 21 May 1984.
39. UMBC/Correspondence, E. Rawdon Smith (Ministry of Information, Malet Street, London WC1) to Betjeman, 28 May 1941.
40. Hillier (2002), pp. 203–4.
41. UMBC/Correspondence, Betjeman to John Lehmann, 12 February 1941; see also Lycett Green (ed.) (1994), p. 279.
42. UMBC/Correspondence, Betjeman to John and Myfanwy Piper, 2 March 1941; see also Lycett Green (ed.) (1994), p. 280.
43. UMBC/Correspondence, Betjeman to John Piper, 17 March 1941 St Patrick's Day; see also Lycett Green (ed.) (1994), p. 283.
44. UMBC/Correspondence, Betjeman to Oliver Stonor, 19 April 1941; see also Lycett Green (ed.) (1994), p. 285.
45. UMBC/Correspondence, Betjeman to John and Myfanwy Piper, 26 May 1941; see also Lycett Green (ed.) (1994), p. 288.
46. UMBC/Correspondence, Betjeman to Douglas Goldring, 14 July 1941; see also Lycett Green (ed.) (1994), p. 293.
47. UMBC/Correspondence, Betjeman to Frank O'Connor, 7 March 1941; see also Lycett Green (ed.) (1994), p. 281.
48. Bevis Hillier, 'Foreword', in John Betjeman, *Uncollected Poems* (London, 1982), p. 2.
49. UMBC/Misc. Memorandum 'Counter Propaganda for Eire', by G.L. Marshall, dated 2 April 1943.
50. UMBC/Correspondence, Betjeman to Oliver Stonor, 27 March 1943; see also Lycett Green (ed.) (1994), p. 313.
51. *Irish Times*, 14 June 1943.
52. 'Fabrics of the Church of Ireland': An address given to the clergymen of the Church of Ireland, 1943, published in Candida Lycett Green (ed.), *Coming Home: An Anthology of Prose* (London, 1997), p. 136.
53. UMBC/Correspondence, Betjeman to Frank Gallagher, 16 June 1943; see also Lycett Green (ed.) (1994), p. 318.
54. UMBC/Correspondence, Betjeman to Mabel Fitzgerald, 20 August 1944; see also Lycett Green (ed.) (1994), p. 245.
55. UMBC/Correspondence, Brian O'Neill to Betjeman, 12 August 1943.
56. UMBC/Correspondence, Betjeman to Frank Longford [Pakenham], 28 February 1946.
57. UMBC/Correspondence, Betjeman to Frank Gallagher, 28 February 1946; see also Lycett Green (ed.) (1994), p. 384.
58. UMBC/Correspondence, Betjeman to P. Morton Shand, 31 October 1952; see also Lycett Green (ed.) (1995), p. 32.
59. UMBC/Correspondence, Betjeman to James Mitchell, 6 June 1974; see also Lycett Green (ed.) (1995), p. 481.

60. UMBC/Correspondence, Betjeman to James Mitchell, 6 June 1974; see also Lycett Green (ed.) (1995), p. 481.

61. UMBC/Correspondence, Betjeman to James Mitchell, 6 June 1974; see also Lycett Green (ed.) (1995), p. 481.

62. UMBC/Correspondence, Betjeman to James Mitchell, 6 June 1974; see also Lycett Green (ed.) (1995), p. 481.

63. See Peter Berresford Ellis, *The Celtic Dawn: A History of Pan Celticism* (London, 1993), pp. 73–4.

64. UMBC/Correspondence, Betjeman to Mary Wilson, 10 November 1971; see also Lycett Green (ed.) (1995), p. 425.

65. UMBC/Correspondence, Betjeman to Penelope Betjeman, 19 August 1955; see also Lycett Green (ed.) (1995), p. 84.

66. John Betjeman, *London's Historic Railway Stations* (London, 1972), p. 126.

67. *Daily Herald*, 2 January 1945.

68. Longford & O'Neill (1970), pp. x–xi.

69. Patrick Taylor-Martin, *John Betjeman: His Life and Work* (London, 1983), p. 81.

70. John Betjeman, *Collected Poems* (London, 1984), p. 121 (from 'Ireland with Emily').

71. Betjeman (1984), p. 122 (from 'Ireland with Emily').

72. Stanford (1961), p. 141.

73. Taylor-Martin (1983), p. 82.

74. Taylor-Martin (1983), p. 82.

75. UMBC/Correspondence, Betjeman to T.S. Eliot, 21 July 1938; see also Lycett Green (ed.) (1994), p. 213.

76. John Betjeman, *Ghastly Good Taste – or, a depressing story of the Rise and Fall of English Architecture* (London, 1933, repub. with additions, 1970), pp. 31–3.

77. Michael Bartholomew, *In Search of H.V. Morton* (London, 2006), p. 121.

78. Bartholomew (2006), p. 137.

79. Bartholomew (2006), p. 137.

80. Bartholomew (2006), pp. 138–9.

81. *Daily Telegraph*, 17 June 1963.

82. John Betjeman, 'Foreword', in L.T.C. Rolt, *Railway Adventure* (London, 1953, nee ed. 1971), p. xx.

83. UMBC/Correspondence, Betjeman to Lady Mander, 2 October 1944.

84. UMBC/Correspondence, Betjeman to Mabel Fitzgerald, 16 October 1944; Betjeman to Geoffrey Taylor, 24 November 1944; see also Lycett Green (ed.) (1994), pp. 348, 350.

85. UMBC/Correspondence, Betjeman to Penelope Betjeman, 10 February 1960.

86. UMBC/Correspondence, Betjeman to John Summerson, 3 May 1958; Betjeman

to Patrick Balfour, 27 October 1952; see also Lycett Green (ed.) (1995), p. 141.

87. UMBC/Correspondence, Betjeman to Anthony Barnes and Jonathan Guinness, 12 June 1947; see also Lycett Green (ed.) (1994), p. 416.

88. UMBC/Correspondence, Betjeman to Patrick Kinross, 28 December 1947; see also Lycett Green (ed.) (1994), p. 428.

89. Vernon Bogdanor, *Devolution in the United Kingdom* (Oxford, 2001), p. 139.

90. UMBC/Correspondence, Betjeman to Patrick Kinross, 28 December 1947; see also Lycett Green (ed.) (1994), p. 428.

91. UMBC/Correspondence, Betjeman to Stuart Piggot, 16 October 1946; see also Lycett Green (ed.) (1994), p. 399.

92. Lycett Green (ed.) (1995), p. 106.

93. UMBC/Correspondence, Betjeman to Candida Betjeman, 26 October 1957; see also Lycett Green (ed.) (1995), p. 135.

94. *Daily Telegraph*, 1 June 1959.

95. *Daily Telegraph*, 1 June 1959.

96. UMBC/Correspondence, Betjeman to H.S. Goodhart-Rendel, 13 July 1949; see also Lycett Green (ed.) (1994), p. 479.

97. John Betjeman, 'The Isle of Man', in Eileen Molony (ed.), *Portraits of Islands* (London, 1951); see also Candida Lycett Green (ed.), *Coming Home: An Anthology* (London, 1997), pp. 295–301, and Candida Lycett Green, *Betjeman's Britain* (London, 1999), pp. 232–9. This essay was based on an earlier talk, 'The Isle of Man', BBC Third Programme, 7 August 1949, which was produced by Eileen Molony. (See Stephen Games [ed.] *Trains and Buttered Toast* [London, 2006], pp. 284–289).

98. Betjeman (1951); Lycett Green (ed.) (1997), pp. 295–6; Lycett Green (ed.) (1999), p. 233.

99. 'Look Stranger – Ellan Vannin', BBC2 Television, 10 December 1970; see also Stephen Games (ed.), *Betjeman's England* (London, 2009), p. 289.

100. William Greenberg, *The Flags of the Forgotten: Nationalism on the Celtic Fringe* (Brighton, 1969), pp. 96–7.

101. *Spectator*, 12 August 1955.

102. *Spectator*, 6 May 1955.

103. Betjeman (1953 & 1970), p. xix.

104. L.J. Sharpe (ed.), *The Rise of Meso Government in Europe* (London, 1993), p. 278.

105. UMBC/Correspondence, Betjeman to Patrick Balfour, 15 April 1930; see also Lycett Green (ed.) (1994), p. 65.

106. Hillier (2002), pp. 571–92.

107. Lycett Green (ed.) (1995), pp. 204–5.

108. *Daily Telegraph*, 20 May 1984.

109. UMBC/Correspondence, Betjeman to Penelope Betjeman, 4 November 1961; see also Lycett Green (ed.) (1995), p. 218.

110. UMBC/Correspondence, Betjeman to Penelope Betjeman, 7 November 1961; see also Lycett Green (ed.) (1995), p. 220.

111. *Bathurst Free Press*, 11 January 1851.

112. Philip Payton, *The Cornish Overseas: A History of Cornwall's Great Emigration* (Fowey, 2005), pp. 228–231.

113. Exeter University Library Special Collections [EUL] Rowse Collection MS113/3/temp/ Box 30, Betjeman to A.L. Rowse, 1 December 1961.

114. Patricia Lay, *One and All: The Cornish in New South Wales* (Qeanbeyan [NSW], 1998), p. 5, pp. 15–16.

115. Payton (2005), p. 172.

116. Payton (2005), pp. 164–5.

117. Payton (2005), pp. 161–3.

118. UMBC/Misc. *Report on John Betjeman's Australia Tour 1 Nov – 7 Dec 1961.*

119. UMBC/Correspondence, Betjeman to Norman Williams and Patsy Zeppel, February 1963; see also Lycett Green (ed.) (1995), p. 242.

120. UMBC/Correspondence, Betjeman to Candida Betjeman, 29 September 1971; see also Lycett Green (ed.) (1995), p. 421.

121. Barry Humphries, *My Life as Me: A Memoir* (Camberwell [Vic], 2002), pp. 292–5.

122. UMBC/Correspondence, Betjeman to Candida Betjeman, 29 September 1971; see also Lycett Green (ed.) (1995), p. 421.

123. UMBC/Correspondence, Betjeman to Candida Betjeman, 9 October 1971; see also Lycett Green (ed.) (1995), p. 422.

124. UMBC/Correspondence, Betjeman to Mary Wilson, 17 October 1971; see also Lycett Green (ed.) (1995), p. 424.

125. UMBC/Correspondence, Betjeman to Mary Wilson, 10 November 1971; see also Lycett Green (ed.) (1995), p. 425.

126. UMBC/Correspondence, Betjeman to Candida Betjeman, 17 October 1971; see also Lycett Green (ed.) (1995), p. 423.

127. UMBC/Correspondence, Betjeman to Mary Wilson, 17 October 1971; see also Lycett Green (ed.) (1995), p. 424.

128. Betjeman (1984), p. 399 ('Back from Australia').

Chapter Six: Cornwall as Liberation

1. John Betjeman, *Collected Poems* (London, 1984), p. 66 (from 'Trebetherick').

2. John Betjeman, *Old Lights for New Chancels* (London, 1940).

3. John Betjeman, *Cornwall Illustrated in a Series of Views* (London, 1934).

4. A.N. Wilson, *Betjeman* (London, 2006), p. 7.

5. 'Beside the Sea', BBC2 Television, 25 December 1969; see also Stephen Games (ed.), *Betjeman's England* (London, 2009), p. 67.

6. John Hurst, 'Literature in Cornwall', in Philip Payton (ed.), *Cornwall Since the War: The Contemporary History of a European Region* (Redruth, 1993), p. 293.

7. Hurst (1993), p. 293.

8. *Mail* (West Hartlepool), 19 May 1984.

9. Candida Lycett Green, *John Betjeman: Letters, Volume One: 1926–1951* (London, 1994), p. 6.

10. Patrick Taylor-Martin, *John Betjeman: His Life and Work* (London, 1983), p. 23.

11. John Betjeman, *Summoned by Bells* (London, 1960), pp. 33–4.

12. John Betjeman (1960), p. 34.

13. Greg Morse, *John Betjeman: Reading the Victorians* (Brighton, 2008), p. 171.

14. Hugo Williams (ed.), *John Betjeman: Poems Selected by Hugo Williams* (London, 2006), p. xv.

15. Betjeman (1960), p. 35.

16. Betjeman (1960), pp. 36–7.

17. Betjeman (1960), p. 36.

18. Betjeman (1960), p. 39–40.

19. Wilson (2006), p. 31.

20. Jon Stallworthy, 'Betjeman Voices', *The Betjemanian: Journal of the Betjeman Society*, 21, 2009/10, p. 8.

21. Betjeman (1960), p. 44–5.

22. Betjeman (1960), p. 45.

23. Bevis Hillier, *Young Betjeman* (London, 1988), p. 125.

24. 'Victorian Provincial Life', BBC West of England Home Service, 24 May 1949; see also Stephen Games (ed.), *Trains and Buttered Toast* (London, 2006), p. 37.

25. Denys Val Baker, *The Timeless Land: The Creative Spirit in Cornwall* (Bath, 1973), pp. 7, 9.

26. Brenda Maddox, *The Married Man: A Life of D.H. Lawrence* (London, 1994), p. 227.

27. Philip Payton, *D.H. Lawrence and Cornwall* (St Agnes, 2009).

28. Jim Hosking, *Boskenna and the Paynters: The Fortunes of a Cornish Family from 1760* (Penzance, 1999), p. 95.

29. Claud Morris, *Confessions of a Cornishman* (Fowey, 2001), p. 142.

30. Patrick Marnham, *Wild Mary: A Life of Mary Wesley* (London, 2006), p. 75.

31. Hillier (1986), p. 124.

32. Betjeman (1984), p. 303 (frm 'Old Friends'); John Betjeman, *High and Low* (London, 1966).

33. Betjeman (1984), p. 169 (from 'North Coast Recollections').

34. Betjeman (1984), p. 170 (from 'North Coast Recollections').

35. Betjeman (1960), pp. 89–90.

36. Uffington Museum Betjeman Collection [UMBC]/Correspondence, Betjeman to Patrick Balfour, 5 August 1929; see also Lycett Green (1994), p. 59.

37. Lycett Green (1994), p. 46.

38. Taylor-Martin (1983), p. 17.

39. Betjeman (1960), p. 11.

40. Betjeman (1984), p. 97 (from 'On a Portrait of a Deaf Man').

41. Betjeman (1960), p. 19.

42. Betjeman (1960), p. 11.

43. Betjeman (1960), p. 16.

44. Taylor-Martin (1983), p. 30.

45. Betjeman (1960), p. 84.

46. Betjeman (1960), pp. 84–5.

47. Betjeman (1960), pp. 80–1.

48. UMBC/Correspondence, Betjeman to Patrick Balfour, 5 August 1929; see also Lycett Green (ed.) (1994), pp. 58–9.

49. UMBC/Correspondence, Betjeman to Pierce Syncott, 21 June 1926; see also Lycett Green (ed.) (1994), p. 27.

50. UMBC/Correspondence, Betjeman to Pierce Synott, 6 September 1927; see also Lycett Green (ed.) (1994), p. 33.

51. UMBC/Correspondence, Betjeman to Pierce Synott, 3 October 1927; see also Lycett Green (ed.) (1994), p. 34.

52. UMBC/Correspondence, Betjeman to Patrick Balfour, 4 April 1942); see also Lycett Green (ed.) (1994), p. 103.

53. Betjeman (1934), p. 37.

54. Betjeman (1934), p. 6.

55. UMBC/Misc. Chronology of John Betjeman's Life.

56. A.L. Rowse, *Friends and Contemporaries* (London, 1989), p. 75.

57. Rowse (1989), p. 96.

58. Philip Payton, *A.L. Rowse and Cornwall: A Paradoxical Patriot* (Exeter, 2005b), especially chapters 5 and 6.

59. Payton (2005b), chapters 8 and 9.

60. UMBC/Correspondence, A.L. Rowse to Betjeman, 5 May 1943 (originals of all UMBC Rowse correspondence are in MacPherson Library Special Collections, University of Victoria [Canada]).

61. UMBC/Correspondence, A.L. Rowse to Betjeman, 5 May 1943.

62. *Tatler*, 15 July 1942.

63. UMBC/Correspondence, A.L. Rowse to Betjeman, 5 May 1943.

64. UMBC/Correspondence, A.L. Rowse to Betjeman, 5 May 1943.

65. UMBC/Correspondence, A.L. Rowse to Betjeman, n.d. c.1953.

66. UMBC/Correspondence, A.L. Rowse to Betjeman, 1 January 1946.

67. A.L. Rowse, *A Cornish Childhood: Autobiography of a Cornishman* (London, 1942), p. 139.

68. Rowse (1942), pp. 160, 227, 116,76.

69. Rowse (1960), p. 105.

70. UMBC/Correspondence, A.L. Rowse to Betjeman, 30 July 1945.

71. UMBC/Correspondence, A.L. Rowse to Betjeman, 13 May 194[?].

72. UMBC/Correspondence, A.L. Rowse to Betjeman, 1 January 1946.

73. UMBC/Correspondence, A.L. Rowse to Betjeman, late 1948 (probably November).

74. UMBC/Correspondence, A.L. Rowse to Betjeman, 12 July 1949.

75. UMBC/Correspondence, A.L. Rowse to Betjeman, 1 January 1946.

76. UMBC/Correspondence, A.L. Rowse to Betjeman, 13 May 194[?]; n.d. c.1953.

77. Bevis Hillier, *John Betjeman: New Fame, New Love* (London, 2002), pp. 477–8; UMBC/Correspondence, A.L. Rowse to Betjeman, 23 August 1948; A.L. Rowse to Betjeman, 13 May 194[?].

78. UMBC/Correspondence, A.L. Rowse to Betjeman, 17 February 1949.

79. UMBC/Correspondence, A.L. Rowse to Betjeman, 11 June 1949.

80. A.L. Rowse, *A Cornish Anthology* (London, 1968), pp. 265–6.

81. UMBC/Correspondence, Betjeman to Penelope Betjeman, 10 February 1960.

82. Exeter University Library Special Collections [EUL] MS113/3 Correspondence/temp/Box 30, Betjeman to A.L. Rowse, 25 December 1958.

83. A.L. Rowse, *A Life: Collected Poems* (Edinburgh, 1981), p. 202.

84. EUL MS113/3 Correspondence/temp/Box 30, Betjeman to A.L. Rowse, 21 March 1967.

85. EUL MS113/3/temp/Box 30, Betjeman to A.L. Rowse, 22 May 1975; Betjeman to A.L. Rowse, 22 October 1977.

86. EUL MS113/3temp/Box 30, Betjeman to A.L. Rowse, 1 September 1980.

87. Rowse, (1981), p. 1.

88. UMBC/Correspondence, A.L. Rowse to Betjeman, n.d. c.1953.

89. A.L. Rowse, *Memories and Glimpses* (London, 1986), p. 480.

90. Rowse (1986), pp. 480–1.

91. John Betjeman, *Cornwall: A Shell Guide* (London, 1964), p. 9.

92. A.L. Rowse, *Oxford in the History of the Nation* (London, 1975), p. 183.

93. Betjeman (1964), p. 32.

94. Betjeman (1964), p. 62.

95. Stallworthy (2009/10), p. 15.

96. Rowse (1986), p. 485.

97. Rowse (1986), p. 479.

98. Rowse (1986), p. 482.

99. A.L. Rowse, *Portraits and Views: Literary and Historical* (London, 1979), p. 87.

100. Rowse (1986) p. 501.

101. UMBC/Correspondence, 2 November 1950; see also Lycett Green (1994), p. 522.

102. Rowse (1986), pp. 477–8.

103. Rowse (1986), p. 478, 481.

104. A.L. Rowse, *Friends and Contemporaries* (London, 1989), p. 178.

105. Rowse (1986), p. 501.

106. UMBC/Correspondence, A.L. Rowse to Betjeman, late 1948.

107. EUL MS113/2 Journals and notebooks/5/3, 18 August 1956.

108. EUL MS113/3 Correspondence/temp//Box30, Penelope Betjeman to A.L. Rowse, 12 July n.d.

109. See Payton (2005b), chapters 9 and 10.

110. Rowse (1986), p. 502.

111. John Betjeman and A.L. Rowse, *Victorian and Edwardian Cornwall from Old Photographs* (London, 1974), dustcover notes.

112. EUL MS113/3 Correspondence/temp/Box 30, Betjeman to A.L. Rowse, 22 July 1974.

113. UMBC/Correspondence, Betjeman to A.L. Rowse, 2 August 1976.

114. Valerie Jacob, *Tregonissey to Trenarren: The Cornish Years of A.L. Rowse* (St Austell, 2001), p. 81.

115. UMBC/Correspondence, Betjeman to Duncan Fallowell, 29 November 1966; see also Candida Lycett Green (ed.) *John Betjeman: Letters, Volume Two: 1951 to 1984* (London, 1995), p. 326.

116. UMBC/Correspondence, Betjeman to Anne Barnes, 9 September 1948; see also Lycett Green (ed.) (1994), p. 485.

117. A.L. Rowse, *Friends and Contemporaries* (London, 1989), pp. 62–3.

118. UMBC/Correspondence, Betjeman to Anne Barnes, 9 September 1948; see also Lycett Green (ed.) (1994), p. 485.

119. Rowse (1986), p. 394.

120. Lycett Green (ed.) (1994), p. 372.

121. UMBC/Correspondence, Betjeman to Anne Barnes, 11 August 1951.

122. UMBC/Correspondence, Betjeman to Cecil Beaton, 1 September 1952; see also Lycett Green (ed). (1995), p. 30.

123. UMBC/Correspondence, Betjeman to Elizabeth Bowen, 25 February 1964; see also Lycett Green (ed.) (1995), p. 271.

124. UMBC/Misc. Chronology of John Betjeman's Life.

125. UMBC/Correspondence, Betjeman to Laurence Whistler, 13 August 1956; see also Lycett Green (ed.) (1995), p. 95.

126. UMBC/Correspondence, Betjeman to Peggy Thomas, 26 September 1958; see also Lycett Green (ed.) (1995), p. 146.

127. Hillier (2002), p. 340.

128. UMBC/Correspondence, Betjeman to Alan Pryce Jones, 11 March 1948; see also Lycett Green (ed.) (1994), p. 442.

129. UMBC/Correspondence, Betjeman to Anne Channel, 29 June 1951; see also Lycett Green (ed.) (1994), p. 537.

130. UMBC/Correspondence, A.L. Rowse to Betjeman, n.d. c.1953.

131. UMBC/Correspondence, Penelope Betjeman to Betjeman, n.d. c.1960; see also Wilson (2006), p. 252.

132. UMBC/Correspondence, Betjeman to Wilhelmine Creswell, 10 December 1936; see also Lycett Green (ed.), p. 162.

133. *Daily Telegraph*, 18 January 2007.

134. UMBC/Correspondence, Betjeman to Michael Redington, n.d.

135. Hillier (2002), p. 458.

136. Lycett Green (ed.) (1995), p. x.

137. Lycett Green (ed.) (1995), p. 9.

138. *Daily Telegraph*, 18 January 2007.

139. Rowse (1986), pp. 272, 480.

140. Rowse (1986), p. 480.

141. Wilson (2006), p. 207.

142. UMBC/Correspondence, Betjeman to T.S. Eliot, 18 October 1963; see also Lycett Green (ed.) (1995), p. 263.

143. UMBC/Correspondence, Betjeman to Elsie Avril, 15 January 1968; see also Lycett Green (ed.) (1994), p. 347.

144. UMBC/Correspondence, Betjeman to Mary Wilson, 14 January 1969; 6 April 1969; 19 June 1970; see also Lycett Green (ed.) (1995), pp. 358, 363, 401.

145. Betjeman (1964), pp. 5–6.

146. UMBC/Correspondence, Betjeman to Penelope Betjeman, 4 September 1980; see Lycett Green (ed.) (1995), p. 564.

147. UMBC/Misc. Medical Records.

148. UMBC/Correspondence, Betjeman to Wilhelmine Harrod, 15 February 1974; see also Lycett Green (ed.) (1995), p. 374.

149. UMBC/Correspondence, Penelope Betjeman to Betjeman, 20 December [1956].

150. UMBC/Correspondence, Penelope Betjeman to Betjeman, 13 June 1961.

151. UMBC/Correspondence, Penelope Betjeman to Betjeman, n.d.

152. *Listener*, 17 August 1972.

153. *The Times*, 11 October 1972.

154. *New York Times*, 11 October 1972.

155. Lycett Green (ed.) (1995), p. 438.

156. UMBC/Correspondence, Betjeman to David Astor, 17 September 1974; see also Lycett Green (ed.), p. 485.
157. Lycett Green (ed.) (1995), p. 553.
158. 'Time With Betjeman' (7), BBC2 Television, 27 March 1983.
159. Lycett Green (ed.) (1995), pp. 581–2.

Chapter Seven: John Betjeman Goes Native

1. John Betjeman (ed. Nigel Kerr), *Guide to English Parish Churches* (London, 1958, new edn. 1993), p. 125.
2. *Evening Standard*, 8 May 1936.
3. ' Beauty in Trust', BBC Television, 4 August 1959; see also Stephen Games (ed.), *Betjeman's England* (London, 2009), p36; 'Birds Eye View', BBC2 Television, 25 December 1969; see also Stephen Games (ed.), *Tennis Whites and Teacakes* (London, 2007), p. 232.
4. 'Birds Eye View', 25 December 1969; see also Games (ed.) (2009), p. 68.
5. Betjeman (1958 & 1993), p. 125.
6. 'The Parson Hawker of Morwenstow', BBC West of England Programme, 7 February 1939; see also Stephen Games (ed.), *Trains and Buttered Toast* (London, 2006), p. 161.
7. John Betjeman, *Cornwall in a Series of Views* (London, 1934), p. 15.
8. C. Hamilton Ellis, *Four Main Lines* (London, 1950), p. 173.
9. C. Hamilton Ellis, *British Railway History 1877–1947* (London, 1959), cited in Bryan Morgan (ed.),.
   The Railway-Lover's Companion (London, 1963), p. 118.
10. Betjeman (1934), p. 50.
11. Betjeman (1934), p. 50.
12. Betjeman (1934), p. 50.
13. Betjeman (1934), p. 17–8.
14. William S. Peterson, *John Betjeman: A Bibliography* (Oxford, 2006), p. 15.
15. J.C. Trewin and H.J. Wilmot, *London-Bodmin: An Exchange of Letters between J.C. Trewin and H.J. Wilmot* (London, 1950).
16. Peterson (2006), pp. 17–8.
17. John Betjeman, *Cornwall: A Shell Guide* (London, 1964), pp. 7–8.
18. Betjeman (1958 & 1993), p. 125.
19. Patrick Taylor-Martin, *John Betjeman: His Life and Work* (London, 1983), p. 24.
20. John Betjeman, 'T Trebetherick', in Michael Williams (ed.), *Both Sides of Tamar: A West Country Alphabet* (Bodmin, 1975), pp. 93–4.
21. Betjeman (1934), p. 6.
22. Betjeman (1975), p. 95.

23. Michael Williams, *People and Places in Cornwall* (Bodmin, 1985), pp.12–13.

24. A.L. Rowse, *Memories and Glimpses* (London, 1986), p. 496.

25. Exeter University Library Special Collections [EUL] MS113/3/temp/Box 30, Betjeman to A.L. Rowse, n.d. c.1960; UMBC/Correspondence, Betjeman to Norman Williams and Patsy Zeppel, n.d. February 1963; see also Candida Lycett Green, *John Betjeman: Letters, Volume Two: 1951–1984* (London, 1995), p. 243.

26. 'Beside the Seaside', 25 December 1969; see also Games (ed.) (2009), p. 69.

27. 'Plymouth', BBC West of England Programme, 26 April 1927; see also Games (ed.) (2006), p. 65.

28. Cited in Hillier (2002), p. 256.

29. 'Beauty in Trust', BBC Television, 4 August 1959; see also Games (2009), p. 35.

30. http://www.camelotintl.com/heritage/counties/england/cornwall.html (18 September 2008).

31. 'Crofton Pumping Station', ITV, 11 November 1955; see also Games (ed.) (2009), pp. 253–4. When the beam engine was restored some fifteen years later, Betjeman was invited to perform the ceremonial restarting – see *The Times*, 22 August 1970.

32. 'One Man's County', ITV, 22 January 1964; see also John Betjeman, *Betjeman's Cornwall* (London, 1984a), p. 25, and Candida Lycett Green (ed.), *Betjeman's Britain* (London, 1999), p. 40.

33. 'One Man's County', 22 January 1964; see also Betjeman (1984a), p. 26, and Lycett Green (ed.) (1999), p. 41.

34. 'One Man's County', 22 January 1964; see also Betjeman (1984a), p. 26, and Lycett Green (ed.) (1999), p. 41.

35. John Betjeman, *Cornwall: A Shell Guide* (London, 1964), p. 53.

36. Betjeman (1964), p. 106.

37. Betjeman (1964), p. 118.

38. Betjeman (1964), p. 14.

39. 'One Man's County', 22 January 1964; see also Betjeman (1984a), p. 26, and Lycett Green (ed.) (1999), p. 41.

40. *The Times*, 17 July 1970.

41. Rowse (1986), p. 494.

42. Rowse (1986), p. 494.

43. Rowse (1986), pp. 494–5.

44. Rowse (1986), p. 495.

45. 'Visitors', BBC West of England Programme, 22 April 1938; see also Games (ed.) (2006), p. 99.

46. UMBC/Misc. John Betjeman's Address Book, 1950s.

47. UMBC/Misc. John Betjeman's Christmas Card List, 1964.

48. *The Times*, 18 June 1964.

49. 'Beauty in Trust', 4 August 1959; see also Games (ed.) (2009), p. 35.

50. 'Beauty in Trust', 4 August 1959; see also Games (ed.) (2009), pp. 36–7.

51. 'Beauty in Trust', 4 August 1959; see also Games (ed.) (2009), p41.

52. *The Times*, 2 June 1967.

53. Bernard Deacon, Dick Cole and Garry Tregidga, *Mebyon Kernow and Cornish Nationalism* (Cardiff, 2003), pp. 79–80.

54. *Western Daily Press*, 23 May 1984.

55. John Betjeman, *Collected Poems* (London, 1984b), p. 350 (from 'Harvest Hymn').

56. UMBC/Correspondence, 22 February 1978; see also Lycett Green (ed.) (1995), p. 534.

57. Cited in David Henshaw, *The Great Railway Conspiracy: The Fall and Rise of Britain's Railways Since the 1950s* (Hawes, 1991), p. 80.

58. 'Let's Imagine a Branch Line Railway', BBC Television, 29 March 1963; this was in 1994 published as a video cassette recording by Home Vision Entertainment.

59. Robin Atthill, *The Somerset and Dorset Railway* (Newton Abbot, 2nd edn 1985), p. 16.

60. UMBC/Correspondence, Gilbert Nelson to John Betjeman, 22 February 1964.

61. UMBC/Correspondence, Betjeman to Gilbert Nelson, 10 March 1964; see also Lycett Green (ed.) (1995), p. 273.

62. Henshaw (1991), p. 192.

63. Stephen Austin, *The Southern Railway's Withered Arm: A View from the Past* (London, 1998), p. 7.

64. 'Coast and Country', BBC West of England Home Service, 7 September 1949, published in John Betjeman, *First and Last Loves* (London, 1952), p. 207; see also Betjeman (1984a), p. 84; Lycett Green (1999), p. 60.

65. UMBC/Correspondence, A.W.T. David (Railway Development Association) to Betjeman, 31 March 1966.

66. Mebyon Kernow, *What Cornishmen Can Do: The Economic Possibilities before Cornwall* (Redruth, 1968), pp. 23, 19–20.

67. Stephen Austin, *Portrait of the Atlantic Coast Express* (London, 1997), p. 23.

68. *The Times*, 20 September 1982.

69. Alan Clarke, *The Tories: Conservatives and the Nation State 1922–1997* (London, 1998), p. 314.

70. *Daily Herald*, 8 March 1961.

71. David Childs, *Britain Since 1945: A Political History* (London, 1984), p. 290, offers a more academic assessment of changing support for the Conservatives during the Thatcher era.

72. Betjeman (1984a), p. 7 (from 'The City'); p. 23 (from 'Slough'); pp. 385–6 (from 'Executive').

73. *Daily Herald*, 8 March 1961.

74. UMBC/Correspondence, Betjeman to David Attenbrough, 13 July 1954; Betjeman to unidentified recipient, 13 November 1950; Betjeman to Nicholas Bentley, 6 November 1952.

75. *Spectator*, 18 June 1954.

76. Rowse (1986), p. 476.

77. *Cornish Nation*, November 1968; see also *Cornish Nation*, September 1972.

78. *Cornish Nation*, November 1968.

79. *Cornish Nation*, January-February 1969.

80. Oriel Malet (ed.), *Daphne du Maurier: Letters from Menabilly – Portrait of a Friendship* (New York, 1992), p. 212.

81. Malet (ed.) (1992), p. 225.

82. Daphne du Maurier, *Vanishing Cornwall: The Spirit and History of Cornwall* (London, 1967), p. 200.

83. Geoffrey Moorhouse, *Britain in the Sixties: The Other England* (London, 1964), p. 41.

84. See Philip Payton, *A.L. Rowse and Cornwall: A Paradoxical Patriot* (Exeter, 2005), pp. 221, 234.

85. Sally Beauman, 'Rebecca', in Helen Taylor (ed.), *The Daphne du Maurier Companion* (London, 2007), p. 47.

86. Hillier (2002), p. 245.

87. Margaret Foster, *Daphne du Maurier* (London, 1993), p. 244.

88. Anthony Kilmister and Donald Lenox, *My Favourite Betjeman* (London, 1985).

89. Betjeman (1984a), p. 295 (from 'Cornish Cliffs').

90. UMBC/Correspondence, Betjeman to William Plomer, 5 December 1960; see also Lycett Green (ed.) (1995), p. 194.

91. Betjeman (1984a), p. 179 (from 'The Town Clerk's Views').

92. See Ronald Perry, with Ken Dean, Bryan Brown and David Shaw, *Counterurbanisation: Inter-National Case Studies of Socio-Economic Change in Rural Areas* (Norwich, 1986).

93. Cole, Deacon & Tregidga (2002), pp. 48–51.

94. *Cornish Nation*, December 1971.

95. 'Muses With Milligan', BBC2, 3 March 1965.

96. Betjeman & Kerr (1958&1993), p. 125.

97. *Cornish Nation*, March 1973.

98. UMBC/Correspondence, Kennedy to The Architectural Press Ltd., 23 July 1934.

99. UMBC /Correspondence, William G. West to Betjeman, 9 March 1974.

100. UMBC/Correspondence, R.W. Nicholls to Betjeman, 31 August 1965.

101. UMBC/Correspondence, Paul Richards to Betjeman, 21 March 1983.

102. UMBC/Correspondence, W.C. Worden to Betjeman, 24 March 1983.

103. UMBC/Correspondence, Vivien Hircock to Betjeman, n.d. c.1983.

104. UMBC/Correspondence, Anon to Betjeman, n.d. c.1983.

105. UMBC/Correspondence, Muriel Williams to Betjeman, 28 March 1983.

106. UMBC/Correspondence, Frank Sutton to Betjeman, 30 March 1983.

107. Chris Nancollas, 'Reflections of an Exile', *An Baner Kernewek/The Cornish Banner*, February 2008,p.12.

108. James Whetter, 'John Betjeman and Cornwall', *An Baner Kernewek/The Cornish Banner*, November 2006, p. 21.

109. Donald R. Rawe, *Padstow's 'Obby 'Oss and May Day Festivities: A Study in Folklore and Tradition* (Padstow, 1971).

110. *Cornish Scene*, Summer 1988, p. 72.

111. Betjeman (1964), p. 121.

112. Bert Biscoe, *'Mercifully Preserved': A Fictional Account of the visit to Truro by Sir John Betjeman during which he saved Walsingham Place from demolition* (Truro, 2006), pp. 1–3.

113. UMBC/Correspondence, Betjeman to Norman Williams and Patsy Zeppel, February 1963; see also Lycett Green (ed.) (1995), p. 243.

114. *Western Morning News*, 23 May 1984.

115. *Sunday Independent* (Plymouth), 20 May 1984.

116. Cited in Whetter, *An BanerKernewek/The Cornish Banner*, p. 21.

Epilogue: 'When People talk to me about "The British" ... I Give Up'

1. *Scotsman*, 9 June 1984.

2. A.L. Rowse, *Portraits and Views: Literary and Historical* (London, 1979), p. 95.

3. John Betjeman, 'Coming Home', BBC Home Service, 15 February 1943; published in the *Listener*, 11 March 1953; see also Candida Lycett Green (ed.), *Coming Home: An Anthology of Prose* (London, 1997), p. 141.

4. Candida Lycett Green (ed.), *Betjeman's Britain* (London, 1999).

5. John Baxendale, *Priestley's England: J.B. Priestley and English Culture* (Manchester, 2007), p. 4.

6. John Betjeman, 'Francis Johnston', in Myfanwy Evans (ed.), *The Pavilion: A Contemporary Collection of British Art and Architecture* (London, 1946), republished in Lycett Green (ed.) (1997), p. 117.

7. *Tablet*, 20 April 1968.

8. Richard Rose, *The United Kingdom as a Multi-National State* (Glasgow, 1970).

9. Norman Davies, *The Isles: A History* (London, 1999).

10. Arthur Aughey, *The Politics of Englishness* (Manchester, 2007), p. 153.

11. Tom Nairn, *After Britain: New Labour and the Return of Scotland* (London, 2000), p. 14.

12. Michael Williams, *People and Places in Cornwall* (Bodmin, 1985), p. 9.

13. *Western Morning News*, 23 May 1984.

14. A.L. Rowse, *Memories and Glimpses* (London, 1986), p. 510.

Further Reading

Works by John Betjeman

Selected verse:

Mount Zion (London, 1931).

Continual Dew (London, 1937).

Old Lights for New Chancels (London, 1940).

New Bats in Old Belfries (London, 1945).

A Few Late Chrysanthemums (London, 1954).

Poems in the Porch (London, 1954).

John Betjeman's Collected Poems (London, 1958; sixth edition 2001).

Summoned by Bells (London, 1960).

High and Low (London, 1966).

A Nip in the Air (London, 1974).

Uncollected Poems (London, 1982).

Selected prose:

Ghastly Good Taste (London, 1933).

Cornwall Illustrated in a Series of Views [a Shell Guide] (London, 1934).

Devon – Compiled with Many Illustrations [a Shell Guide] (London, 1936).

Devon: A Shell Guide (London, 1955).

Collins Guide to English Parish Churches (London, 1958; fourth edition 1993).

First and Last Loves (London, 1960).

Cornwall: A Shell Guide (London, 1964).

London's Historic Railway Stations (London, 1972).

Betjeman's Cornwall (London, 1984).

(edited with) Geoffrey Taylor, *English, Scottish and Welsh Landscape 1700–1860* (London, 1944).

(with) A.L. Rowse, *Victorian and Edwardian Cornwall from Old Photographs* (London, 1972).

Works about John Betjeman (including anthologies)

Bert Biscoe, 'Mercifully Preserved': A Fictional Account of a Visit to Truro by Sir John Betjeman during which he saved Walsingham Place from Demolition (Truro, 2006).

Dennis Brown, John Betjeman (Plymouth, 1996).

Jane Cooper and Sharon Smith, The White Horse and the Village of Uffington (Uffington, 2004).

Frank Delaney, Betjeman Country (London, 1983).

Stephen Games (ed.), Trains and Buttered Toast: Betjeman's Best BBC Radio Talks (London, 2006).

Stephen Games (ed.), Tennis Whites and Teacakes: An Anthology of Betjeman's Prose, Verse and Occasional Writing (London, 2007).

Stephen Games (ed.), Sweet Songs of Zion: Betjeman Radio Poems about English Hymn-writing (London, 2007).

Stephen Games (ed.), Betjeman's England: Betjeman's Best Topographical Television Programmes (London, 2009).

Kevin Gardner (ed.), Faith and Doubt of John Betjeman: An Anthology of Betjeman's Religious Work (London, 2005).

Kevin Gardner (ed.), Poems in the Porch: The Radio Poems of John Betjeman (London, 2008).

Kevin Gardner, John Betjeman: Writing the Public Life (Waco, Texas, 2010).

Bevis Hillier, John Betjeman: A Life in Pictures (London, 1984).

Bevis Hillier, Young Betjeman (London, 1988).

Bevis Hillier, John Betjeman: New Fame, New Love (London, 2002).

Bevis Hillier, Betjeman: The Bonus of Laughter (London, 2004).

Bevis Hillier, Betjeman: The Biography (London, 2006).

Candida Lycett Green, (ed.) John Betjeman: Letters, Volume One: 1926 to 1951 (London, 1994).

Candida Lycett Green (ed.), John Betjeman: Letters, Volume Two: 1951 to 1984 (London, 1995).

Candida Lycett Green (ed.), Coming Home: An Anthology of Prose (London, 1997).

Candida Lycett Green (ed.), Betjeman's Britain (London, 1999).

Greg Morse, John Betjeman: Reading the Victorians (Brighton, 2008).

Timothy Mowl, Stylistic Cold Wars: Betjeman versus Pevsner (London, 2000).

Philip Payton, 'John Betjeman and the Holy Grail: One Man's Celtic Quest', in Philip Payton (ed.), Cornish Studies: Fifteen (Exeter, 2007), pp. 185–208.

William S. Petersen (ed.), John Betjeman: A Bibliography (Oxford, 2006).

A.L. Rowse, 'The Poetry of John Betjeman', in Portraits and Views: Literary and Historical (London, 1979), pp. 87–95.

A.L. Rowse, 'The Real Betjeman', in Memories and Glimpses (London, 1986), pp. 477–510.

Derek Stanford, *John Betjeman: A Study* (London, 1961).

Patrick Taylor-Martin, *John Betjeman: His Life and Work* (London, 1983).

A.N. Wilson, *Betjeman* (London, 2006).

Works about Cornwall

Bernard Deacon, *Cornwall: A Concise History* (Cardiff, 2007).

Alan M. Kent, *The Literature of Cornwall* (Bristol, 2000).

Philip Payton (ed.), *Cornwall Since the War* (Redruth, 1993).

Philip Payton, *Cornwall: A History* (Fowey, 2004).

Philip Payton, *The Cornish Overseas: A History of Cornwall's 'Great Emigration'* (Fowey, 2005).

Philip Payton, *A.L. Rowse and Cornwall: A Paradoxical Patriot* (Exeter, 2005; paperback 2007).

Philip Payton, *D.H. Lawrence and Cornwall* (St Agnes, 2009).

Donald R. Rawe, *Padstow's 'Obby 'Oss and May Day Festivities: A Study in Folklore and Tradition* (Padstow, 1971).

A.L. Rowse, *A Life: Collected Poems* (Edinburgh, 1981).

Michael Williams, *People and Places in Cornwall* (Bodmin, 1986).

Index